PETERBOROUGH UNITED
Who's Who?

DESERT ISLAND FOOTBALL HISTORIES

PETERBOROUGH UNITED WHO'S WHO?

Series Editor: Clive Leatherdale

Matt Hill

Desert Island Books

First Published in 2002

DESERT ISLAND BOOKS LIMITED
89 Park Street, Westcliff-on-Sea, Essex SS0 7PD
United Kingdom
www.desertislandbooks.com

© 2002 Matt Hill

British Library Cataloguing-in-Publication Data
A catalogue record for this book is available from the British Library

ISBN 1-874287-48-1

Printed in Great Britain
by
The Cromwell Press, Trowbridge, Wiltshire

Photographs in this book are reproduced by kind permission of
the Peterborough *Evening Telegraph* and *Herald & Post*

~ *Preface* ~

Matt Hill – what would we do without people like Matt? Matt has been a loyal supporter of Peterborough United over countless seasons and if you want any facts or figures on Posh, then Matt's your man!

I was delighted to be invited to help launch Matt's first publication, *Peterborough United: The Modern Era*, in 2001. It is, therefore, an even greater privilege to be asked to write the Preface to this second book. I shall enjoy reading Matt's entries on the 499 players he details who played between 1960 and the present day and I'm particularly looking forward to seeing what he's written about the lads I played with from 1968 to 1981. Now, I could tell you a tale or two about one or two players, but that's another story . . .

Having played over 500 games for Posh, I was lucky enough to witness some tremendous performances by some great players – Freddie Hill, a skilful midfielder who read the game well and had the funniest dry wit that kept the changing rooms ringing with laughter; my old pal, Jim Hall, and the inimitable John Cozens, two magnificent centre forwards; Chris Turner, a tireless centre-half if ever there was one, who I believe could and should have played at the very highest level and who then returned to become Posh's most successful manager; Jack Carmichael – tough, uncompromising, solid as a rock.

And then, later, 'King' Kenny Charlery, an outstanding centre-forward who is still scoring great goals today; Simon Davies and Matthew Etherington, players with great futures who are a credit to the Posh Youth Scheme.

We all have our favourites. Sit back and enjoy this fascinating insight into the multitude of personalities and abilities that make up *Peterborough United: Who's Who?*

And, if ever you meet up with Chris Turner, Jack Carmichael and I on a Saturday night in Peterborough, feel free to enlighten us on your favourite players – and why.

TOMMY ROBSON

~ *Author's Note* ~

It is often claimed that a football club would be nothing without its supporters. Whilst that is undoubtedly true, the same could obviously be said about players. They are what football revolves around. By and large, fans remain loyal, permanent fixtures of their club, but players come and go, moving regularly from one club to another. This book aims to provide a definitive list of the 499 players, good, bad and indifferent, who have donned a Posh shirt in competitive action since the club entered the Football League in 1960 up to the close of 2001-02.

I have not attempted to grade or judge any of the players featured, or to suggest who has been the club's greatest servant. I'll leave that for you, the reader, to decide. Of course, not all those featured have been 'Posh greats' and some will be remembered, no less fondly perhaps, for being anything but.

In the four years it has taken me to produce this book I have interviewed or spoken to many of the former players who feature in the pages that follow. Some have since become friends, others have been genuinely perplexed as to why I should be interested in them, but all, without exception, have proved themselves to be courteous and helpful. To all those players, and indeed all those who have played their part in the Peterborough United story, thank you.

I would also like to offer my heartfelt thanks to my friend Simon Curtis, without whose help this book would not have been possible. Simon's gift of a personal computer played a huge part in turning a pipedream into reality. There are many others who have helped me complete what has been a marathon project. Alan Swann of the *Evening Telegraph* and Sue Lamb of the *Herald & Post* deserve special mention for allowing me access to their picture libraries. Thanks are also due to Mike Davage for checking and correcting early manuscripts, and for putting me in touch with many former players. Mick Robinson is another who deserves praise for the speed and enthusiasm with which he helped me produce accurate playing records for every player. I must also thank Tommy Robson for writing the preface, Mick Bratley of posh.net, Sean Ingham for providing priceless old photos and Peter French for his computer wizardry. Nor must I forget to mention Clive Leatherdale for commissioning the project.

My wife Jo continues to give me fantastic support, in addition to helping me realise that there is more to life than football.

Dedication

I dedicate this work to the memory of my cousin Sarah Nelson. Sarah died on 22 March 1999 in Farcet, Peterborough, aged 14.

MATT HILL

ADAMS, George Robert
Wing-half   *Born Hackney, 28 September 1947*

A stocky Londoner, Adams was signed aged 18 from Chelsea by Gordon Clark in July 1966. Unable to make the first team at Stamford Bridge, Adams' two-year Posh career was only slightly more productive. Debuting in a 0-2 League Cup home defeat by Northampton in September 1966, he had just a few more games before Norman Rigby released him in 1968. Legend has it that Adams was once a victim of manager Clark's acerbic wit. The unhappy lad asked his manager why he was in the reserves, to be told 'because we haven't got an 'A' team'!

Season	League			FA Cup			League Cup			Other			Total		
	Aps	Sub	Gls	Aps	Sub	Gls	Aps	Sub	Gls	Aps	Sub	Gls	Aps	Sub	Gls
1966-67	7	2	1		1		1						8	3	1
1967-68	6	1	1	1									7	1	1
Total	13	3	2	1	1		1						15	4	2

ADCOCK, Anthony Charles (Tony)
Forward   *Bethnal Green, 27 February 1963*

Red-haired striker Tony Adcock came to prominence with Colchester United in the early 1980s. In six seasons he scored over 100 goals, earning a £85,000 move to Manchester City in June 1987. He played 15 League games for City, scoring five goals, including a hat-trick in a 10-1 win over Huddersfield, before returning to the lower Leagues with Northampton and Bradford City. He joined Posh, initially on loan from Northampton, in December 1991. His ball control and keen vision, allied to his coolness in front of goal, earned Tony a permanent contract. Hero worship soon followed, as Adcock became an integral part of Chris Turner's promoted side. With Posh elevated to the new First Division, Adcock went from strength to strength, hitting 19 goals in his first full season to finish as the club's leading goalscorer. In 1993-94 he became locked in a wage dispute but still managed 12 League goals for a side that finished bottom. Tony left London Road in 1994, whereupon he had an injury-plagued spell with Luton before returning to his first club, Colchester, for the 1995-96 season. After scoring his 200th goal in League football during 1996-97, Tony retired in 1999 following a short spell with non-League Heybridge Swifts.

Season	League			FA Cup			League Cup			Other			Total		
	Aps	Sub	Gls	Aps	Sub	Gls	Aps	Sub	Gls	Aps	Sub	Gls	Aps	Sub	Gls
1991-92	23	1	7							3			26	1	7
1992-93	44	1	16	3		1	3		2			1	50	2	19
1993-94	40	2	12	2			5		1			1	47	4	13
Total	107	4	35	5		1	8		3	3		2	123	7	39

ALLARDYCE, Craig Samuel
Central Defender   Bolton, 9 June 1975

Son of Bolton stalwart Sam Allardyce, tall, robust defender Craig gained League experience with Preston and Blackpool before being invited to London Road for a trial by Barry Fry in 1998-99. After debuting in a 2-1 win at Hartlepool in September 1998, he made three further appearances before joining Mansfield in December, but later dropped out of the Football League with Boston.

Season	League			FA Cup			League Cup			Other			Total		
	Aps	Sub	Gls	Aps	Sub	Gls	Aps	Sub	Gls	Aps	Sub	Gls	Aps	Sub	Gls
1998-99	4												4		

ALLEN, Kenneth Richard (Kenny)
Goalkeeper   Thornaby, 12 January 1948

John Wile signed 6ft 4in Allen on a non-contract basis in December 1983 as cover for David Seaman. Formerly with Hartlepool, WBA, Bournemouth and South African side Hellenic, the experienced goalkeeper played once for Posh in an Associate Members Cup defeat at Wrexham in February 1984. He moved to IFK Gothenburg, Swindon and Torquay, with whom he experienced an unhappy return to London Road in April 1987, being wrestled to the ground by angry Posh fans whilst leaving the field. After quitting the professional game in 1989, Kenny had spells with non-League Bath and Salisbury.

Season	League			FA Cup			League Cup			Other			Total		
	Aps	Sub	Gls	Aps	Sub	Gls	Aps	Sub	Gls	Aps	Sub	Gls	Aps	Sub	Gls
1983-84										1			1		

ANDERSON, John
Goalkeeper   Barrhead, 8 December 1929

Prior to signing for Posh in July 1960, Anderson had spent over a decade with Leicester, where he played 261 League games and won a full Scottish cap. He spent just one season at London Road, his only senior appearance coming in a 1-4 defeat at Preston in Posh's first ever League Cup-tie. Upon his release in 1961, Anderson returned to the Midlands for spells with non-League Nuneaton and Bedworth United.

Season	League			FA Cup			League Cup			Other			Total		
	Aps	Sub	Gls	Aps	Sub	Gls	Aps	Sub	Gls	Aps	Sub	Gls	Aps	Sub	Gls
1960-61							1						1		

ANDERSON, Trevor
Forward   Belfast, 3 March 1951

A skilful Ulsterman who won four of his 22 caps for Northern Ireland as a Posh player, Anderson began his League career with Manchester United, where he was hailed as 'the new George Best'. He made 19

League appearances in two seasons at Old Trafford before joining Swindon in November 1974. Trevor scored 35 goals in 131 League games for the Robins – prompting John Barnwell to pay £20,000 to bring him to London Road in December 1977. After making his debut in a 0-0 draw at Hereford on Boxing Day, he figured in every match that season as Posh missed out on promotion on goal-difference. After relegation to Division Four a year later, Anderson returned to Northern Ireland to join Linfield, whom he later managed. No longer involved in football, he works as a clerk at Belfast City hospital.

Season	League			FA Cup			League Cup			Other			Total		
	Aps	Sub	Gls	Aps	Sub	Gls	Aps	Sub	Gls	Aps	Sub	Gls	Aps	Sub	Gls
1977-78	26		5										26		5
1978-79	23		1	1		1	8						32		2
Total	49		6	1		1	8						58		7

ANDREWS, Gary Michael
Defender *Nottingham, 12 May 1968*

Andrews began with Brian Clough's Nottingham Forest in September 1985, but after just one League Cup appearance in three years he accepted Mick Jones' offer of a first-team place with Posh. He made his League debut in a 1-1 home draw with Lincoln in September 1988 and performed a variety of defensive roles before being released in 1990.

Season	League			FA Cup			League Cup			Other			Total		
	Aps	Sub	Gls	Aps	Sub	Gls	Aps	Sub	Gls	Aps	Sub	Gls	Aps	Sub	Gls
1988-89	33			3			2			2			40		
1989-90	9	1		1		1	1			2		1	13	1	2
Total	42	1		4		1	3			4		1	53	1	2

ANDREWS, Wayne Michael Hill
Forward *Paddington, 25 November 1977*

Andrews made an explosive start to his three-month London Road loan spell from Watford, scoring four goals on his debut in the 5-2 thrashing of Barnet in February 1999. That was as many goals as he had scored in three seasons at Vicarage Road, where he made 28 League appearances. The rest of his time with Posh brought just one more goal – in a 2-0 win at Plymouth – as injury restricted his progress. Following his subsequent release from Watford, Wayne plied his trade with St Albans, Aldershot and Chesham but is now with Oldham.

Season	League			FA Cup			League Cup			Other			Total		
	Aps	Sub	Gls	Aps	Sub	Gls	Aps	Sub	Gls	Aps	Sub	Gls	Aps	Sub	Gls
1998-99	8	2	5										8	2	5

ANSAH, Andrew (Andy)

Forward   *Lewisham, 19 March 1969*

A lively little forward who made his name in Southend's meteoric rise through the divisions in the 1990s, Ansah made two substitute appearances during a brief trial period with Posh in March 1996. After helping record a 3-1 home victory over Crewe, Andy scored in a 1-1 draw at Shrewsbury on his 27th birthday before leaving to try his luck with Gillingham. That move was also short-lived, and after appearing twice for Leyton Orient in 1996-97 he moved into the non-League arena with Hayes, Bromley and Heybridge Swifts. He returned to League soccer with Brighton and Brentford and later played for Farnborough Town.

Season	League			FA Cup			League Cup			Other			Total		
	Aps	Sub	Gls	Aps	Sub	Gls	Aps	Sub	Gls	Aps	Sub	Gls	Aps	Sub	Gls
1995-96		2	1											2	1

ANTHROBUS, Stephen Anthony (Steve)

Forward   *Lewisham, 10 November 1968*

Well-travelled Steve Anthrobus made little impact during an injury-riddled loan spell from Premier League Wimbledon in 1993-94. A big, bustling striker whose career began at Millwall, he wore Posh's No 9 shirt in Division One matches at Portsmouth and Birmingham. Two seasons later he scored against Posh for Shrewsbury. He left Gay Meadow for Crewe in 1997 before joining Oxford two years later.

Season	League			FA Cup			League Cup			Other			Total		
	Aps	Sub	Gls	Aps	Sub	Gls	Aps	Sub	Gls	Aps	Sub	Gls	Aps	Sub	Gls
1993-94	2												2		

ASHLEY, Kevin Mark

Right-back   *Birmingham, 31 December 1968*

A diminutive full-back whose career was blighted by injury, Ashley came through the ranks at Birmingham, where his accomplished displays led to a £500,000 move to Wolves in September 1990. Injuries enabled Posh boss John Still to sign him on a free transfer in August 1994. After showing promise at London Road, further injuries and loss of form saw him lose his place. In 1996 he briefly served Doncaster before moving to non-League with Telford and Bromsgrove Rovers.

Season	League			FA Cup			League Cup			Other			Total		
	Aps	Sub	Gls	Aps	Sub	Gls	Aps	Sub	Gls	Aps	Sub	Gls	Aps	Sub	Gls
1994-95	27			2			2						31		
1995-96	9			2			1			2			14		
Total	36			4			3			2			45		

ASTBURY, Michael John (Mike)

Goalkeeper   *Leeds, 22 January 1964*

Astbury was a reliable, agile goalkeeper signed on loan from York by John Wile after regular custodian John Turner broke his leg in an FA Cup clash with Leeds in 1986. Mike helped Posh defeat Carlisle in the next round before having his loan extended. Posh's run came to an end in a fifth round replay at Brighton. After returning to York, Astbury signed for Darlington, for whom he played 38 League games, before ending his professional career with spells at Chester and Chesterfield.

Season	League			FA Cup			League Cup			Other			Total		
	Aps	Sub	Gls	Aps	Sub	Gls	Aps	Sub	Gls	Aps	Sub	Gls	Aps	Sub	Gls
1985-86	4			3						1			8		

BANHAM, Roy

Centre-half   *Nottingham, 30 October 1936*

Banham joined Posh in July 1958 from Nottingham Forest and was a regular in the final season in the Midland League. He lost his place to Jim Rayner once League football arrived at London Road, but stayed two more years with Posh, providing reliable defensive cover until his release on a free transfer to Southern League Bedford. After subsequent spells at King's Lynn and Grantham – then managed by former Posh team-mate Terry Bly – Roy tried management with March Town.

Season	League			FA Cup			League Cup			Other			Total		
	Aps	Sub	Gls	Aps	Sub	Gls	Aps	Sub	Gls	Aps	Sub	Gls	Aps	Sub	Gls
1960-61	12			3									15		
1961-62	4			1									5		
Total	16			4									20		

BARBER, Frederick (Fred)

Goalkeeper   *Ferryhill, 26 August 1963*

Fred's party-piece of taking to the field wearing a mask and bowing to the crowd earned him national fame and, on a bizarre day in Bradford, the attentions of the West Yorkshire police who claimed he was inciting the crowd! Popular keeper Fred clocked up almost 100 appearances in three spells with Posh between 1989 and 1995. He first arrived on loan from Walsall in October 1989 and built up a good rapport after conceding only three goals in six matches. Although allowed to return to Fellows Park, Fred was back on a permanent basis in August 1991 after Posh boss Chris Turner answered his 'come and get me' call and paid the Saddlers' £25,000 asking price. Fred performed heroically in 1991-92 as Posh defeated Wimbledon, Newcastle and Liverpool in the League Cup prior to securing promotion to Division One via the play-offs. That Wembley win over Stockport was his last game for over a year on account of the emerging Ian Bennett, but Barber was recalled when Bennett joined Birmingham in December 1993. It was, therefore, a surprise when Fred joined Luton in August 1994, but within four months he was back on loan until breaking his collar-bone. In 1996 he joined Kidderminster, ending a League career that had begun at Darlington 15 years earlier. These days Fred is a goalkeeping coach.

Season	League			FA Cup			League Cup			Other			Total		
	Aps	Sub	Gls	Aps	Sub	Gls	Aps	Sub	Gls	Aps	Sub	Gls	Aps	Sub	Gls
1989-90	6												6		
1991-92	39			3			8			8			59		
1993-94	24			2						2			27		
1994-95	5												5		
Total	74			5			8			10			97		

BARKER, Richard Joseph (Richie)
Inside-forward   *Derby, 23 November 1939*
A former Derby and Notts County forward, Barker was signed by Jim Iley in September 1971 and made his debut in a 2-1 home win over Gillingham. He scored Posh's 1,000th League goal in a 5-2 success at Cambridge in April 1972. Breaking his leg in a reserve game, he retired from League football but moved into management with Shrewsbury, Stoke, and, more recently, as assistant boss at Sheffield Wednesday.

Season	League			FA Cup			League Cup			Other			Total		
	Aps	Sub	Gls	Aps	Sub	Gls	Aps	Sub	Gls	Aps	Sub	Gls	Aps	Sub	Gls
1971-72	36		9	4		2							40		11

BARNARD, Leigh Kenneth
Midfielder   *Eastbourne, 29 October 1958*
Barnard had six seasons with Portsmouth before Peter Morris signed him on loan in March 1982. Debuting as a substitute in a 2-1 win at Torquay, he appeared twice more from the bench before tasting 90 minutes' action in a 0-4 mauling at Sheffield United. Swindon snapped him up on a free transfer and he made over 200 League appearances for them before ending his League career at Cardiff in the early 1990s.

Season	League			FA Cup			League Cup			Other			Total		
	Aps	Sub	Gls	Aps	Sub	Gls	Aps	Sub	Gls	Aps	Sub	Gls	Aps	Sub	Gls
1981-82	1	3											1	3	

BARNES, David Oswald (Bobby)
Winger   *Kingston, 17 December 1962*
Born in Kingston-upon-Thames, Barnes grew up in the Wanstead area of East London. It was with West Ham that he burst onto the scene in the early 1980s. After making over 50 appearances for the Hammers he went to Scunthorpe (on loan), Aldershot, Swindon, Bournemouth and Northampton. A wide-man with an eye for goal, Bobby signed for Posh in February 1992 in time to boost the club's promotion bid. With his skills and crossing ability, he was a revelation on the left, helping

Posh to a club-record nine consecutive League wins. A knee injury ruled him out of the last few games before manager Chris Turner – aware of Bobby's match-winning potential – gambled on his fitness for the second-leg play-off semi-final at Huddersfield. Bobby came up trumps, providing the cross for Steve Cooper to head Posh's last-gasp winner. Barnes gave another fine performance in the Wembley final with Stockport. One of his final contributions came in December 1993 when, following his dismissal in a League Cup-tie at Portsmouth, he paid his statutory £50 club fine in penny coins. Knowing chairman Chris Turner was suffering with back trouble, Bobby bagged up the money and dumped it in Turner's office. Unable to command a regular place during 1993-94, Bobby left the club in January 1994 for Partick Thistle, for whom he debuted before a 55,000 crowd at Ibrox. Bobby served two years in Hong Kong before quitting football to work as a financial advisor. He now combines his football knowledge and business acumen as an advisor for the Players' Football Association.

Season	League			FA Cup			League Cup			Other			Total		
	Aps	Sub	Gls	Aps	Sub	Gls	Aps	Sub	Gls	Aps	Sub	Gls	Aps	Sub	Gls
1991-92	15		5							2			17		5
1992-93	22	4	3	1			4			1			27	5	3
1993-94	5	3	1					3					5	6	1
Total	42	76	9	1			4	3		3			49	11	9

BARNES, Charles Ronald (Ron)

Outside-right   *Bolton, 21 February 1936, Died 1991*

A stylish wide player, Ron Barnes began his career as understudy to Stanley Matthews at Blackpool. Struggling to make headway, he moved to Rochdale, having made just nine League appearances for the Seasiders. He also had spells with Wrexham and Norwich before coming to London Road. Ron made his Posh debut on the opening day of 1964-65 and contributed to the club's record run to the FA Cup quarter-final that season. In January 1966 he moved on to Torquay, where he appeared regularly until taking his talents to South Africa in 1969.

Season	League			FA Cup			League Cup			Other			Total		
	Aps	Sub	Gls	Aps	Sub	Gls	Aps	Sub	Gls	Aps	Sub	Gls	Aps	Sub	Gls
1964-65	20		3	7		1	2						29		4
1965-66	19		3	2			3						24		3
Total	39		6	9		1	5						53		7

BARRON, James (Jim)

Goalkeeper   *Tantobie, 19 October 1943*

Free-transfer Jim came to Posh in August 1977 from Connecticut Bi-Centennials in the North American Soccer League. A veteran of some 400 League games, he had previously served Wolves, Chelsea, Oxford, Nottingham Forest and Swindon. He shared goalkeeping duties with

Keith Waugh in 1977-78, when Posh conceded just 33 League goals to set a new Third Division record, prior to taking up a coaching position. He returned to first-team duty after a two-year break when stepping in for the injured Waugh in a 5-2 home defeat of Southend in October 1980. The following summer Jim took the assistant manager's job at his first club, Wolves. He has also been manager at Cheltenham and been coach at Aston Villa and reserve team boss at Birmingham.

Season	League			FA Cup			League Cup			Other			Total		
	Aps	Sub	Gls	Aps	Sub	Gls	Aps	Sub	Gls	Aps	Sub	Gls	Aps	Sub	Gls
1977-78	20			5			1						26		
1980-81	1												1		
Total	21			5			1						27		

BASHAM, Michael (Mike)
Defender   *Barking, 27 September 1973*

Basham began as a West Ham trainee. After a loan spell at Colchester he signed for Swansea in March 1994, making 29 League appearances and being part of the Swans side that lifted the Autoglass Trophy at Wembley in 1994. Given a trial by Posh manager Mick Halsall in December 1995, Basham was offered full-time terms after impressing with some tough-tackling displays. He failed to live up to his potential and was released in August 1997 to link up with former Posh colleagues at Barnet. Mike joined York on a free transfer in March 2001.

Season	League			FA Cup			League Cup			Other			Total		
	Aps	Sub	Gls	Aps	Sub	Gls	Aps	Sub	Gls	Aps	Sub	Gls	Aps	Sub	Gls
1995-96	13	1	1										13	1	1
1996-97	4	1		1			1						5	2	
Total	17	2	1	1			1						18	3	1

BEASLEY, Andrew (Andy)
Goalkeeper   *Sedgley, 5 February 1964*

A former Luton apprentice, Andy Beasley helped Posh during a goalkeeping crisis in 1986-87 when John Wile had no cover for the injured John Turner. Arriving on loan from Mansfield, Beasley kept a clean sheet in his first two games. Posh followed a 2-0 win over Southend with a 0-0 draw in a League Cup-tie at Colchester. The signing of Kevin Shoemake signalled his return to Field Mill. Andy stayed with the Stags until July 1993, after which he appeared for Doncaster and Chesterfield. Beasley is now an Academy coach at Nottingham Forest.

Season	League			FA Cup			League Cup			Other			Total		
	Aps	Sub	Gls	Aps	Sub	Gls	Aps	Sub	Gls	Aps	Sub	Gls	Aps	Sub	Gls
1986-87	7						3						10		

BEATTIE, Richard Scott (Dick)

Goalkeeper   Glasgow, 24 October 1936, Died 1990

A Scottish Under-23 cap, athletic keeper Beattie arrived in June 1962 with a fine pedigree, having spent five years at Celtic before making 122 League appearances in three seasons with Portsmouth. His Posh career was undistinguished and after being displaced by Brian Ronson he returned north to St Mirren in January 1963. Implicated in the football betting scandals of the early 1960s, Dick served a nine-month prison sentence before going abroad, working as a welder in Algiers.

Season	League			FA Cup			League Cup			Other			Total		
	Aps	Sub	Gls	Aps	Sub	Gls	Aps	Sub	Gls	Aps	Sub	Gls	Aps	Sub	Gls
1962-63	10												10		

BEECH, Kenneth (Kenny)

Midfield   Stoke, 18 March 1958

A tough-tackling, blond midfielder, Beech joined Posh from Walsall in August 1983. He began at Port Vale, where he played 199 League and Cup games. In his early Posh days he cracked a rib and punctured a lung during a defeat at Hereford which sidelined him for two months, but he returned for the remainder of the season. Unable to stake a regular place in 1984-85, he was given a free transfer to Stafford Rangers.

Season	League			FA Cup			League Cup			Other			Total		
	Aps	Sub	Gls	Aps	Sub	Gls	Aps	Sub	Gls	Aps	Sub	Gls	Aps	Sub	Gls
1983-84	38		3	1			2			1			42		3
1984-85	20	2	2	2			1						23	2	2
Total	58	2	5	3			3			1			65	2	5

BEESLEY, Michael Albert (Mike)

Inside-forward   Epping Forest, 10 June 1942

Beesley appeared in a couple of first-team games for West Ham in 1960-61 before making his mark with Southend. He scored 34 goals in 79 league games, then signed for Posh in July 1965. Manager Gordon Clark should have paid £3,000 for Beesley, but picked him up for nothing after Southend failed to register him with the Football League. Beesley made history as Posh's first substitute when he replaced Harry Orr in a 4-2 win at Oldham. After 23 League and two cup appearances in two seasons, Beasley rejoined Southend, quitting football in 1971.

Season	League			FA Cup			League Cup			Other			Total		
	Aps	Sub	Gls	Aps	Sub	Gls	Aps	Sub	Gls	Aps	Sub	Gls	Aps	Sub	Gls
1965-66	9	1	1				1		1				10	1	2
1966-67	14	1	2	1									15	1	2
Total	23	2	3	1			1		1				25	2	4

BENJAMIN, Ian Tracey

Forward   *Nottingham, 11 December 1961*

A tall, rangy striker, Benjamin came to prominence in the late 1970s when sold by Sheffield United to WBA for £125,000, at the time making him English football's second most expensive teenager. But Ian featured only twice in First Division action before being released to Notts County. Injuries meant he never represented County in League action. In August 1982 Benjamin was signed by Posh manager Martin Wilkinson for £5,000 and scored on his debut in an opening-day draw at Stockport. Despite being Posh's only ever-present in 1982-83, 'Benji' never truly fulfilled his potential and was released on a free transfer to Northampton by John Wile in May 1984. To Posh's embarrassment, Ian prospered as one the finest target-men in the lower leagues. He won a Fourth Division championship medal with the Cobblers in 1987 before embarking on a nomadic circuit with Cambridge, Chester, Exeter, Southend, Luton and Brentford, ending his League career with Wigan in 1994-95. He played a total of 483 League games, scoring 127 goals. Spells in non-League football followed as Kettering, Chelmsford and Raunds Town all benefited from Ian's experience. Now a postman in Kettering, 'Benji' has served spells managing non-League Corby Town, Warboys Town, Soham Town Rangers, and Wisbech Town.

Season	League			FA Cup			League Cup			Other			Total		
	Aps	Sub	Gls	Aps	Sub	Gls	Aps	Sub	Gls	Aps	Sub	Gls	Aps	Sub	Gls
1982-83	46		6	4			4		1				54		7
1983-84	31	3	8	1			3	1					35	4	8
Total	77	3	14	5			7	1	1				89	4	15

BENNETT, Ian Michael

Goalkeeper   *Worksop, 10 October 1971*

Ian was in a long line of Posh goalkeeping heroes who moved on to better things. Signed on a free transfer from Newcastle in March 1991, 'Benno' waited a year for his Posh debut – a televised 3-3 Autoglass Trophy semi-final at Stoke City – but made the No 1 jersey his own in 1992-93, following promotion to Division One. His agility and positional sense, added to a neat habit of saving penalties, made him a target for several big clubs and his £325,000 transfer to Birmingham in December 1993 came as a huge disappointment to London Road fans. In his first full season at St Andrews, Ian was ever-present in Barry Fry's side that won the Second Division and the Auto Windscreens Shield at Wembley. Bennett has made in excess of 250 League appearances for Birmingham and was part of the side that suffered play-off semi-final heartache for the third successive season in 2000-01.

Season	League			FA Cup			League Cup			Other			Total		
	Aps	Sub	Gls	Aps	Sub	Gls	Aps	Sub	Gls	Aps	Sub	Gls	Aps	Sub	Gls
1991-92	7									2			9		
1992-93	46			3			4			2			55		
1993-94	19						6						25		
Total	72			3			10			4			89		

BENNETT, Richard John (Dick)
Wing-half   *Northampton, 16 February 1945*

Dick Bennett was an England Youth international who signed from non-League Wellingborough in August 1963. He spent a couple of seasons with Posh, playing four League games, but was released in 1965.

Season	League			FA Cup			League Cup			Other			Total		
	Aps	Sub	Gls	Aps	Sub	Gls	Aps	Sub	Gls	Aps	Sub	Gls	Aps	Sub	Gls
1963-64	3												3		
1964-65	1												1		
Total	4												4		

BENNING, Paul Martin
Defender   *Hayes, 7 June 1963*

Plucked from non-League Hayes by Noel Cantwell in December 1987, Benning debuted as a substitute in a 0-4 Sherpa Van Trophy defeat at Wolves in February 1988. He had to wait two more months for his League debut in a 2-1 home win over Exeter, and although playing in the next game at Burnley he was released. After a spell with Australian side Gosnells City he returned to Hayes, and has since turned out for various non-League sides, including Aylesbury, Sutton and Harrow.

Season	League			FA Cup			League Cup			Other			Total		
	Aps	Sub	Gls	Aps	Sub	Gls	Aps	Sub	Gls	Aps	Sub	Gls	Aps	Sub	Gls
1987-88	2									1			2	1	

BERRY, George Frederick
Central Defender   *West Germany, 19 November 1957*

Famous from his Afro hairstyle days at Wolves in the 1970s, George became only the second black player capped by Wales, in 1979 against West Germany – ironically the country where he was born! He earned five full caps and played in the top flight with Stoke before becoming a cult figure during a brief but memorable spell at London Road. He arrived on a free transfer in 1990 and, despite being sent off at Cardiff, 'Denzil' won the fans' affections with his whole-hearted displays. His finest moment came on 11 May 1991, when he scored the equaliser at Chesterfield that secured promotion to the Third Division after an absence of twelve years. Many at London Road were sad to see chain-smoking George leave in August 1991 for Preston, for whom he made four League appearances, the first of which was back at Posh on the opening day of 1991-92. After a year with Stafford Rangers, Berry quit playing. He now works for the Players' Football Association.

Season	League			FA Cup			League Cup			Other			Total		
	Aps	Sub	Gls	Aps	Sub	Gls	Aps	Sub	Gls	Aps	Sub	Gls	Aps	Sub	Gls
1990-91	28	4	6				1			1		1	30	4	7

BILLINGTON, David
Midfielder   *Oxford, 15 October 1979*

Billington was a month short of his 17th birthday when Barry Fry sent him on as a sub in a Coca-Cola Cup-tie at Southampton in September 1996. David's assured display earned a League debut at Watford three days later. To complete a fairytale week, he kept his place for the return leg against the Saints. Although making only four more appearances, Billington's progress had not gone unnoticed and in March 1997 Sheffield Wednesday paid a staggering £1 million for him, plus youth-team colleague Mark McKeever. Progress was hampered by a knee injury and, after several comebacks, including a short period back at Posh in 2000-01, 'Billo' quit the professional game on medical advice.

Season	League			FA Cup			League Cup			Other			Total		
	Aps	Sub	Gls	Aps	Sub	Gls	Aps	Sub	Gls	Aps	Sub	Gls	Aps	Sub	Gls
1996-97	2	3					1	1					3	4	

BIRKS, Graham
Left-back   *Sheffield, 25 January 1942*

A strong left-back who signed from Sheffield Wednesday in May 1964 (along with keeper Tony Read), Birks was a regular in his first season, when his tough tackling helped Gordon Clark's team reach the last eight of the FA Cup. He lost his place to Ian Crawford the following season and, shortly after scoring his only goal, in a FA Cup defeat at Shrewsbury, he transferred to Southend in January 1966. He made 139 League appearances for them and a further 73 for Chester, before spending two years with South African side Port Elizabeth City. Upon his return to England in 1974, he played for non-League Fleetwood, Worksop and Buxton, then worked as a sales manager for a brewery. Now retired, Graham travels as a caddy for a professional golfer.

Season	League			FA Cup			League Cup			Other			Total		
	Aps	Sub	Gls	Aps	Sub	Gls	Aps	Sub	Gls	Aps	Sub	Gls	Aps	Sub	Gls
1964-65	32			7			1						40		
1965-66	2			1		1							3		1
Total	34			8		1	1						43		1

BLOUNT, Mark
Defender   *Derby, 5 January 1974*

Equally comfortable in central defence or at full-back, Mark began his career with his home-town club Derby, from where he joined non-

League Gresley Rovers, before being sold in February 1995 for £12,500 to Sheffield United. He made some 20 appearances for the Blades before coming to Posh on a non-contract basis the following season. Debuting at right-back in a 0-0 draw at Swansea in April 1996, Blount appeared occasionally before joining Gresley and then Burton Albion.

Season	League			FA Cup			League Cup			Other			Total		
	Aps	Sub	Gls	Aps	Sub	Gls	Aps	Sub	Gls	Aps	Sub	Gls	Aps	Sub	Gls
1995-96	4	1											4	1	

BLY, Terence Geoffrey (Terry)
Centre-forward   Fincham, 22 October 1935

Goal-machine Bly signed in June 1960 from Second Division Norwich, whom he had helped to the semi-finals of the FA Cup. Despite scoring 31 goals in 57 League games for Norwich, few anticipated the impact he would have on Posh's debut season as a League club. Bly opened his account in Posh's first ever Football League game, at home to Wrexham, before bagging a hat-trick in a 4-1 home win over Crystal Palace watched by 21,000. A brave centre-forward who possessed the instinct of being in the right place at the right time, Terry hit the net at a phenomenal rate as Jimmy Hagan's side raced to the Fourth Division championship at the first time of asking. Bly finished the campaign in style, scoring a *seventh* hat-trick on the last day against Barrow to take his tally to 52 League goals – still a club and Fourth Division record. He added a more modest 29 goals in Division Three in 1961-62 before controversially leaving London Road for Jimmy Hill's Coventry in a £10,000 deal. His rich scoring vein continued at Highfield Road, where he found the net 26 times in 32 League matches. Terry finished his professional career with Notts County in 1964 before starting a 15-year spell managing Grantham, where he lives and owns a sports shop.

Season	League			FA Cup			League Cup			Other			Total		
	Aps	Sub	Gls	Aps	Sub	Gls	Aps	Sub	Gls	Aps	Sub	Gls	Aps	Sub	Gls
1960-61	46		52	5		2	1						52		54
1961-62	42		29	6		4	1						49		33
Total	88		81	11		6	2						101		87

BOARDMAN, Craig George
Central Defender   Nottingham, 30 November 1970

After spending four fruitless years at Nottingham Forest, Craig joined Posh in August 1993, but his only appearance came in a 1-3 defeat at WBA in the short-lived Anglo-Italian Cup in September 1993. He transferred to Conference side Halifax, where his displays earned him a move back into the full-time game with Scarborough in August 1995. Injury prompted a return to non-League Stalybridge a year later.

Season	League			FA Cup			League Cup			Other			Total		
	Aps	Sub	Gls	Aps	Sub	Gls	Aps	Sub	Gls	Aps	Sub	Gls	Aps	Sub	Gls
1993-94										1			1		

BODLEY, Michael John (Mick)
Central Defender   Hayes, 14 September 1967

Mick began with Chelsea in the late 1980s but after six First Division games joined Northampton for £50,000 in January 1989. Within nine months Mick had dropped out of League football to team up with Barry Fry at Barnet, making a swift return to the Football League when Barnet won the Conference in 1991. Bodley followed Fry to Southend in July 1993 and linked up with Fry again at London Road three years later. Strong in the air and firm in the tackle, the big defender was prone to costly errors. Fry kept faith, however, early in 1998 making Bodley skipper, which position he held until his contract was cancelled by mutual consent in March 1999. Returning to the non-League with Dagenham & Redbridge, postman Mick now plays for Ryman League Canvey Island, with whom he won the FA Trophy in 2001.

Season	League			FA Cup			League Cup			Other			Total		
	Aps	Sub	Gls	Aps	Sub	Gls	Aps	Sub	Gls	Aps	Sub	Gls	Aps	Sub	Gls
1996-97	31			5			3			4			43		
1997-98	31		1	2			4			2			39		1
1998-99	24			1			2						27		
Total	86		1	8			9			6			109		1

BOOTHROYD, Adrian Neil (Adi)
Full-back   Bradford, 8 February 1971

An affable Yorkshireman whose career was cut short by injury, Adi began as a trainee at Huddersfield, where he made his debut in 1989-90. Two years with Bristol Rovers followed before he moved to Hearts. A return to England saw him make 102 League appearances in three seasons with Mansfield prior to signing for Posh in July 1996-97. He gave good performances at right-back until a broken leg in an Easter Monday fixture at Notts County forced his retirement, aged just 27. Boothroyd remained at London Road as coach to the youngsters in the Posh Academy, efforts that earned him a similar post at Norwich.

Season	League			FA Cup			League Cup			Other			Total		
	Aps	Sub	Gls	Aps	Sub	Gls	Aps	Sub	Gls	Aps	Sub	Gls	Aps	Sub	Gls
1996-97	24	2	1	4	1		2			4			34	3	1

BRACE, Stuart Clive
Winger   Taunton, 21 September 1942

After playing for Plymouth and Watford, Brace first showed his potential with Mansfield in the mid-1960s. He left Field Mill for Posh in November 1967 and debuted as a right-winger in a 3-2 home win over

Grimsby. He struggled to build a rapport with Posh fans, who never forgave him for missing three sitters in a 0-1 FA Cup defeat by Portsmouth in January 1968, even though he had netted in the previous two rounds. Brace had better luck after leaving Posh for Grimsby in October 1968. He hit 81 goals in 206 League appearances, and added 112 games and 37 goals to his tally during a three-year spell with Southend, prior to his retirement from League football in 1976.

Season	League			FA Cup			League Cup			Other			Total		
	Aps	Sub	Gls	Aps	Sub	Gls	Aps	Sub	Gls	Aps	Sub	Gls	Aps	Sub	Gls
1967-68	15		4	3		2							18		6
1968-69	7	1	2				2						9	1	2
Total	22	1	6	3		2	2						27	1	8

BRADFORD, David William
Midfield   *Manchester, 22 February 1953*

Hailing from the north-west, Bradford played 64 League games for Blackburn in the early 1970s prior to joining Sheffield United. He spent a month on loan at Posh under Noel Cantwell, playing four times in 1976-77. In February 1977 he moved from Bramhall Lane to WBA, after which he played in the United States for Detroit Express and Washington Diplomats. He returned to England with Coventry in 1981-82, but later played for Tulsa Roughnecks and Seattle Sounders.

Season	League			FA Cup			League Cup			Other			Total		
	Aps	Sub	Gls	Aps	Sub	Gls	Aps	Sub	Gls	Aps	Sub	Gls	Aps	Sub	Gls
1976-77	4												4		

BRADLEY, Keith
Full-back   *Ellesmere Port, 31 January 1946*

Bradley was a reliable right-back who won a Fourth Division championship medal with Posh in 1973-74. Keith initially arrived on loan in November 1972, but his displays persuaded Noel Cantwell to pay Aston Villa £4,000 to cement the deal. He had been a servant to Villa for almost ten years, making close to 150 appearances, among them a Wembley League Cup final defeat by Spurs in 1971. An unsung hero, Bradley rarely had a bad game. He finished his League career in 1976, returning to the Midlands. He coached Birmingham in the 1980s.

Season	League			FA Cup			League Cup			Other			Total		
	Aps	Sub	Gls	Aps	Sub	Gls	Aps	Sub	Gls	Aps	Sub	Gls	Aps	Sub	Gls
1972-73	23			1									24		
1973-74	36			4			2						42		
1974-75	38			7		1	1						46		1
1975-76	9	3			1		3						12	4	
Total	106	3		12	1	1	6						124	4	1

BRADSHAW, Darren Shaun
Defender/Midfielder   Sheffield, 19 March 1967

Tall, comfortable in possession, Bradshaw was equally at home in defence or midfield during Posh's two First Division seasons in the 1990s. Starting his League career with Chesterfield in 1987, Darren had spells with York and Newcastle before signing for Posh on a free transfer in August 1992. He had to wait before claiming a regular place in Chris Turner's promoted side, but played 34 League games in his first season before becoming a consistent force during the 1993-94 relegation battle. Bradshaw announced his intention to leave after the drop was confirmed and, following a loan spell with Plymouth, signed for Blackpool for £35,000 in October 1994. Three years later he joined Rushden & Diamonds, where he made almost 100 Conference appearances before switching to Stevenage in February 2001. A further move took Darren to Worksop in time for the 2001-02 season.

Season	League			FA Cup			League Cup			Other			Total		
	Aps	Sub	Gls	Aps	Sub	Gls	Aps	Sub	Gls	Aps	Sub	Gls	Aps	Sub	Gls
1992-93	32	2		3			1						36	2	
1993-94	38	1	1	1			6		1	2			47	1	2
Total	70	3	1	4			7		1	2			83	3	2

BRADSHAW, Paul William
Goalkeeper   Altrincham, 28 April 1956

A highly regarded teenager at Blackburn, Bradshaw earned England Under-21 honours before moving to Wolves for £150,000 in September 1977. He played 200 League games for Wolves and had two spells with WBA either side of stints with Bristol Rovers, Newport, and Walsall, where he also acted as coach. After signing for Posh in September 1990 and debuting in a 1-3 League Cup defeat at QPR, Paul played a major role in helping the side gain promotion to Division Three in 1990-91, whereupon he surprisingly retired from League football. A spell at Kettering followed before he took up employment with one of his former clubs, Wolves, as a security supervisor.

Season	League			FA Cup			League Cup			Other			Total		
	Aps	Sub	Gls	Aps	Sub	Gls	Aps	Sub	Gls	Aps	Sub	Gls	Aps	Sub	Gls
1990-91	39			5			2			1			47		

BREEN, Gary Patrick
Central Defender   London, 12 December 1973

A Londoner of Irish descent, Breen gained Republic of Ireland Under-21 caps whilst at London Road. A tall, elegant central defender who could bring the ball forward, this former Maidstone and Gillingham man was seen as one of manager John Still's better signings when costing £70,000 in August 1994. He played well in the Posh rearguard until February 1996, when Barry Fry poached him for Birmingham in a deal that saw Ken Charley return to Posh for a third spell. Gary soon gained full international honours, and a year later he moved up again, signing for Premier League Coventry. While some may have been surprised at the speed of his rise, his confident displays in a Sky Blue shirt made him a regular for the Republic of Ireland, for whom he starred, and scored against Saudi Arabia, in the 2002 World Cup finals.

Season	League			FA Cup			League Cup			Other			Total		
	Aps	Sub	Gls	Aps	Sub	Gls	Aps	Sub	Gls	Aps	Sub	Gls	Aps	Sub	Gls
1994-95	43	1	1	2			2			3		1	50	1	2
1995-96	25			4			4			3			36		
Total	68	1	1	6			6			6		1	86	1	2

BREMNER, Kevin Johnston
Forward   *Banff, 7 October 1957*

Younger brother of former Aston Villa star Des, Kevin Bremner set a Football League record in 1982-83 when scoring for five different clubs. He would find the net consistently during a much-travelled career that took him to Colchester, Millwall, Reading and Brighton amongst others, before joining Posh in July 1990. London Road fans never saw the best of him as his twelve-month stay was plagued by injury. After scoring three times in League Cup-ties with Fulham and again on his home debut against Carlisle – a string of injuries sidelined him for most of the season. He returned to his native Scotland in July 1991 to join Dundee but by 1995 was youth-team coach at Gillingham.

Season	League			FA Cup			League Cup			Other			Total		
	Aps	Sub	Gls	Aps	Sub	Gls	Aps	Sub	Gls	Aps	Sub	Gls	Aps	Sub	Gls
1990-91	13	4	3	3			2		3	2			20	4	6

BRISSETT, Jason Curtis
Winger   *Redbridge, 7 September 1974*

Much was expected of this tricky wide player, who began as an Arsenal trainee. He arrived at London Road on a free transfer in June 1993. A petulant character, he was nearly thrown out after repeated disciplinary problems, but was reprieved by Posh boss Lil Fuccillo. Dogged by inconsistency, Brissett's finest moment in a Posh shirt came on 8 January 1994 when he scored the goal that nearly knocked Spurs out of the FA Cup before a full house at London Road. Such bounty was rare, and Jason joined Second Division Bournemouth in December 1994. He graced Wembley in the 1998 Auto-Windscreen final, and has also served Walsall, Cheltenham, Leyton Orient and Stevenage.

Season	League			FA Cup			League Cup			Other			Total		
	Aps	Sub	Gls	Aps	Sub	Gls	Aps	Sub	Gls	Aps	Sub	Gls	Aps	Sub	Gls
1993-94	23	7		2		1	4	1	1	2			31	8	2
1994-95	4	1			1		1			1	1	1	6	3	1
Total	27	8		2	1	1	5	1	1	3	1	1	37	11	3

BROOKES, Eric

Left-back   *Mapplewell, 3 February 1944*

Eric was a former England youth and schoolboy international who came through the ranks at Barnsley, where he played 325 League games during the 1960s. He had two seasons at Northampton before ending his professional career at London Road. He made his Posh debut against Southend on the opening day of 1971-72 and stayed until 1973, when Noel Cantwell released him on a free transfer. He subsequently appeared for March Town and Ely City. Eric still lives in Peterborough, employed by local engineering firm Perkins.

Season	League			FA Cup			League Cup			Other			Total		
	Aps	Sub	Gls	Aps	Sub	Gls	Aps	Sub	Gls	Aps	Sub	Gls	Aps	Sub	Gls
1971-72	18	1		4			1						23	1	
1972-73	23		1	3			1						27		1
Total	41	1	1	7			2						50	1	1

BROUGHTON, Drewe Oliver

Forward   *Hitchin, 25 October 1978*

Unwanted by Norwich, for whom he had scored once in nine League games, Broughton was pursued by Posh and Third Division rivals Brentford, with the Bees winning the race for the 20-year-old's signature in October 1998. Bizarrely, Drewe signed for Posh a month later, having made just one sub appearance for Ron Noades' team. Tall, athletic and a willing runner, he was pitched into the first team by Barry Fry, alongside fellow newcomer Steve Butler and loanee striker Leon McKenzie in a three-pronged attack. Three goals in five games suggested Drewe might boost Posh's promotion bid, but injuries and loss of form saw him warming the substitutes' bench towards the end of the season. He made little impact during 1999-2000 and spent the latter part of the season on loan to Nuneaton Borough. The following season saw Drewe loaned to Dagenham & Redbridge, Stevenage, and Kidderminster, who bought him for £50,000 in February 2001.

Season	League			FA Cup			League Cup			Other			Total		
	Aps	Sub	Gls	Aps	Sub	Gls	Aps	Sub	Gls	Aps	Sub	Gls	Aps	Sub	Gls
1998-99	14	11	7							1	1	1	15	12	8
1999-00	5	5	1				2						7	5	1
Total	19	16	8				2			1	1	1	22	17	9

BRYANT, Paul

Right-back   *Bromley, 10 January 1969*

A former Bretton Woods schoolboy, Paul signed YTS forms for Posh in 1985. He made his only first-team appearance in the closing weeks of 1985-86 when John Wile let him loose in a Freight Rover Trophy home tie against Aldershot. Impressive displays at youth and reserve-team level earned Bryant a professional contract, but he was released in November 1987 with Posh in financial crisis. He served Stamford and King's Lynn before a two-year spell with Finnish side Oravais IF. After returning to England in 1991, Paul enhanced his reputation in non-League circles, helping Stamford lift the United Counties League title in 1997 and 1998, before moving on to Yaxley and Blackstones.

Season	League			FA Cup			League Cup			Other			Total		
	Aps	Sub	Gls	Aps	Sub	Gls	Aps	Sub	Gls	Aps	Sub	Gls	Aps	Sub	Gls
1985-86										1			1		

BUCHANAN, David
Forward   *Newcastle, 23 June 1962*

A tricky little forward, Buchanan burst on to the scene aged 16 with Leicester at the same time as Gary Lineker, but Buchanan's progress was dogged by injury. He totalled 33 League games, scoring seven goals, before arriving at London Road on a free transfer in August 1983 via a loan spell at Northampton. A debut goal in a 3-1 Posh win against Hartlepool on the opening day was followed by two more in a 3-0 success against Mansfield. But John Wile soon opted for the power of new signings Ray Hankin and Alan Waddle over Buchanan's more cunning style. The young striker then fell victim to a leg fracture. Released in the summer, Dave resurrected himself with Blyth Spartans which prompted a return to League action with Sunderland, for whom he top-scored in 1986-87. Released from Roker in 1988, he joined York, prior to ending his career with Newcastle Blue Star and Whitley Bay.

Season	League			FA Cup			League Cup			Other			Total		
	Aps	Sub	Gls	Aps	Sub	Gls	Aps	Sub	Gls	Aps	Sub	Gls	Aps	Sub	Gls
1983-84	13	3	4	1			4			1			18	4	4

BULLARD, James (Jimmy)
Midfielder   *Newham, 23 October 1978*

London-born Bullard arrived at London Road on a free transfer from West Ham in July 2001. An energetic midfielder whose strength and stamina belies his slight frame, Jimmy was a big hit in his first season. Debuting at Swindon on the opening day of 2001-02, Jimmy was relegated to the bench for the next half-dozen matches but following a fine display in a League Cup-tie with Coventry he became a regular. Fans warmed to his industry and passing skills, not to mention his knack of scoring from distance. Long-range strikes against Bournemouth, Bristol City and Wrexham – all scored within ten days in September – alerted bigger clubs to Jimmy's talents, but despite interest from Ipswich and Leicester, he remained at London Road to become one of Barry Fry's best ever signings.

Season	League			FA Cup			League Cup			Other			Total		
	Aps	Sub	Gls	Aps	Sub	Gls	Aps	Sub	Gls	Aps	Sub	Gls	Aps	Sub	Gls
2001-02	36	4	8	5		1	1			2		2	44	4	11

BULLIMORE, Wayne Alan
Midfielder   *Mansfield, 12 September 1970*

A ball-playing midfielder, Bullimore was signed by Barry Fry in March 1997 on a free transfer from Bradford City, having served Barnsley, Stockport, and Scunthorpe after failing to make the grade at Manchester United. Despite showing nice touches when given a central midfield role, Wayne had few opportunities at London Road. With just a few games under his belt, he returned north to Scarborough in March 1998, then dropped out of the Football League to join Barrow.

Season	League			FA Cup			League Cup			Other			Total		
	Aps	Sub	Gls	Aps	Sub	Gls	Aps	Sub	Gls	Aps	Sub	Gls	Aps	Sub	Gls
1996-97	2	4											2	4	
1997-98	8	7	1		1			3			1		9	11	1
Total	10	11	1		1			3			1		11	15	1

BURTON, Kenneth Owen (Ollie)
Full-back   *Sheffield, 11 February 1950*

One of the first of Noel Cantwell's many loan signings, Burton had four outings in March 1973 before returning to his home-town team Sheffield Wednesday. He later made his mark at Chesterfield, playing 237 League games between 1973 and 1979. He spent 1980-81 with Halifax before hanging up his boots. He is now a Sheffield postman.

Season	League			FA Cup			League Cup			Other			Total		
	Aps	Sub	Gls	Aps	Sub	Gls	Aps	Sub	Gls	Aps	Sub	Gls	Aps	Sub	Gls
1972-73	3	1											3	1	

BUTLER, Geoffrey (Geoff)
Full-back   *Middlesbrough, 29 September 1946*

Peter Morris brought this experienced 34-year-old to London Road as player-coach. Geoff had signed for his local club Middlesbrough in 1964 and served Chelsea and Sunderland before enjoying longer spells with Norwich and Bournemouth, from where Posh poached him in August 1981. His first appearance came at Hull the following month and he established himself at right-back prior to leaving London Road, along with Morris, at the end of 1981-82. In February 1983, Geoff became manager of Salisbury, a job he held until his dismissal in 2001.

Season	League			FA Cup			League Cup			Other			Total		
	Aps	Sub	Gls	Aps	Sub	Gls	Aps	Sub	Gls	Aps	Sub	Gls	Aps	Sub	Gls
1981-82	39			3									42		

BUTLER, Steven (Steve)
Forward   *Birmingham, 27 January 1962*

A former Cambridge United favourite, veteran front-man Steve Butler struggled after joining Posh as player-coach in November 1998. Asked to replace Jimmy Quinn as target-man, Butler arrived with 120 League goals under his belt from his time with Brentford, Maidstone, Watford, Cambridge and Gillingham. Although his link-up play was good, he rarely posed a goalscoring threat and the crowd turned on him. Barry Fry stayed faithful until February 1999, when Butler was loaned to Stevenage. Butler joined Gillingham as player-coach for 1999-2000 and scored a Wembley play-off goal that took the Gills to Division One. Butler later followed Gills' manager Peter Taylor to Leicester.

Season	League			FA Cup			League Cup			Other			Total		
	Aps	Sub	Gls	Aps	Sub	Gls	Aps	Sub	Gls	Aps	Sub	Gls	Aps	Sub	Gls
1998-99	13	1	2	1						1		1	15	1	3

BUTLIN, Barry Desmond
Forward   *Roliston, 9 November 1949*

Butlin joined Posh in August 1977, listing Derby, Notts County, Luton, Nottingham Forest, Brighton and Reading as former clubs. A striker of slender frame, he spent two mediocre seasons at London Road, despite scoring four goals in his first six games. Following relegation to the Fourth Division in 1978-79, Butlin spend two seasons with Sheffield United. He now works as a financial adviser in Nottingham.

Season	League			FA Cup			League Cup			Other			Total		
	Aps	Sub	Gls	Aps	Sub	Gls	Aps	Sub	Gls	Aps	Sub	Gls	Aps	Sub	Gls
1977-78	34		7	3			2						39		7
1978-79	30		5	1		1	7		1				38		7
Total	64		12	4		1	9		1				77		14

BUTTERWORTH, Garry
Left-back   *Whittlesey, 8 September 1969*

Butterworth was a local discovery from Whittlesey who came through the ranks. He began as a YTS player in 1986-87, making his League debut in a 1-1 draw at Halifax on the last day of the season. He played more frequently the next season and was given a professional contract in June 1988, winning a regular place in 1989-90, from when he made rapid progress. He was voted Player of the Season in 1990-91, after switching from midfield to left-back. The following season was perhaps the most successful in Posh history, but not for Butterworth, who was dropped in favour of new signing Ronnie Robinson. An unused substitute 24 times that season, Garry was released to Dagenham & Redbridge after Posh's 1992 play-off success. Two years later Rushden & Diamonds paid £20,000 to take him to Nene Park, where he earned international recognition with England's semi-professional side. Garry was instrumental in the Diamonds winning the Conference in 2001.

Season	League			FA Cup			League Cup			Other			Total		
	Aps	Sub	Gls	Aps	Sub	Gls	Aps	Sub	Gls	Aps	Sub	Gls	Aps	Sub	Gls
1986-87		1												1	
1987-88	6	5									2		6	7	
1988-89	6	2											6	2	
1989-90	29	10	2	3						3			35	10	2
1990-91	46			5			4			1			56		
1991-92	14	5	1		1		4	1		2	3		20	10	1
Total	101	23	3	8	1		8	1		6	5		123	30	3

BYATT, Dennis John

Central Defender   Hillingdon, 8 August 1958

A free-transfer from Fulham, Byatt spent 1978-79 with Posh but made
little impact. Released by Peter Morris in the summer, he switched to
Northampton where he fared better, making 47 League appearances in
two seasons. He joined Wealdstone in 1981 and captained them in
1985 to an unprecedented double of FA Trophy and Gola League title.

Season	League			FA Cup			League Cup			Other			Total		
	Aps	Sub	Gls	Aps	Sub	Gls	Aps	Sub	Gls	Aps	Sub	Gls	Aps	Sub	Gls
1978-79	2	1											2	1	

BYRNE, Johnny

Inside-forward   Cambuslang, 25 May 1939

Byrne arrived at London Road as a little-known front player in 1965,
having been a nondescript player with Preston, Tranmere, Barnsley,
Hibs and Queen of the South. Posh chief Gordon Clark obviously saw
potential and his faith was vindicated when Byrne hit three hat-tricks
within the first two months of 1965-66 – two of them in the run to the
semi-final of the League Cup. He also bagged 19 League goals that season, which helped fans recover from the departure of Derek Dougan.
Although the goals never again flowed so freely, Byrne formed a useful partnership with John Fairbrother and was ever present from April
1966 until his farewell in December 1967 – a run of 89 League and Cup
games. He joined Northampton in a player exchange with Jim Hall.

Season	League			FA Cup			League Cup			Other			Total		
	Aps	Sub	Gls	Aps	Sub	Gls	Aps	Sub	Gls	Aps	Sub	Gls	Aps	Sub	Gls
1965-66	36	1	19	1			6		6				43	1	25
1966-67	46		6	4		1	3		1				53		8
1967-68	24		3	1		1	1		1				26		5
Total	106	1	28	6		2	10		8				122	1	38

Ernie Moss v Rotherham, August 1976

Bert Murray v Middlesbrough
FA Cup, February 1975

Jon Nixon scores against Middlesbrough in the FA Cup, February 1975

Andy Parkinson

Tony Adcock v Tranmere, May 1993

Martin Carruthers

Richard Forsyth

Steve Earle (left) v Barnet in the FA Cup, November 1977

Jimmy Quinn v Scunthorpe
August 1997   Jim Walker

CAMP, Steven (Steve)

Forward   *Manchester, 8 February 1954*

One of John Barnwell's first signings, teenage striker Steve Camp had served Leatherhead and Fulham, for whom he played five League games. The former bank clerk got off to a flying debut with Posh when scoring twice in a 4-1 League Cup defeat of Bradford City in August 1977, but the signing of Barry Butlin meant Camp saw little first-team action. He returned briefly in March 1978, scoring his only League goal in a 1-0 home win over Colchester. Released by Posh in 1978, Camp rejoined Leatherhead. He is now a bank manager in Sutton, Surrey.

Season	League			FA Cup			League Cup			Other			Total		
	Aps	Sub	Gls	Aps	Sub	Gls	Aps	Sub	Gls	Aps	Sub	Gls	Aps	Sub	Gls
1977-78	6	1	1				3		2				9	1	3

CARMICHAEL, John (Jack)

Central Defender   *Newcastle, 11 November 1948*

A great servant to Posh, Carmichael cost a bargain £4,000 from Arsenal in January 1971. In a London Road career spanning 12 years, 'Jolly Jack' made over 400 appearances for the club – a total bettered only by Tommy Robson. Although born in Newcastle, Jack, whose grandfather played for Clyde and Sunderland, moved to Glasgow aged two and was spotted by the Gunners playing for junior club Possil Park. Despite skippering Arsenal's reserves to two Football Combination titles, Bertie Mee let him leave for Posh, initially on loan. Debuting in a 1-0 victory over Southport, he was ever-present in his first two full seasons, forming a strong central defensive partnership with Chris Turner, and appointed club captain. Jack compensated for any lack of finesse with relentless enthusiasm, consistency and terrific will to win. He missed out on a Fourth Division championship medal in 1973-74 – understudying Mick Jones – but regained his place to earn the Player of the Season award in the next two seasons. In 1976-77 he again played in every match and reached another milestone when, having switched to midfield, he broke his goalscoring duck. That strike, in a 4-0 FA Cup win at Tranmere, was followed a week later by his first League goal, at home to Sheffield Wednesday. In the early 1980s Jack followed former boss Noel Cantwell to play for New England Teamen, but returned to Posh in January 1983. He later served non-League Stamford, whom he briefly managed in 1990-91. More recently Jack was landlord of the King's Head public house in Weldon, near Corby.

Season	League			FA Cup			League Cup			Other			Total		
	Aps	Sub	Gls	Aps	Sub	Gls	Aps	Sub	Gls	Aps	Sub	Gls	Aps	Sub	Gls
1970-71	17												17		
1971-72	46			4			1						51		
1972-73	46			4			1						51		
1973-74	9	13		1	3		1						10	17	

Season	League			FA Cup			League Cup			Other			Total		
	Aps	Sub	Gls	Aps	Sub	Gls	Aps	Sub	Gls	Aps	Sub	Gls	Aps	Sub	Gls
1974-75	33	2		8									41	2	
1975-76	45	1		5			4						54	1	
1976-77	46		4	2		1	5						53		5
1977-78	27	3		4		1	4						35	3	1
1978-79	25	2		1			7						33	2	
1979-80	37		1	1			6						44		1
1982-83	5	1											5	1	
Total	336	22	5	30	3	2	28		1				394	26	7

CARR, Ashley

Midfielder   *Crowland, 15 August 1968*

Progressing through the ranks, Ashley was given his League debut by Noel Cantwell at Halifax on the last day of 1986-87. A tidy midfielder with good skills, Carr proved a useful squad member over the next two seasons before being released. He went on to be a successful non-League player with Holbeach, Wisbech and Raunds Town.

Season	League			FA Cup			League Cup			Other			Total		
	Aps	Sub	Gls	Aps	Sub	Gls	Aps	Sub	Gls	Aps	Sub	Gls	Aps	Sub	Gls
1986-87	1												1		
1987-88	8	5		1		1	1		1	1	2	1	11	9	1
1988-89		1								1			1	1	
Total	9	6		1		1	1		1	2	2	1	13	10	1

CARRUTHERS, Martin George

Forward   *Nottingham, 7 August 1972*

A former Aston Villa apprentice, pacy striker Carruthers arrived in November 1996 from Stoke, who had signed him from Villa for £300,000 three years earlier. Fry paid Stoke just £75,000 and Martin looked a bargain. Hard-working and full of running, he made a quick impact before injury ruled him out of the last three months of the 1996-97 relegation season. The following season he built a devastating partnership with veteran Jimmy Quinn, equalling Jim Hall's club record of scoring in six consecutive League games. But as Posh's form dipped after Christmas, so Martin's goals dried up and injury struck again. Struggling for form in 1998-99, he was loaned out to York before joining Darlington for an undisclosed fee on transfer deadline day. He was on the move again six months later, joining Southend, where he finished 1999-2000 as top scorer with 19 goals in all competitions. Martin has since joined for Scunthorpe in a £20,000 deal.

Season	League			FA Cup			League Cup			Other			Total		
	Aps	Sub	Gls	Aps	Sub	Gls	Aps	Sub	Gls	Aps	Sub	Gls	Aps	Sub	Gls
1996-97	13	1	4	3		2				2			18	1	6
1997-98	37	2	15	3		2	3	1	1	3			46	3	18
1998-99	13	1	2				2		1	1			16	1	3
Total	63	4	21	6		4	5	1	2	6			80	5	27

CARTER, Darren Stephen (Danny)
> *Winger*   *Hackney, 29 June 1969*

Discovered playing for non-League Billericay Town in 1988, Danny made over 200 League and Cup appearances for Leyton Orient before John Still signed him for £25,000 in June 1995. The winger suffered with injuries and a loss of form during his two years with Posh. Given few opportunities under Barry Fry, Carter left the club in 1997, taking his talents to Wales with Barry Town and Merthyr Tydfil.

Season	League Aps	Sub	Gls	FA Cup Aps	Sub	Gls	League Cup Aps	Sub	Gls	Other Aps	Sub	Gls	Total Aps	Sub	Gls
1995-96	30	7	1	2			3			3			38	7	1
1996-97	3	5			1			2					3	8	
Total	33	12	1	2	1		3	2		3			41	15	1

CARTER, Ian Noel
> *Full-back*   *Birmingham, 20 September 1967*

Born in England, Carter was raised in Canada, whom he represented in the 1994 World Cup qualifiers. A resolute defender with two good feet, he signed in January 1994 from Toronto Blizzard and debuted in a 0-1 home defeat by Wolves. He returned to Canada that summer.

Season	League Aps	Sub	Gls	FA Cup Aps	Sub	Gls	League Cup Aps	Sub	Gls	Other Aps	Sub	Gls	Total Aps	Sub	Gls
1993-94	9	2		1									10	2	

CASSELLS, Keith Barrington
> *Forward*   *Islington, 17 July 1957*

London-born Cassells played eight games for Peter Morris's side in early 1980 while on loan from Watford. A fast, skilful front-man, he found success with Oxford the following season. This paved the way in March 1982 for a big-money move to Southampton, for whom he played 19 First Division games, before ending his career in the lower Leagues with Brentford and Mansfield. Keith is now in the police force.

Season	League Aps	Sub	Gls	FA Cup Aps	Sub	Gls	League Cup Aps	Sub	Gls	Other Aps	Sub	Gls	Total Aps	Sub	Gls
1979-80	8												8		

CASSIDY, Francis James Augustine
> *Midfielder*   *Watford, 20 August 1964*

Francis spent two fruitless years with his home-town club, Watford, prior to his free-transfer signing by John Wile in August 1984. An unused sub for the first game of 1984-85, Francis debuted a week later in a 0-1 League defeat at Hereford. He enjoyed considerable success that season, popping up in forward positions to score goals. He lost his place for much of 1985-86, though he replaced injured skipper Trevor

Quow during that season's cup run. Cassidy later served non-League Bishop's Stortford, Aylesbury, Yeading and Hemel Hempstead.

Season	League			FA Cup			League Cup			Other			Total		
	Aps	Sub	Gls	Aps	Sub	Gls	Aps	Sub	Gls	Aps	Sub	Gls	Aps	Sub	Gls
1984-85	31		7	1			1		1				33		8
1985-86	13	2	2	6		1	1			1		1	21	3	3
Total	44	2	9	7		1	2		1	1		1	54	3	11

CASTLE, Stephen Charles (Steve)
Midfielder   *Ilford, 17 May 1966*

Arriving as player-coach from Barry Fry's former club, Birmingham, in May 1997, Castle – a committed performer – had gained much experience with Leyton Orient and Plymouth. He debuted for Posh as captain in the 0-1 home defeat by Scunthorpe on the opening day of 1997-98. Plagued by injury, he reserved his best displays for Sky TV, scoring twice in an FA Cup-tie at Swansea, then heading the winner at home to League leaders Notts County. He was influential in midfield in 1998-99, alongside home-grown kids Simon Davies and Matthew Etherington, and further endeared himself to the fans with a long-range goal in the home win over rivals Cambridge. Dubbed 'Captain Marvel' by Fry, Castle's grit, not to mention his vital goals from midfield, helped lead the club into Division Two in 1999-2000. Out of contract after the Wembley play-off final, and with former club Leyton Orient wanting to recruit him, Castle returned to Brisbane Road.

Season	League			FA Cup			League Cup			Other			Total		
	Aps	Sub	Gls	Aps	Sub	Gls	Aps	Sub	Gls	Aps	Sub	Gls	Aps	Sub	Gls
1997-98	34	3	3	2	1	2	4			2	1	1	42	5	6
1998-99	26		4	1			1	1		1			29	1	4
1999-00	36	4	10	1			2			3			42	4	10
Total	96	7	17	4	1	2	7	1		6	1	1	113	10	20

CAVENER, Philip (Phil)
Winger   *Tynemouth, 2 June 1961*

A fair-haired winger, Cavener started with Burnley in the late 1970s. He was loaned to Bradford City and briefly served Gillingham before joining Northampton in August 1984. After nearly 50 League games for the Cobblers he joined Posh on a non-contract basis in March 1986. His stay was brief. He went to Kettering, then became assistant manager at Arlesey. Phil now runs a health centre and lives in Sandy, Beds.

Season	League			FA Cup			League Cup			Other			Total		
	Aps	Sub	Gls	Aps	Sub	Gls	Aps	Sub	Gls	Aps	Sub	Gls	Aps	Sub	Gls
1985-86	9	1								1			10	1	

CHAPPLE, Philip Richard (Phil)

Central Defender   Norwich, 26 November 1966

Norwich-born Phil began his career at Carrow Road but it was only after a move to Cambridge United in March 1988 that he came to prominence. He was a key member of the U's side under John Beck in the early 1990s, winning a Third Division championship medal in 1990-91. After 187 League appearances for Posh's closest rivals, he moved to Charlton in a £100,000 deal in August 1993. Vastly experienced, a fine tackler and dominant in the air, Chapple came to Posh as a free transfer in June 1998. Injuries kept him out throughout 1998-99, apart from League and Auto Windscreen victories over Leyton Orient in December. Chapple tasted action at the start of 1999-2000, before further injuries struck. Accepting that his playing days were over, he switched to coaching the reserves in 2000-01 before being promoted to first-team coach following Wayne Turner's resignation in March 2002.

Season	League			FA Cup			League Cup			Other			Total		
	Aps	Sub	Gls	Aps	Sub	Gls	Aps	Sub	Gls	Aps	Sub	Gls	Aps	Sub	Gls
1998-99	1									1			2		
1999-00	15	1	1	1						1			17	1	1
Total	16	1	1	1						2			19	1	1

CHARD, Philip John (Phil)

Midfielder/Full-back   Corby, 16 October 1960

Progressing through the ranks, Corby lad Chard first played in Posh's first team as an 18-year-old in 1979. He notched almost 200 appearances in various positions before signing for Northampton in August 1985. After starting in midfield, Chard was converted to right-back by John Wile in 1983-84, when he also became an ace penalty taker. He continued in defence in his last season with Posh, but reverted to midfield – a role Chard preferred – after joining the Cobblers. Ironically, his first game for his new club was a League Cup-tie at London Road. Phil helped Northampton storm to the Fourth Division championship in 1987, before playing a small part in Wolves' revival. In October 1989 he returned to Northampton, where he later had a spell as manager.

Season	League			FA Cup			League Cup			Other			Total		
	Aps	Sub	Gls	Aps	Sub	Gls	Aps	Sub	Gls	Aps	Sub	Gls	Aps	Sub	Gls
1978-79	5	1	1										5	1	1
1979-80	15	5	2	1			4	1	1				20	6	3
1981-82	31	8	3	3		1	1	1					35	9	4
1982-83	39	5	4	2			4						45	5	4
1983-84	38		7	1			4		1	1			44		8
1984-85	25		1	2			2						29		1
Total	153	19	18	9		1	15	2	2	1			178	21	21

CHARLERY, Kenneth Leroy (Ken)

Forward *Stepney, 28 November 1964*

Two fine goals at Wembley in May 1992 elevated Charlery to hero status. Fans christened him 'King Kenny'. Signed with Gary Cooper from Maidstone in March 1991, Ken began the first of three spells with Posh, struggling to break into the side that ended 1990-91 with promotion to the old Third Division. Although signed as a winger, the former Fisher Athletic, Billericay and Beckton player emerged as a potent striker the following season, opening his account in a 2-1 League Cup win at Wimbledon. After scoring the winner against Newcastle in the next round, Ken's rich form continued throughout Posh's greatest ever season – culminating in his Wembley play-off destruction of Stockport. Chris Turner's side made a strong start in the new Division One, but Charlery was unexpectedly sold to Watford in October 1992 for a club record £350,000. He stayed a year at Vicarage Road – scoring 13 League goals in 48 games for the Hornets – but was back with Posh in December 1993 to assist their futile fight against the drop. In 1994-95 he was top scorer and winner of the Player of the Season award – adding to the one he received in 1992. Although in his 30s, Charlery appeared in his prime, so his departure in July 1995 to Barry Fry's Birmingham came as a blow, despite the £350,000 fee received. But after just 17 League games for Birmingham, he returned to Posh again in February 1996, signed as player-coach by Mick Halsall in a deal that saw defender Gary Breen move to St Andrews. Kenny's third and least successful stint at London Road saw a run of 24 goalless League games and brought about his sale to Stockport in March 1997. He played ten times for County before becoming Barnet's record signing that summer. Ken scored 38 League goals in 124 appearances for the Bees and made a late entry on the international stage with St Lucia before winding down his career with Boston United and Dagenham & Redbridge. His form in the Conference earned him further international recognition, this time representing England's semi-professional team.

Season	League Aps	Sub	Gls	FA Cup Aps	Sub	Gls	League Cup Aps	Sub	Gls	Other Aps	Sub	Gls	Total Aps	Sub	Gls
1990-91	2	2											2	2	
1991-92	33	4	16	3		1	6		2	11		7	53	4	26
1992-93	10		3				4		3	1			15		6
1993-94	26		8	1	1	1							27	1	9
1994-95	44		16	1		2	2			1		1	48		19
1995-96	19		7							1			20		7
1996-97	36	1	5	6		6	4		1	5		1	51	1	13
Total	170	7	55	11	1	10	16		6	19		9	216	8	80

CHRISTIE, Derrick Hugh Michael

Winger *Bletchley, 15 March 1957*

A speedy wide-man capable of operating on either flank, Christie's injuries restricted his chances. Signed from Cardiff in August 1986, he had made his mark with Northampton and Cambridge, playing over 100 games for each. His Posh debut came in a League Cup-tie at Colchester, but after a few more games he was released in the summer. He works as a government clerk, living in Deeping St James.

Season	League			FA Cup			League Cup			Other			Total		
	Aps	Sub	Gls	Aps	Sub	Gls	Aps	Sub	Gls	Aps	Sub	Gls	Aps	Sub	Gls
1986-87	6	2		1			1	1			1		8	4	

CLAMP, Harold Edward (Eddie)
Wing-half   *Coalville, 14 September 1934, Died 1995*
Former England international Eddie Clamp spent six months with Posh in the twilight of a career that saw him win two League championship medals with Wolves in the late 1950s. He also served Arsenal and Stoke before appearing for Posh in 1964-65. Unable to turn back the clock, Clamp was released on a free transfer by Gordon Clark and joined Worcester City. On retiring from football, Eddie worked as a self-employed builder in Wolverhampton. He died in December 1995.

Season	League			FA Cup			League Cup			Other			Total		
	Aps	Sub	Gls	Aps	Sub	Gls	Aps	Sub	Gls	Aps	Sub	Gls	Aps	Sub	Gls
1964-65	8												8		

CLARK, Simon
Defender   *Boston, 12 March 1967*
A late starter, Clark debuted aged 27 in a 1-4 defeat at Bristol City in the final match of 1993-94. A no-nonsense competitor, he learned his trade with non-League Boston, Holbeach, King's Lynn, Hendon and Stevenage before becoming John Still's first signing. Clark performed various defensive roles before Barry Fry sold him for a nominal fee to Leyton Orient in June 1997. Simon made 98 League appearances for the O's before joining Colchester on a free transfer in June 2000. At London Road in 2000-01 he was sent off in Colchester's 1-3 defeat.

Season	League			FA Cup			League Cup			Other			Total		
	Aps	Sub	Gls	Aps	Sub	Gls	Aps	Sub	Gls	Aps	Sub	Gls	Aps	Sub	Gls
1993-94	1												1		
1994-95	32			2			2				1		37	1	
1995-96	39	1	1	4			3			4		1	49	1	2
1996-97	30	4	2	6						3			39	4	2
Total	102	5	3	12			5			7	1	1	126	6	4

CLARKE, Andrew Weston (Andy)
Forward   *Islington, 22 July 1967*
Andy Clarke became part of Posh folklore when scoring the goal that clinched promotion to Division Two at Wembley in May 2000. His winner against Darlington was the 18th goal by the ex-Wimbledon

striker in a successful first season with Posh. Barry Fry got his man in May 1999 after the pacy forward had been loaned to Port Vale and Northampton. Clarke joined the Dons from Fry's Barnet in February 1991 for £250,000 – a then record fee for a non-League player – and scored 17 times in 171 Premiership appearances, more than half as substitute. A hamstring injury delayed his Posh debut until coming on as sub at Mansfield in September. His first goal was an unstoppable 30-yard looping drive against Brighton in the FA Cup. Posh fans took to Clarke's hard-working, spirited play, while opposing defenders were perplexed by his pace and skill. Although losing form in 2000-01, Clarke's eleven goals were exceeded only by Leon McKenzie. In February 2002 Clarke learned he had tested positive for cannabis following a random drug test carried out after Posh's Christmas game at Cambridge. He escaped with a two-month ban after the authorities took into account his previously exemplary record. Fry responded by offering a three-year contract which the player signed in May 2002.

Season	League			FA Cup			League Cup			Other			Total		
	Aps	Sub	Gls	Aps	Sub	Gls	Aps	Sub	Gls	Aps	Sub	Gls	Aps	Sub	Gls
1999-00	33	4	15	2		1				4		2	39	4	18
2000-01	36	6	9	4		1	1		1	1			42	6	11
2001-02	19	9	5	5	1	2	1	1	1	1			26	11	8
Total	88	19	29	11	1	4	2	1	2	6		2	107	21	37

CLARKE, Colin John

Forward   *Newry, 30 October 1962*

Few could have predicted what lay ahead for Clarke while the young Irishman was learning his trade over three indifferent years at London Road. Signed as a teenager by Peter Morris in July 1981, after impressing for Ipswich against Posh in Tommy Robson's testimonial, Clarke never really showed his potential. After being loaned to Gillingham, he joined Tranmere on a free transfer in July 1984, whereupon his career took off. Clarke bagged 22 League goals and, after hitting a further 26 for Third Division Bournemouth the following season, he went to the 1986 World Cup in Mexico with Northern Ireland. His displays in those finals led to a £400,000 move to First Division Southampton in June 1986. Undaunted by top-flight defences, Clarke scored 20 League goals in his first season at The Dell, including a hat-trick on his debut against QPR. He later signed for QPR for a club record £800,000, using his strength and power to good effect, before finishing his League career back on the south coast with Portsmouth. Colin made the last of his 38 international appearances in 1992, by which time his 13 goals had established a new record for Northern Ireland. After quitting football to run a restaurant near Newbury, Berkshire, Colin returned to the game as coach to American clubs San Jose Flash and Dallas Burn.

Season	League Aps	Sub	Gls	FA Cup Aps	Sub	Gls	League Cup Aps	Sub	Gls	Other Aps	Sub	Gls	Total Aps	Sub	Gls
1981-82	22	5	4				2						24	5	4
1982-83	37		9	4		2	1		1				42		12
1983-84	17	1	5				4	1	1				22	1	6
Total	76	6	18	4		2	7	2	1				88	6	22

CLARKE, Lee

Forward   *Peterborough, 28 July 1983*

The son of former Posh and Northern Ireland striker Colin Clarke, Peterborough-born Lee was signed from United Counties League outfit Yaxley in November 2001 after a three-month trial period. Strong in possession and good with both feet, Clarke has regularly found the net for the Under-19 and reserve sides. He made his first-team debut as a sub in an Auto Windscreens fixture at Bristol City in December 2001, before coming on in a Second Division game at Colchester that month.

Season	League Aps	Sub	Gls	FA Cup Aps	Sub	Gls	League Cup Aps	Sub	Gls	Other Aps	Sub	Gls	Total Aps	Sub	Gls
2001-02		1									1			2	

CLAYTON, Gary

Right-back/Midfielder   *Sheffield, 2 February 1963*

Within days of becoming manager in January 1991, Chris Turner went to one of his former clubs, Cambridge, to take Gary Clayton on loan. Thrust into the first team, the Yorkshire-born former Doncaster player helped achieve a 1-0 win at Walsall. Clayton kept his place in Posh's next three matches before returning to the Abbey, becoming a regular in the U's Division One side. After switching to midfield, in February 1994 he joined Huddersfield before moving to Plymouth and Torquay.

Season	League Aps	Sub	Gls	FA Cup Aps	Sub	Gls	League Cup Aps	Sub	Gls	Other Aps	Sub	Gls	Total Aps	Sub	Gls
1990-91	4												4		

CLEAVER, Christopher William (Chris)

Forward   *Hitchin, 24 March 1979*

Striker Chris rose through the ranks to make his first-team debut as a 17-year-old in October 1996. An enthusiastic front runner with a good work-rate, his best run was early in 1998 when scoring in home wins over Rochdale and Exeter. Given few opportunities in 1998-99, he was loaned for three months to Grantham Town, and the following season to Cambridge City. Chris was released at the end of the campaign, whereupon he tried his luck in Finland with TP55 based in Seinajoki.

Season	League			FA Cup			League Cup			Other			Total		
	Aps	Sub	Gls	Aps	Sub	Gls	Aps	Sub	Gls	Aps	Sub	Gls	Aps	Sub	Gls
1996-97	6	7	1	1						1			7	8	1
1997-98	4	10	2				2				2		4	14	2
1998-99		2		1										3	
Total	10	19	3	2			2			1	2		11	25	3

CLISS, Anthony (Tony)
Winger   *March, 22 September 1959*

A local lad from Manea, Tony's career started well with a goal on his home debut against Cambridge in November 1977. A winger who could also play 'in the hole', Cliss spent five years with Posh, enjoying his best spell in 1979-80 under Peter Morris. He hit seven goals that season, including one in an Easter home game with Stockport, when his wayward shot squeezed through the side-netting. Tony left Posh for Crewe in December 1982, teaming up again with Morris, before playing for Dario Gradi's emerging side of the mid-1980s. Cliss made 113 League appearances for the Alex until a knee injury forced his retirement in 1987. Cliss now works as a postman in March.

Season	League			FA Cup			League Cup			Other			Total		
	Aps	Sub	Gls	Aps	Sub	Gls	Aps	Sub	Gls	Aps	Sub	Gls	Aps	Sub	Gls
1977-78	3		1										3		1
1978-79	15	4	2										15	4	2
1979-80	34		7	1									35		7
1980-81	10	12	1		1		4						14	13	1
1981-82	2	2			1								2	3	
1982-83	1	2						1					1	3	
Total	65	20	11	1	2		4	1					70	23	11

CODNER, Robert Andrew George
Midfielder   *Walthamstow, 23 January 1965*

Codner failed to deliver with Spurs and Leicester in the early 1980s but after starring for non-League Barnet he was signed by Brighton in September 1988 for £125,000. He played nearly 300 games for the Seagulls until his release in 1995. During 1995-96 he had trials with Birmingham, Luton and Reading, and saw non-League action with Crawley, Woking and Ilkeston, before spending two weeks at London Road. He had a second spell at Barnet in March 1996, which lasted a year before he tried his luck with Southend, Stevenage and Kettering.

Season	League			FA Cup			League Cup			Other			Total		
	Aps	Sub	Gls	Aps	Sub	Gls	Aps	Sub	Gls	Aps	Sub	Gls	Aps	Sub	Gls
1995-96	1	1											1	1	

COLLINS, Stephen Mark (Steve)
Midfielder   *Stamford, 21 March 1962*

One of a string a fine players developed through the ranks in the late 1970s, Stamford lad Collins debuted in 1978-79 under Peter Morris.

Used sparingly at first, Steve claimed a regular spot in 1981-82, keeping the experienced Ian Phillips out of the side. The 1982-83 campaign was undoubtedly Collins' best. After being ever present he was sold for a small fee to Southend, for whom he made 51 League appearances. He then had a brief spell with Lincoln before rejoining Posh on a free transfer in December 1985. His second spell with the club saw him perform a utility role, his all-action style earning him the nickname 'Psycho'. He suffered a near fatal injury against Northampton in January 1987. Knocked cold following a collision with Cobblers' goalkeeper Peter Gleasure, Steve swallowed his own tongue until physio Bill Harvey came to his rescue. On making a full recovery, Collins took his total number of Posh appearances past 250 before being released in 1989. He then played in the Conference with Kettering and Boston prior to serving Corby, Rothwell Town and Mirrlees Blackstone. He joined home-town club Stamford in 1996 and helped them win promotion to the Dr Martens League a couple of years later.

Season	League			FA Cup			League Cup			Other			Total		
	Aps	Sub	Gls	Aps	Sub	Gls	Aps	Sub	Gls	Aps	Sub	Gls	Aps	Sub	Gls
1978-79	5												5		
1979-80	8			1			3						12		
1980-81	1												1		
1981-82	34		1	3			2						39		1
1982-83	44	2		4			4						52	2	
1985-86	21	1								1			22	1	
1986-87	26	1		1			3			2			32	1	
1987-88	39		1	2			4			4			49		1
1988-89	28	6	1	4			3	1		2			37	7	1
Total	206	10	3	15			19	1		9			249	11	3

CONMY, Oliver Martin (Ollie)

Winger   *Mulrany, 13 November 1939*

A Republic of Ireland international who won all five of his caps while with Posh, Conmy gave eight years service from 1964 until retiring in 1972. Beforehand, Ollie had spent five years with Huddersfield where he tasted League action on just three occasions. In his first season at London Road he helped Gordon Clark's team reach the quarter-finals of the FA Cup, creating chances for Derek Dougan and Peter Deakin. The following season Posh reached the semi-finals of the League Cup, with Conmy scoring in early-round victories over Newcastle and First Division leaders Burnley. Diminutive yet dynamic, Ollie's first touch gave him time on the ball, and in the late 1960s he was arguably the club's most influential player. Though less of a regular during his last two seasons, Ollie's performances seldom slackened and he signed off with a goal in his farewell match as Posh beat Reading 3-2 at home in May 1972. At that time, only Brian Wright had more appearances to his name. Ollie played part-time for Cambridge City whilst employed as a civil servant, before returning briefly to Posh as youth-team coach in the late 1970s. Now retired, the genial Irishman with the Yorkshire brogue – his family settled in Dewsbury when he was eight – moved from Peterborough to Southport in 2001.

Season	League			FA Cup			League Cup			Other			Total		
	Aps	Sub	Gls	Aps	Sub	Gls	Aps	Sub	Gls	Aps	Sub	Gls	Aps	Sub	Gls
1964-65	29		3	7			1						37		3
1965-66	25	1	7	1			5		4				31	1	11
1966-67	32	1	3	4		2	3						39	1	5
1967-68	41		9	3		1	1		1				45		11
1968-69	42		3	1			5						48		3
1969-70	35	2	2	4		1							39	2	3
1970-71	19	6	1	1									20	6	1
1971-72	28	2	6	4			1		1				33	2	7
Total	251	12	34	25		4	16		6				292	12	44

CONNOR, Daniel (Dan)
Goalkeeper   *Dublin, 31 January 1981*

Injuries to senior keepers Mark Tyler and Bart Griemink forced Barry Fry to give Eire Under-18 cap Connor his debut at Brighton in January 1999. The young Dubliner, one day short of his 18th birthday, performed well enough in a 0-1 defeat to keep his place at home to Barnet. Dan's season ended wretchedly, however, when he broke a leg in the Under-19s' final match of the campaign against Crewe. He made a full recovery and, after returning to Academy duty, received another taste of Third Division action as a sub for the injured Tyler at Cheltenham in February 2000. Tyler's consistency over the last two seasons meant Connor's only starts have been restricted to cup competitions.

Season	League			FA Cup			League Cup			Other			Total		
	Aps	Sub	Gls	Aps	Sub	Gls	Aps	Sub	Gls	Aps	Sub	Gls	Aps	Sub	Gls
1998-99	2												2		
1999-00		1												1	
2000-01										2			2		
2001-02		1					1						1	1	
Total	2	2					1			2			5	2	

COOKE, Joseph (Joe)
Forward   *Dominica (WI), 15 February 1955*

Caretaker boss Billy Hails signed Joe from Bradford City in January 1979 in a £20,000 deal that saw midfielder Lammie Robertson move the other way. Big Joe made his debut at home to Chester. Posh won 2-1 to end a worst-ever run of 17 winless League games. Despite Joe's aerial threat and occasional goal, relegation meant he left the club. After two years at Oxford he joined Exeter, before returning to Valley Parade where he was converted to centre-half. Spells with Rochdale and Wrexham followed until his retirement in 1988.

Season	League			FA Cup			League Cup			Other			Total		
	Aps	Sub	Gls	Aps	Sub	Gls	Aps	Sub	Gls	Aps	Sub	Gls	Aps	Sub	Gls
1978-79	18		5										18		5

COOKE, Robert Leslie (Robbie)

Forward　　　　　　　　*Rotherham, 16 February 1957*

Twice released as a lad by Mansfield, Cooke signed from non-League Grantham in May 1980 and netted in each of his first four games for Posh at the start of 1980-81. With his speed, first touch and clinical finishing, Robbie emerged as a lethal marksman in Peter Morris's side that narrowly missed promotion to Division Three in 1981 and 1982. He is remembered for his goals during Posh's FA Cup run in 1980-81, particularly his winner at Notts County in round four. After heading Posh's scoring chart in his first two seasons, his form dipped following Martin Wilkinson's appointment as manager in 1982-83. Following a loan spell at Luton, Cooke joined Second Division Cambridge in February 1983 for £12,000. Later, with Brentford, he hit the net 53 times in 123 League appearances and helped the Bees to the final of the 1985 Freight Rover Trophy, scoring in their 1-3 Wembley defeat by Wigan. After finishing his League career at Millwall in 1988, his goals for Kettering helped them reach round four of the 1989 FA Cup. A year later he was the Conference's top marksman, his 28 goals eclipsing Sutton's Efan Ekoku, Enfield's Paul Furlong, and Andy Clarke of Barnet. On leaving Bourne Town in 1992, Cooke became player-manager at Warboys Town, returning to Kettering in 1998 as assistant boss to Peter Morris. Robbie worked for Peterborough-based travel giants Thomas Cook, but now scouts full-time for Everton.

Season	League			FA Cup			League Cup			Other			Total		
	Aps	Sub	Gls	Aps	Sub	Gls	Aps	Sub	Gls	Aps	Sub	Gls	Aps	Sub	Gls
1980-81	46		22	6		4	4		3				56		29
1981-82	46		24	3		3	2		1				51		28
1982-83	23		5	4		3	3		3				30		11
Total	115		51	13		10	9		7				137		68

COOKSEY, Scott Andrew

Goalkeeper　　　　　　　*Birmingham, 24 June 1972*

After failing to break through with Derby and Shrewsbury, 6ft 3in Cooksey's goalkeeping with non-League Bromsgrove led to Posh buying him for £25,000 in December 1993. He debuted four months later in a 1-5 thrashing at Charlton. At the start of 1994-95 Cooksey was handed the No 1 jersey following the sale of Fred Barber, but his blunders saw him barracked and cost him his place. Although he returned before Christmas, he spent the rest of the season loaned to Conference sides Welling and Stalybridge. Released in 1995, he joined Hednesford and was voted Player of the Year for 1996-97. He returned to League side Shrewsbury before returning to the Conference with Hereford.

Season	League			FA Cup			League Cup			Other			Total		
	Aps	Sub	Gls	Aps	Sub	Gls	Aps	Sub	Gls	Aps	Sub	Gls	Aps	Sub	Gls
1993-94	3												3		
1994-95	12			2			2			1			17		
Total	15			2			2			1			20		

COOPER, Gary

Midfielder   *Hammersmith, 20 November 1965*

A tenacious midfielder with a trusty left foot, London-born Cooper spent three years with Posh, during which his ball-playing was over-shadowed by his antics. Released by QPR after just one First Division appearance, the former England Schoolboy and Youth international had a spell with Fisher Athletic before helping Maidstone acquire League status in 1989. He joined Posh, along with Ken Charlery, in a combined £40,000 deal on transfer deadline day in 1991. Cooper made only a few appearances as Posh won promotion that year, but became a regular in central midfield in 1991-92. He missed out on a Wembley play-off owing to his mysterious 'disappearance' during the closing weeks of the campaign. Reprieved by Chris Turner, Cooper starred in Division One in 1992-93, lifting the Supporters' Club Player of the Season trophy and briefly wearing the captain's armband. The follow-ing season, with Posh propping up the division, Cooper's poor dis-plays drew flak from supporters. After an unsavoury clash with fans following a home defeat by Bristol City, he played just once more before joining Birmingham in December 1993. He won a Second Division championship medal with the Blues in 1994-95 before drop-ping into non-League football with Welling United and Kingstonian.

Season	League			FA Cup			League Cup			Other			Total		
	Aps	Sub	Gls	Aps	Sub	Gls	Aps	Sub	Gls	Aps	Sub	Gls	Aps	Sub	Gls
1990-91	2	4	1										2	4	1
1991-92	33		4	3		2	6			7			49		6
1992-93	35		3	2			3		1	1			41		4
1993-94	13	1	2				3			1		1	17	1	3
Total	83	5	10	5		2	12		1	9		1	109	5	14

COOPER, Ronald (Ron)

Full-back   *Peterborough, 28 August 1938*

Ron Cooper was the first locally born player to make an impact for Posh after achieving League status in 1960. Although tasting Midland League action with the club in 1959, he had to wait until 1963-64 for his League debut – a 4-0 home victory over Colchester. Ron went on to appear in 150 League and Cup games, mainly as a tough, reliable right-back. Ron left London Road after a decade's service in 1968 and was rewarded with a testimonial watched by 5,000 fans against Derby, who won 4-2 with manager Brian Clough playing and scoring a goal. Ron later had a spell as manager of Bourne Town in the late 1970s.

Season	League			FA Cup			League Cup			Other			Total		
	Aps	Sub	Gls	Aps	Sub	Gls	Aps	Sub	Gls	Aps	Sub	Gls	Aps	Sub	Gls
1963-64	21		1	2									23		1
1964-65	19			7									26		
1965-66	16												16		
1966-67	39			4			1						44		
1967-68	37			3			1						41		
Total	132		1	16			2						150		1

COOPER, Stephen Brian (Steve)

Forward   *Birmingham, 22 June 1964*

A tall fair striker, good in the air, Cooper's name entered Posh folklore with the goal that took the club to Wembley in 1992. A loanee from Tranmere in March 1992, he made most of his appearances from the subs' bench, as on that glorious night at Huddersfield when his diving header gave Posh a last-gasp play-off semi-final winner. Despite his elevation to cult status, 'Zebedee' (because of his jumping prowess) was not offered a contract by Chris Turner and returned to Tranmere after sitting out the Wembley triumph over Stockport. Prior to joining Rovers in December 1990, Cooper had served Halifax, Newport, Plymouth and Barnsley after starting out with his home-town club Birmingham in 1982. He continued his wanderings when joining York in August 1993, then Airdrie. His goals helped the Diamonds reach the 1995 Scottish Cup final. After a brief spell with Ayr, injury forced Cooper's retirement from professional football in 1999-2000.

Season	League			FA Cup			League Cup			Other			Total		
	Aps	Sub	Gls	Aps	Sub	Gls	Aps	Sub	Gls	Aps	Sub	Gls	Aps	Sub	Gls
1991-92	2	7								4	1		2	11	1

CORDER, Peter Robert

Goalkeeper   *Loughton, 12 June 1966*

Corder made his Football League debut, aged 19, while on loan from Spurs in October 1985, but Posh slipped to a 1-3 defeat at Cambridge. In the next match, at Tranmere, John Wile's team were thrashed 0-7 – the club's worst ever League defeat. Regular custodian John Turner was recalled for the 1-1 home draw with Exeter, while Corder returned to White Hart Lane before drifting out of League football. He played for Nuneaton, Boston on loan, Corby, Stamford, Holbeach and Raunds Town. He later combined employment for Budget Insurance in Peterborough with part-time work as a sports massage therapist – his clients included the Zimbabwe Cricket team and Peterborough United. Corder has now settled into a full-time role at London Road.

Season	League			FA Cup			League Cup			Other			Total		
	Aps	Sub	Gls	Aps	Sub	Gls	Aps	Sub	Gls	Aps	Sub	Gls	Aps	Sub	Gls
1985-86	2												2		

CORNER, David Edward
Central Defender   Sunderland, 15 May 1966

Tall, red-haired centre-back David Corner began his career in the early 1980s at his home-town club, Sunderland, playing in the 1985 League Cup final when a teenager. Loaned to Posh late in 1987-88, his arrival coincided with Posh conceding just three goals in nine games. A cash crisis ruled out a permanent move and, after returning to Roker Park, David joined Leyton Orient in July 1988. He later helped Darlington win the Conference and Division Four in successive seasons.

Season	League			FA Cup			League Cup			Other			Total		
	Aps	Sub	Gls	Aps	Sub	Gls	Aps	Sub	Gls	Aps	Sub	Gls	Aps	Sub	Gls
1987-88	9												9		

CORNFORTH, John Michael
Midfielder   Whitley Bay, 7 October 1967

Midfielder Cornforth spent a month on loan from Wycombe in 1997-98, debuting in a 1-0 win at one of his former clubs, Swansea, before playing his first home game against new-boys Macclesfield. He went back to Adams Park having shown little of the ability that earlier in his career earned him two Welsh caps and a £350,000 move from Swansea to Birmingham. After time with Cardiff and Scunthorpe, Exeter signed him in February 2000. Cornforth is now manager at St James Park.

Season	League			FA Cup			League Cup			Other			Total		
	Aps	Sub	Gls	Aps	Sub	Gls	Aps	Sub	Gls	Aps	Sub	Gls	Aps	Sub	Gls
1997-98	3	1											3	1	

COSTELLO, Peter
Forward   Halifax, 31 October 1969

A lively little striker, Yorkshire-born Costello signed from Rochdale for £30,000 in March 1991 – one of Chris Turner's six record-breaking transfer deadline signings. Peter played a few games before the end of the season without scoring, and was then frozen out by the wealth of forward talent at the club. After netting three times in cup competitions, Costello left for Lincoln early in 1992-93. He played in Hong Kong before returning to help Boston into the Football League in 2002.

Season	League			FA Cup			League Cup			Other			Total		
	Aps	Sub	Gls	Aps	Sub	Gls	Aps	Sub	Gls	Aps	Sub	Gls	Aps	Sub	Gls
1990-91	3	2											3	2	
1991-92		1						1		1	1	2	1	3	2
1992-93		2					1	1	1	1			2	3	1
Total	3	5					1	2	1	2	1	2	6	8	3

COWAN, Thomas (Tom)

Defender   *Belshill, 28 August 1969*

An uncompromising full-back, capable of playing either left or right, Cowan came on loan from the unlikely source of Cambridge United's reserves in January 2002. Fry's injury-hit squad meant he was thrust into Second Division action, despite not having graced Cambridge's first team since September. Cowan played a few games, scoring in a 2-3 home defeat by Wrexham, then returned to the Abbey. In May 2002 he joined York, his seventh English League club since starting out with Clyde and Rangers. He has also served Sheffield United, Stoke (on loan), Huddersfield and Burnley in a 14-year professional career.

Season	League			FA Cup			League Cup			Other			Total		
	Aps	Sub	Gls	Aps	Sub	Gls	Aps	Sub	Gls	Aps	Sub	Gls	Aps	Sub	Gls
2001-02	4	1	1										4	1	1

COZENS, John William

Forward   *Hammersmith, 14 May 1946*

Londoner Cozens entered the professional game late when joining Notts County as a 24-year-old from Hillingdon Borough for £7,000 in 1970. A prolific goalscorer in the Southern League, he was given few opportunities until 1971-72 when he made his mark with 17 goals in 37 matches. Overlooked by the Magpies the following season, he became Noel Cantwell's first signing in a £8,000 deal in December 1972. Cantwell's desire to sign Cozens in time for an FA Cup-tie at Bishops Stortford meant the player was unaware of Posh's precarious League position and even where Peterborough was! John scored important goals as Posh battled clear of the re-election zone, and captained the side that won the Fourth Division title in 1973-74. Ever-present that season, he led the line alongside Jim Hall and top scored with 25 League and cup goals, including two crucial efforts in the title-decider with Gillingham, which Posh won 4-2 at London Road. A big-time player, Cozens had earlier hit Posh's goal in the FA Cup home defeat by Leeds, watched by 28,000 fans. A knee injury forced him to miss most of the following season, but in 1975-76 he added to his store of FA Cup goals at Manchester United. Despite further injuries, he was again top scorer in 1976-77, then was surprisingly sold to Cambridge for £2,000 in November 1977. After helping the U's to promotion to the Second Division ahead of Posh in 1978, injury forced John's retirement in 1980. He stayed a further five years at the Abbey as both coach and assistant manager, then appeared as a veteran striker with Ramsey Town in the United Counties League, before managing Bourne Town and King's Lynn. In later years John has undertaken roles in local football, most recently at Stamford, where he was in charge in 1998-99.

Season	League			FA Cup			League Cup			Other			Total		
	Aps	Sub	Gls	Aps	Sub	Gls	Aps	Sub	Gls	Aps	Sub	Gls	Aps	Sub	Gls
1972-73	24		10	3		1							27		11
1973-74	46		19	4		6	2						52		25
1974-75	4		1				1						5		1
1975-76	21		3	3	1	2	1	1	1				25	2	6
1976-77	25	4	7	2		1	4	1	2				31	5	10
1977-78	7	1	1										7	1	1
Total	127	5	41	12	1	10	8	2	3				147	8	54

CRAWFORD, John (Ian)

Full-back/Winger   Edinburgh, 14 July 1934

Edinburgh-born Crawford helped Hearts win the 1956 Scottish Cup with two goals in the final against Celtic watched by a 133,000 crowd at Hampden. Two Scottish championships followed before he signed for West Ham in 1961. Capped at Under-23 level, Ian scored five goals in 24 League games before moving to Scunthorpe in February 1963. He arrived at London Road in 1964 as manager Gordon Clark presided over a busy close season. Debuting at Exeter in the opening game of 1964-65 – one of five newcomers in the side – Ian was a creative talent at home on either wing. He switched to left-back before the end of the campaign and stayed there for two seasons. Injury ruled out most of 1967-68, but he returned the next season, bowing out after a 0-1 home defeat by Doncaster in April 1969. He became youth-team coach at Everton, then Arsenal, before making his managerial mark in Norway.

Season	League			FA Cup			League Cup			Other			Total		
	Aps	Sub	Gls	Aps	Sub	Gls	Aps	Sub	Gls	Aps	Sub	Gls	Aps	Sub	Gls
1964-65	34		5	2			2						38		5
1965-66	46		1	2			6						54		1
1966-67	46			4			3						53		
1967-68	9						1						10		
1968-69	37			1			3						41		
Total	172		6	9			15						196		6

CRICHTON, Paul Andrew

Goalkeeper   Pontefract, 3 October 1965

An agile goalkeeper with quick reactions, Crichton first came to Posh on loan from Nottingham Forest in March 1987. Despite being beaten just twice in four games, he was returned to Forest by Noel Cantwell. Having already helped out at Notts County and Darlington, Crichton had additional spells with Swindon, Rotherham and Torquay before rejoining Posh on a full contract in November 1988. He made the No 1 jersey his own, but had to contest it with Tony Godden in 1989-90. He left for regular first-team action at struggling Doncaster. Released by Rovers on a free transfer, Crichton earned Grimsby's Player of the Season award in 1993-94. He joined WBA in 1996, then Aston Villa and Burnley, before signing for Norwich for £150,000 in June 2001.

Season	League			FA Cup			League Cup			Other			Total		
	Aps	Sub	Gls	Aps	Sub	Gls	Aps	Sub	Gls	Aps	Sub	Gls	Aps	Sub	Gls
1986-87	4												4		
1988-89	31			4						2			37		
1989-90	16			1						1			18		
Total	51			5						3			59		

CROSBY, Philip Alan (Phil)

Left-back/Central Defender   Leeds, 9 November 1962

Phil Crosby signed for Second Division Grimsby in September 1980, but only after moving to Rotherham three years later did he come of age as a reliable full-back. A former England Youth cap, he made 183 League appearances for the Millers and helped them to the Division Four title in 1989 before joining Posh in August for £42,500. In his two seasons with Posh, Phil did well at left-back or in central defence and was voted fans' Player of the Year in the 1990-91 promotion-winning season. Homesick for the north, he joined York in July 1991.

Season	League			FA Cup			League Cup			Other			Total		
	Aps	Sub	Gls	Aps	Sub	Gls	Aps	Sub	Gls	Aps	Sub	Gls	Aps	Sub	Gls
1989-90	40	2		3			2			2	1		47	2	
1990-91	45			5			4			1			55		
Total	85	2		8			6			3	1		102	2	

CROWE, Victor Herbert (Vic)

Wing-half   Abercynon, 31 January 1932

An inspirational leader, Vic Crowe played 294 League games in ten years at Aston Villa before joining Posh in July 1964. Capped 16 times by Wales, Crowe cost £4,000 and his experience was pivotal to the record-breaking run to the FA Cup last eight. After skippering the side to wins over Arsenal and Swansea, Vic was carried off with a torn calf muscle at Chelsea after just two minutes, following a challenge on Bert Murray – later to play for Posh – and by the time he limped back Posh were 0-3 down. Crowe even scored a consolation goal before Chelsea ran out 5-1 winners. The following season he led the side to the semi-finals of the League Cup and briefly ran the team when Gordon Clark became general manager. That arrangement was dropped before 1966-67, and Vic shortly left Posh to take charge of American side Atlanta. He returned to England four years later to become manager of Aston Villa before returning to the USA as manager of Portland Timbers.

Season	League			FA Cup			League Cup			Other			Total		
	Aps	Sub	Gls	Aps	Sub	Gls	Aps	Sub	Gls	Aps	Sub	Gls	Aps	Sub	Gls
1964-65	27			8		2	1						36		2
1965-66	26			1			5		1				32		1
1966-67	3						3						6		
Total	56			9		2	9		1				74		3

CULLEN, David Jonathan (Jon)

Midfielder   *Durham, 10 January 1973*

A tall midfielder with neat passing, Cullen started out at Doncaster, making nine League appearances after signing in 1991. Spells with non-League Spennymoor and Morpeth followed before he resumed his League career with Hartlepool in March 1997. Jon's twelve League goals in 34 games earned him a £250,000 move to Sheffield United in January 1998. Things didn't work out, but Cullen impressed Barry Fry during loan spells at Shrewsbury and Halifax, and signed for £35,000 in March 2000. Cullen did his bit in Posh's successful Third Division promotion bid, scoring crucial goals during the run-in. He played in the Wembley play-off final against Darlington despite missing the semi-finals through suspension – following a dismissal at Brighton. Unable to recreate his early form during 2000-01, he spent the end of the season loaned to Carlisle and seemed destined for a permanent return north. Instead, Cullen spent most of 2001-02 fighting for fitness.

Season	League			FA Cup			League Cup			Other			Total		
	Aps	Sub	Gls	Aps	Sub	Gls	Aps	Sub	Gls	Aps	Sub	Gls	Aps	Sub	Gls
1999-00	12	1	3							1			13	1	3
2000-01	12	6	1	1					1	2		1	15	7	2
2000-01	10	3	1		2		1			1			12	5	1
Total	34	10	5	1	2		1	1		4		1	40	13	6

CULPIN, Paul

Forward   *Kirby Muxloe, 8 February 1962*

After failing to make the grade at Leicester in the early 1980s, Culpin joined Nuneaton Borough, where his goals attracted attention. First Division Coventry signed him in June 1985 for £50,000 – a then enormous sum for a non-League player. He struggled to make an impact, and after scoring just two League goals in nine outings moved on to Northampton in October 1987. Paul quickly found his feet, hitting 24 goals in 63 League games in a prolific partnership with Tony Adcock. After two years at the County Ground he was bought by new Posh boss Mark Lawrenson for £40,000. Culpin debuted in a 4-3 victory over Exeter and scored his first goal a week later in a 2-1 win at Rochdale. A natural finisher, Culpin top scored as Posh won promotion to the Third Division in 1990-91, despite starting only 21 League games. The subsequent front pairing of his former team-mate Adcock and Ken Charlery relegated Paul to the bench the following season, giving him little chance to justify his 'I'll blast us up the League' quote. He left Posh in March 1992, joining Hereford on a non-contract basis.

Season	League			FA Cup			League Cup			Other			Total		
	Aps	Sub	Gls	Aps	Sub	Gls	Aps	Sub	Gls	Aps	Sub	Gls	Aps	Sub	Gls
1989-90	9	3	2	2	1					1			12	4	2
1990-91	21	7	10	2	1	2	3		1	2		1	28	8	14

1991-92		7	2		3	1		2			12	3
Total	30	17	14	4	5	3	3	2	1	3	1	40	24	19

CUNNINGHAM, David
Winger   *Kirkcaldy, 10 August 1953*

Scottish winger Cunningham was 'borrowed' by John Barnwell from Swindon in November 1978. Southend and Hartlepool had already had him on loan. Cunningham played four games for Posh, scoring in a 2-3 defeat at Plymouth. He joined Aston Villa, then Hereford for a club-record fee. He ended his League career at Newport. He moved into the non-League arena with Trowbridge Town in 1981.

Season	League			FA Cup			League Cup			Other			Total		
	Aps	Sub	Gls	Aps	Sub	Gls	Aps	Sub	Gls	Aps	Sub	Gls	Aps	Sub	Gls
1978-79	4		1										4		1

CURTIS, Andrew (Andy)
Winger   *Rotherham, 2 December 1972*

A promising wide player, Andy's professional career was cut short by injury. Despite playing only twelve Fourth Division games for York, his potential was clear to Chris Turner, who signed him in September 1992. After debuting in an Anglo-Italian Cup defeat at Wolves, Curtis had to wait until January 1993 for his first League start. He showed subtle skills and a turn of pace in a 1-0 home win over Southend before scoring his first goal in a 3-2 win at big spenders Derby a week later. Sadly for Andy, a broken leg sustained in pre-season ruled him out of 1993-94, which led to his eventual release from London Road in 1995.

Season	League			FA Cup			League Cup			Other			Total		
	Aps	Sub	Gls	Aps	Sub	Gls	Aps	Sub	Gls	Aps	Sub	Gls	Aps	Sub	Gls
1992-93	8	3	1				1			1			9	4	1

CURTIS, Hamish
Left-back   *Peterborough, 26 May 1973*

Local lad Curtis had a startling debut – his one and only game being the Rumbelows Cup quarter-final replay defeat at Middlesbrough in 1992. A product of Posh's youth policy, Hamish had spent much of 1991-92 on loan to Spalding and Kettering before receiving his surprise call-up at a packed Ayresome Park, and the 18-year-old full-back stuck to the task of marking England Under-21 international winger Stuart Ripley. Released the following summer, Hamish represented several local non-League sides, and was part of a large contingent of former Posh players to help Stamford into the Dr Martens League in 1998.

Season	League			FA Cup			League Cup			Other			Total		
	Aps	Sub	Gls	Aps	Sub	Gls	Aps	Sub	Gls	Aps	Sub	Gls	Aps	Sub	Gls
1991-92							1						1		

CUSACK, Nicholas John (Nick)

Forward   *Maltby, 24 December 1965*

Spotted by Leicester boss David Pleat when playing for non-League Alvechurch, Yorkshire-born Cusack signed for the Foxes in June 1987. He scored once in 16 League games before joining Posh for £40,000 in July 1988. Nick debuted in a 2-2 draw at Carlisle on the opening day of 1988-89 and scored his first goal in a 3-0 League Cup win at WBA. Strong in the air, he led the line well and ended the season as top scorer before transferring to Scottish Premier side Motherwell for £100,000. After returning south with Darlington in January 1992, he served Oxford, Wycombe on loan, Fulham and Swansea, whom he helped to the Third Division title in 1999-2000 as a central defender.

Season	League			FA Cup			League Cup			Other			Total		
	Aps	Sub	Gls	Aps	Sub	Gls	Aps	Sub	Gls	Aps	Sub	Gls	Aps	Sub	Gls
1988-89	44		10	4		1	4		1	2			54		12

Gary Sargent v Sheffield Wednesday, Shipp Cup, July 1977

Steve Castle

Alan Slough v Sheffield Wednesday, Shipp Cup, July 1977

Jim Iley   Dennis Emery

Dave McVay

David Johnson

Ian Benjamin scores against Mansfield, August 1982

David Farrell

Lee Power

DANIELSSON, Helgi
Midfielder   *Valur, 13 July 1981*

Technically gifted, with good close control, Helgi had represented Iceland's Under-18s and Under-21s before breaking into Posh's first team in 2000-01. He first came to notice the previous season when AC Milan invited him to train with them. His long-awaited League chance came at Bristol City as a sub for the last five minutes of a 1-2 defeat in October 2000. He had to wait five months for his next outing, at Port Vale, again from the bench. Used more frequently during 2001-02, Helgi showed great potential and is a player with a bright future.

Season	League			FA Cup			League Cup			Other			Total		
	Aps	Sub	Gls	Aps	Sub	Gls	Aps	Sub	Gls	Aps	Sub	Gls	Aps	Sub	Gls
2000-01	3	3											3	3	
2001-02	20	11	2	1		1	1			2			24	11	3
Total	23	14	2	1		1	1			2			27	14	3

DANZEY, Michael James
Forward   *Widnes, 8 February 1971*

Danzey started out at Nottingham Forest but never made their first team. He was sub twice when loaned to Chester in February 1990. He was loaned to Boston before joining Posh without a contract in January 1991. His only game was as a sub in a 1-1 draw at Halifax in February 1991. He joined St Albans but returned to full-time football in 1992 as a defender with Cambridge United before joining Aylesbury United.

Season	League			FA Cup			League Cup			Other			Total		
	Aps	Sub	Gls	Aps	Sub	Gls	Aps	Sub	Gls	Aps	Sub	Gls	Aps	Sub	Gls
1990-91		1												1	

DARRELL, Michael Alan (Micky)
Midfielder   *Bilston, 14 January 1947*

Signed by Jim Iley on a free transfer from Birmingham in May 1971, blond midfielder Darrell never commanded a regular place in two seasons. He was an unused sub when Posh opened 1971-72 with a 2-0 home win over Southend, but debuted a week later in a 1-1 draw at Newport, when he ousted Tommy Robson from the No 11 shirt. Micky enjoyed his longest run during the last two months of the campaign, but saw little action after Noel Cantwell replaced Iley in October 1972. He was released the following summer.

Season	League			FA Cup			League Cup			Other			Total		
	Aps	Sub	Gls	Aps	Sub	Gls	Aps	Sub	Gls	Aps	Sub	Gls	Aps	Sub	Gls
1971-72	20	6	4	1			1						21	7	4
1972-73	12	4	2										12	4	2
Total	32	10	6	1			1						33	11	6

DAVIES, Simon
Midfielder   *Haverfordwest, 10 October 1979*

A prodigious talent with good vision and range of passes, Davies will surely surpass the 13 Welsh caps won by his uncle, former QPR and Crystal Palace midfielder Ian Evans. 'Digger' burst onto the Third Division scene after starring in Posh's celebrated youth side, debuting in a 1-3 defeat at Hull in January 1998. He became a midfield regular in 1998-99, when his progress was rapid. Missing just three games all season, Davies was voted into the PFA Division Three side (alongside team-mate Matthew Etherington) and won Posh's Player of the Season award. He also earned Welsh caps at Under-18 and Under-21 level. Prior to 1999-2000, Davies (and Etherington) spent a week training at Manchester United, where his professionalism and modesty was praised by Sir Alex Ferguson. Back at Posh, Davies drove in a 30-yard rocket to earn victory at Northampton. In January 2000, Tottenham's combined £1.2 million bid for Davies and Etherington was accepted by chairman Peter Boizot. Davies' value was recorded at £700,000 – Posh's most expensive export. Both players had their Premiership debuts as subs at Anfield in April, making their first full appearances at Manchester United the following month. Davies won his first full Welsh cap against Ukraine in March 2001. His rise continued in 2001-02, when he made 41 League and cup appearances for Spurs, scored seven goals, and became a regular in the Welsh team.

Season	League			FA Cup			League Cup			Other			Total		
	Aps	Sub	Gls	Aps	Sub	Gls	Aps	Sub	Gls	Aps	Sub	Gls	Aps	Sub	Gls
1997-98	4	2								1			5	2	
1998-99	43		4	1			2			2			48		4
1999-00	16		2	2			2						20		2
Total	63	2	6	3			4			3			73	2	6

DAY, William (Billy)
Outside-right   *Middlesbrough, 27 December 1936*

Day played 120 League games for his home-town club Middlesbrough and also saw first-team action at Newcastle before becoming a free-transfer signing by Jack Fairbrother in April 1963. Day appeared in six League games that season but was a victim of new boss Gordon Clark's summer restructuring in 1964. After a stint with non-League Cambridge United, Day returned to Teesside to work as a bookmaker.

Season	League			FA Cup			League Cup			Other			Total		
	Aps	Sub	Gls	Aps	Sub	Gls	Aps	Sub	Gls	Aps	Sub	Gls	Aps	Sub	Gls
1962-63	6		1										6		1
1963-64	12		1										12		1
Total	18		2										18		2

DE SOUZA, Miquel Juan

Forward   *Newham, 11 February 1970*

Barry Fry paid Wycombe £50,000 for De Souza on transfer deadline day 1997 in the hope that the strong front-man would score the goals to save Posh from relegation. Two goals in eight games could not prevent a slide into the basement. The former Birmingham striker started 1997-98 as first choice, but he was injured against Portsmouth in a League Cup-tie and lost his place to Martin Carruthers, whose subsequent partnership with Jimmy Quinn confined Miquel to the bench. Left out again the following season, he was loaned to Southend before joining Rushden & Diamonds in December 1998. Miquel, who has a Portuguese grandfather, spent 2000-01 helping Farnborough to win the Ryman Premier League while studying for a sports science degree.

Season	League			FA Cup			League Cup			Other			Total		
	Aps	Sub	Gls	Aps	Sub	Gls	Aps	Sub	Gls	Aps	Sub	Gls	Aps	Sub	Gls
1996-97	8		2										8		2
1997-98	8	16	3				1	1		1		1	10	17	4
1998-99	3												3		
Total	19	16	5				1	1		1		1	21	17	6

DEAKIN, Peter

Inside-forward   *Normanton, 25 March 1938*

Deakin was the first player to see Posh League action in two spells. He initially arrived from First Division Bolton in June 1964. A neat inside-forward, he figured in the 1964-54 FA Cup run, scoring both goals in the 2-0 win at Swansea that earned a quarter-final at Chelsea. Though signed by Gordon Clark to create openings for others, Deakin hit the net 45 times in his first two seasons. In September 1966 he was transferred to Bradford, where he scored nine goals in 36 League games before re-joining Posh a year later on a part-time basis. His second spell was less distinguished, and after 16 League appearances he joined Brentford, where he ended his playing days. Deakin's involvement with Posh resumed in the 1970s when he set up a youth policy.

Season	League			FA Cup			League Cup			Other			Total		
	Aps	Sub	Gls	Aps	Sub	Gls	Aps	Sub	Gls	Aps	Sub	Gls	Aps	Sub	Gls
1964-65	35		18	8		6	2						45		24
1965-66	33	1	16	2		3	4		2				39	1	21
1966-67	6						1						7		
1967-68	16		1	1		1							17		2
Total	90	1	35	11		10	7		2				108	1	47

DEARDEN, Kevin Charles

Goalkeeper   *Luton, 8 March 1970*

A short but agile goalkeeper, Dearden was on loan from Spurs for the first seven games of 1990-91. Standing in for injured Paul Bradshaw, he conceded only five goals and was on the losing side just once. He had loan spells with seven other clubs prior to joining Brentford on a free transfer in September 1993. He made nearly 250 appearances for the Bees, was loaned to Barnet, then served Wrexham and Torquay.

Season	League			FA Cup			League Cup			Other			Total		
	Aps	Sub	Gls	Aps	Sub	Gls	Aps	Sub	Gls	Aps	Sub	Gls	Aps	Sub	Gls
1990-91	7												7		

DIGHTON, Richard Anthony (Dick)
Goalkeeper   *Corby, 26 July 1951*

A former Coventry apprentice, Dighton played only eight games in three years for Posh, owing to the consistency of regular keeper Mick Drewery. Signed in November 1969, Dighton's League debut came while on loan to Stockport in October 1970. He got his chance with Posh later that season. He made one appearance the following season before being released. He later turned out for Kettering and Stamford.

Season	League			FA Cup			League Cup			Other			Total		
	Aps	Sub	Gls	Aps	Sub	Gls	Aps	Sub	Gls	Aps	Sub	Gls	Aps	Sub	Gls
1970-71	7												7		
1971-72	1												1		
Total	8												8		

DOBSON, Anthony John (Tony)
Defender   *Coventry, 5 February 1969*

After winning England Under-23 caps as a youngster with Coventry, rugged centre-back Dobson's next club was Blackburn, where he made 41 League appearances before joining Portsmouth for £150,000 in September 1993. After losing his place at Fratton Park, he was 'borrowed' in January 1996 by Mick Halsall. Dobson left Portsmouth in August 1997 and had spells with WBA, Gillingham and Northampton. Now out of League football, he plays for Forest Green Rovers.

Season	League			FA Cup			League Cup			Other			Total		
	Aps	Sub	Gls	Aps	Sub	Gls	Aps	Sub	Gls	Aps	Sub	Gls	Aps	Sub	Gls
1995-96	4												4		

DOIG, Russell
Winger   *Millport, 17 January 1964*

John Wile brought this left-sided Scottish winger on a month's loan from Leeds in 1986. Formerly with St Mirren and East Stirling, Doig played the last of his seven games for Posh in a 2-1 home win against Tranmere just days after Wile's dismissal. Returning to Leeds, he made eleven senior appearances before signing for Hartlepool in March 1988. Still living in the Leeds area, Russell is now a taxi driver.

Season	League			FA Cup			League Cup			Other			Total		
	Aps	Sub	Gls	Aps	Sub	Gls	Aps	Sub	Gls	Aps	Sub	Gls	Aps	Sub	Gls
1986-87	7												7		

DONOWA, Brian Louie (Louie)

Winger   *Ipswich, 24 September 1964*

Renowned for his speed, winger Donowa spent the last weeks of 1996-97 on loan from Birmingham. He first hit the headlines at Norwich, where he won England Under-21 caps and a League Cup winners' medal in 1985. He left Carrow Road for a nomadic career that took him to Deportivo La Coruna in Spain and to Dutch side Willem II, before returning to Ipswich, Bristol City and Birmingham, whom he joined in August 1991. At St Andrews, he collected a Second Division champions' medal under Barry Fry in 1995. It was Fry who brought him to Posh in January 1997. Lou scored in three consecutive games, but with Posh at the foot of Division two he lost his early form and was relegated to the bench. After returning to St Andrews, he joined Walsall at the start of 1997-98, then Boston, King's Lynn and Northampton.

Season	League			FA Cup			League Cup			Other			Total		
	Aps	Sub	Gls	Aps	Sub	Gls	Aps	Sub	Gls	Aps	Sub	Gls	Aps	Sub	Gls
1996-97	16	6	1							4	1	2	20	7	3

DOUGAN, Alexander Derek (Derek)

Centre-forward   *Belfast, 20 January 1938*

A colourful character, Derek Dougan captured the hearts of fans during two years at London Road. Belfast-born Dougan courted controversy during his early days at Portsmouth and Blackburn – notably when shaving his head and demanding a transfer on the morning of Rovers' FA Cup final with Wolves in 1960. Brushes with authority at his next club, Aston Villa, prompted him to quit the game and the country. Jack Fairbrother tracked him down in Germany and – despite competition from other clubs – persuaded the enigmatic star to re-launch his career at London Road. The reduced pressure of the Third Division seemed to suit 'The Doog', whose performances struck a balance between showmanship and soccer. He debuted against Wrexham on the opening day of 1963-64, when a 14,000 crowd saw him make a scoring start in a 5-2 win. With his impudent skills and aerial ability, he netted 20 League goals that season to finish as the club's top scorer. The FA Cup took precedence in 1964-65 as Posh reached the quarter-finals for the only time. After hitting hat-tricks in early rounds against Salisbury and Chesterfield, the Irishman hit the equaliser in the 2-1 home win over Arsenal in round four, in front of a then record 30,000 crowd. The good times came to an end in May 1965 when Posh, claiming they couldn't meet Dougan's wage demands, sold him to Leicester for £25,000. He scored 35 times in 68 League games for the Foxes before joining Wolves for £50,000 in March 1967. Legendary status was achieved at Molineux where, in addition to eight years as a player, he emerged as one of the game's senior spokesmen, becoming PFA chairman and media pundit. He had a spell with Kettering before returning to Wolves as chairman and chief executive, negotiating a last-minute deal to save the club from extinction in 1982. 'The Doog' became a marketing and public relations consultant. In 1997, despite a heart attack, he stood as an Independent in Belfast in the General Election.

Season	League			FA Cup			League Cup			Other			Total		
	Aps	Sub	Gls	Aps	Sub	Gls	Aps	Sub	Gls	Aps	Sub	Gls	Aps	Sub	Gls
1963-64	38		20	2			1		1				41		21
1964-65	39		18	8	7		2						49		25
Total	77		38	10	7		3		1				90		46

DOWNES, Robert David (Bobby)
Winger   *Bloxwich, 18 August 1949*

Signed at 18 from WBA by Norman Rigby in September 1967, Downes received rave reviews for his tricky wing-play in the closing weeks of 1967-68. Despite his potential, he was given only sporadic opportunities the following season, prompting a transfer to Rochdale in August 1969. He played 174 League games before featuring in Watford's rise under Graham Taylor in the late 1970s. After finishing his career with Barnsley and Blackpool, Downes became a respected coach, teaming up with Taylor at Aston Villa, Wolves, and finally Watford in 1996. Bobby is now director of youth football at Blackburn.

Season	League			FA Cup			League Cup			Other			Total		
	Aps	Sub	Gls	Aps	Sub	Gls	Aps	Sub	Gls	Aps	Sub	Gls	Aps	Sub	Gls
1967-68	12		2										12		2
1968-69	11	3	1	1		1							12	3	2
Total	23	3	3	1		1							24	3	4

DOYLE, Jeffrey Noel (Jeff)
Midfielder   *Dublin, 25 February 1967*

Signed by John Wile on a free transfer from Coventry in August 1986, Dubliner Jeff spent one season with Posh, where he made little impression. Having failed to break through at Highfield Road, he made his League debut in a Sunday defeat at Northampton in September 1986. He kept his place until Wile's dismissal two months later, after which new boss Noel Cantwell selected him only rarely.

Season	League			FA Cup			League Cup			Other			Total		
	Aps	Sub	Gls	Aps	Sub	Gls	Aps	Sub	Gls	Aps	Sub	Gls	Aps	Sub	Gls
1986-87	13	1		1			2			1	1	1	17	2	1

DOYLE, Robert (Bob)

Midfielder   *Dumbarton, 27 December 1953*

Signed from Barnsley for £20,000 by Noel Cantwell in July 1976, this stylish Scottish midfielder became a Posh favourite. A fine passer, he spent three seasons at London Road, exceeded 150 appearances, was twice voted Player of the Season, and was ever-present in the side that missed promotion to Division Two on goal-difference in 1978. The previous season had seen Bob voted the Third Division's best player by the *People* newspaper. Further testimony to Doyle's talent came when he was sold to Blackpool in July 1979 for £110,000 – a club record fee which was not broken until 1992. He played for three different managers at Blackpool before joining Portsmouth in December 1980. After 177 League appearances, winning a Third Division champions medal in 1983, a final move in August 1985 took him to Hull, where a knee injury ended his career two years later. Bob returned to Peterborough, where he lives by driving for Orton Waterville-based King Brothers.

Season	League			FA Cup			League Cup			Other			Total		
	Aps	Sub	Gls	Aps	Sub	Gls	Aps	Sub	Gls	Aps	Sub	Gls	Aps	Sub	Gls
1976-77	43		5	2			5		1				50		6
1977-78	46		2	5			5						56		2
1978-79	41		3	1			8		1				50		4
Total	130		10	8			18		2				156		12

DREWERY, Michael Stephen (Mick)

Goalkeeper   *Snettisham, 16 January 1949*

Norfolk-born Drewery joined Posh – his only League club – in July 1967, whereupon he spent 18 months understudying Tony Millington. He debuted at home to Halifax in December 1968, but the game was abandoned at half-time due to the icy pitch. His 'official' debut came in a 2-2 draw at Grimsby a week later and he established himself when Millington moved the following summer. Consistency enabled Mick to remain Posh's first-choice keeper for the next four seasons, in which time he missed just eight games and was ever present in 1969-70 and 1972-73. He set a club record seven consecutive clean sheets during Posh's Fourth Division title-winning season of 1973-74, but lost his place when Noel Cantwell 'borrowed' Eric Steele from Newcastle. His last appearance was in the FA Cup-tie with Leeds in January 1974, but he remained with Posh until back injury forced his retirement in 1976.

Season	League			FA Cup			League Cup			Other			Total		
	Aps	Sub	Gls	Aps	Sub	Gls	Aps	Sub	Gls	Aps	Sub	Gls	Aps	Sub	Gls
1968-69	7												7		
1969-70	46			4			2						52		
1970-71	39			2			1						42		
1971-72	45			4			1						50		
1972-73	46			4			1						51		
1973-74	26			4			2						32		
Total	209			18			7						234		

DRURY, Adam James

Left-back   *Cottenham, 29 August 1978*

After debuting in a 0-4 defeat by Oxford in May 1996, Drury grew in confidence to emerge as one of Posh's most consistent performers of recent times. An uncompromising tackler with bags of pace, Adam came to prominence in 1997-98, dislodging the gifted but inconsistent Neil Lewis from the left-back berth to produce performances which earned him the Player of the Season award. After twice dislocating his shoulder, Adam enhanced his reputation in 1998-99 with his consistency and composure – trademarks of most of the youngsters nurtured at London Road by Kit Carson. His first goal was at Brentford in May 1997, and Drury broke his London Road scoring duck with a stunner against Hull in February 2000. Having helped Posh secure promotion to Division Two at Wembley in May, Adam turned in several Man of the Match performances in Division Two. Such displays did not go unnoticed, and his admirers were sorry to see him leave in March 2001 for Norwich – whom he had represented as a schoolboy before following Kit Carson to Posh. Adam has the potential to achieve much.

Season	League			FA Cup			League Cup			Other			Total		
	Aps	Sub	Gls	Aps	Sub	Gls	Aps	Sub	Gls	Aps	Sub	Gls	Aps	Sub	Gls
1995-96		1												1	
1996-97	5		1				1						6		1
1997-98	24	7		1			1			4			30	7	
1998-99	39	1		1			2			2			44	1	
1999-00	41	1	1	2			2			4			49	1	1
2000-01	29			5			2				1		36	1	
Total	138	10	2	9			8			10	1		165	11	2

DUFF, William (Willie)

Goalkeeper   *Winchburgh, 6 February 1935*

After winning League and Cup winners' medals with Hearts, Scottish Under-23 international Duff switched to the English First Division in December 1956 when joining Charlton, playing 213 League games before being brought to Posh by Jack Fairbrother in May 1963. Duff established himself as Posh's regular keeper, behind a defence that had wobbled since Jack Walls' departure a year earlier. Injury restricted Duff's appearances early in 1964-65 but he recovered to help the side reach the last eight of the FA Cup. After missing just three games the following season, he lost his place to Tony Millington in 1966-67 and left the club that summer. Willie lives in North Potomac, America.

Season	League			FA Cup			League Cup			Other			Total		
	Aps	Sub	Gls	Aps	Sub	Gls	Aps	Sub	Gls	Aps	Sub	Gls	Aps	Sub	Gls
1963-64	39			2			1						42		
1964-65	23			5									28		
1965-66	43			2			6						51		
1966-67	13						3						16		
Total	118			9			10						137		

DUNCLIFFE, Michael John (John)

Left-back   *Brighton, 17 September 1947*

Solid and dependable, left-back John Duncliffe signed in July 1970 on a free transfer from Grimsby, with whom he had made over 70 League appearances. Born in Brighton, he had also spent three years with his hometown club. John made his Posh debut in a 0-0 draw at Stockport on the opening day of 1970-71 and remained a regular throughout his three seasons at London Road. By the time of his release to Wisbech at the end of 1972-73, he had exceeded 100 League games to become one of the most popular Posh players. He remained in the Peterborough area after quitting football and now monitors the progress of his son, Jean-Paul, a member of Posh's Under-19 academy side until 2001.

Season	League			FA Cup			League Cup			Other			Total		
	Aps	Sub	Gls	Aps	Sub	Gls	Aps	Sub	Gls	Aps	Sub	Gls	Aps	Sub	Gls
1970-71	44			2			1						47		
1971-72	31						1						32		
1972-73	45			4			1						50		
Total	120			6			3						129		

DUNN, Iain George William

Midfielder   *Howden, 1 April 1970*

A goalscoring midfielder formerly with York and Chesterfield, Dunn spent two weeks on trial during Chris Turner's days as manager. A former England Youth cap, he made just one senior appearance, as a substitute in an Anglo-Italian Cup-tie at Wolves in September 1992. After dropping into non-League football with Goole, Dunn did better with Huddersfield, as part of the side that was promoted to Division One in 1995. He has since turned out for Scunthorpe, Chesterfield – for whom he began a second spell in 1997 – and Gainsborough Trinity.

Season	League			FA Cup			League Cup			Other			Total		
	Aps	Sub	Gls	Aps	Sub	Gls	Aps	Sub	Gls	Aps	Sub	Gls	Aps	Sub	Gls
1992-93											1			1	

DUNNE, James Patrick (Jimmy)

Inside-forward   *Dublin, 16 March 1935*

Jimmy Dunne joined Posh from Dublin side St Patrick's Athletic in July 1960, as Jimmy Hagan prepared for the challenge of League football. A Republic of Ireland cap from his days at Leicester in the 1950s, Dunne made four appearances in two years before joining Bedford Town and Cambridge United – then of the Southern League – in 1962.

Season	League			FA Cup			League Cup			Other			Total		
	Aps	Sub	Gls	Aps	Sub	Gls	Aps	Sub	Gls	Aps	Sub	Gls	Aps	Sub	Gls
1960-61	1		1										1		1
1961-62	3												3		
Total	4		1										4		1

DUNPHY, Nicholas Owen (Nick)

Defender   *Sutton Coldfield, 3 August 1974*

One of several non-League players brought in by John Still during the summer of 1994, Dunphy had previously played for Rushall Olympic, Sutton Coldfield and Hednesford. He made two appearances from the subs' bench before returning to non-League with Cheltenham. He later served Tamworth, Bromsgrove, Walsall Wood and Blakenhall.

Season	League			FA Cup			League Cup			Other			Total		
	Aps	Sub	Gls	Aps	Sub	Gls	Aps	Sub	Gls	Aps	Sub	Gls	Aps	Sub	Gls
1994-95		2												2	

Colin Clarke v Mansfield, May 1983

Terry Bly

Noel Luke

Alan Paris v Southend, August 1986

Bobby Moss

Steve Phillips is fouled by Cambridge's Steve Dowman, January 1987

David Seaman

Ronnie Jepson v Cambridge
April 1990

Ian Ross, 1978-79

From left:
Jeff Lee,
John Winters,
Bob Doyle

EARLE, Stephen John (Steve)

Forward   *Feltham, 1 November 1945*

A former England Youth cap, Earle scored regularly with Fulham and Leicester in the late 1960s and early 70s. He had two games on loan in November 1977 but at 32 he was not the answer to John Barnwell's problems and, following a feeble debut in a 1-0 win over Plymouth, he appeared just once in Division Three before returning to Leicester. He briefly reappeared in City's team before his contract was cancelled in March 1978. Now living in Tulsa, he works as an insurance salesman.

Season	League			FA Cup			League Cup			Other			Total		
	Aps	Sub	Gls	Aps	Sub	Gls	Aps	Sub	Gls	Aps	Sub	Gls	Aps	Sub	Gls
1977-78	1			1									2		

EBDON, Marcus

Midfielder   *Pontypool, 17 October 1970*

A Welsh Under-21 cap, ball-playing midfielder Ebdon's name will be remembered for the exquisite pass from which Ken Charlery scored the winner in the 1992 Wembley play-off final. Marcus was only 21 and much was hoped for from the blond, former Everton apprentice, but in four more years – appearing in nearly 150 League games – his Posh career never really took off. His best displays were in Division Two in 1994-95, when his intricate skills were capped by well-taken goals. He scored in his last League game for Posh in December 1996, in a 1-2 defeat at Chesterfield, who paid £100,000 for him a few months later. He has now passed 150 League appearances for the Spireites.

Season	League			FA Cup			League Cup			Other			Total		
	Aps	Sub	Gls	Aps	Sub	Gls	Aps	Sub	Gls	Aps	Sub	Gls	Aps	Sub	Gls
1991-92	12	3	2		1		2	1		4	1		18	6	2
1992-93	28		4	3			3			2			36		4
1993-94	10			1			2						13		
1994-95	35		6	2			2			3			42		6
1995-96	39		2	4		1	3			2			48		3
1996-97	12	8	1	2	2		2	1					16	11	1
Total	136	11	15	12	3	1	14	2		11	1		173	17	16

EDWARDS, Andrew David (Andy)

Central Defender   *Epping, 17 September 1971*

A reliable central defender, Edwards was signed from Birmingham in November 1996. His League debut was as a 17-year old with Southend in 1988. He appeared in 147 League games for the Shrimpers before re-joining former boss Barry Fry at St Andrews for £450,000 at the start of 1995-96. Nicknamed 'Eagle' after infamous ski jumper Eddie 'The Eagle' Edwards, Andy followed Fry again in November 1996, making his Posh debut in a 6-2 win over Rotherham. He has remained a con-stant in the side ever since, and despite attracting interest from other clubs, has stayed loyal. He surpassed himself in 1999-2000, despite having six different central defensive partners. Often skippering the side, he led Posh up the Wembley steps to lift the Third Division play-off trophy. 'Eagle' maintained his high standards in 2000-01, missing just two Second Division matches on his way to his 200th League appearance for the club, at Swindon in April 2001. In 2001-02 Edwards made 52 faultless appearances at the heart of the Posh defence.

Season	League			FA Cup			League Cup			Other			Total		
	Aps	Sub	Gls	Aps	Sub	Gls	Aps	Sub	Gls	Aps	Sub	Gls	Aps	Sub	Gls
1996-97	25			4						5			34		
1997-98	46		2	3			4			4		1	57		3
1998-99	41		2	1			2			2			46		2
1999-00	44		2	2			2			4			52		2
2000-01	43		1	5	1		2						50		2
2001-02	44		1	5			2			1			52		1
Total	243		8	20	1		12			16		1	291		10

EDWARDS, Matthew David (Matt)
Midfielder   Hammersmith, 15 June 1971

A wide midfielder, Edwards spent two months on loan from Spurs at the end of 1991-92. Although only appearing three times, each match was an occasion. Deputising for the injured Bobby Barnes, Matt played both legs of the Autoglass Trophy area final with Stoke, then in the first leg, play-off semi-final with Huddersfield. Released by Spurs in 1992, Edwards joined Brighton, making 78 League appearances, before having spells with Kettering, Walton & Hersham, and Enfield.

Season	League			FA Cup			League Cup			Other			Total		
	Aps	Sub	Gls	Aps	Sub	Gls	Aps	Sub	Gls	Aps	Sub	Gls	Aps	Sub	Gls
1991-92										3			3		

EMERY, Dennis
Inside-forward   Sandy, 4 October 1933   Died 1986

A Posh 'great', Emery arrived from Eynesbury in 1954 after failing to break through with Spurs. Signed by George Swindin, the slim inside-forward was pivotal to the side that won five consecutive Midland League titles between 1956 and 1960. In that time he hit 166 goals and entertained with his rangy style that took him past opponents. When League football arrived in 1960-61, it was fitting that Emery scored Posh's first League goal in that historic opener against Wrexham. He became the perfect foil for Terry Bly, helping his new team-mate score a record 52 League goals while bagging 15 himself as Posh won the Fourth Division title at the first attempt. The following season, Dennis top-scored with 14 strikes from 19 League games until a road accident cut short his career. He made a comeback 15 months later in an FA Cup-tie at Derby but the sparkle had gone. He played just three more games in 1962-63 before being released to Bedford for £1,500. Dennis passed away aged 52 in 1986 following surgery for ulcerated colitis.

Season	League			FA Cup			League Cup			Other			Total		
	Aps	Sub	Gls	Aps	Sub	Gls	Aps	Sub	Gls	Aps	Sub	Gls	Aps	Sub	Gls
1960-61	46		15	5		2	1						52		17
1961-62	19		14	2		1	1						22		15
1962-63	3			1									4		
Total	68		29	8		3	2						78		32

EMMERSON, Morris
Goalkeeper   *Sunniside, 23 October 1942*

A tall, Durham-born goalkeeper, Emmerson was brought to Posh by Gordon Clark in July 1963. Signed from Middlesbrough as cover for Willie Duff, Morris debuted in March 1964 in a 3-2 win at Luton. He held his place for a further six matches before Duff was recalled.

Season	League			FA Cup			League Cup			Other			Total		
	Aps	Sub	Gls	Aps	Sub	Gls	Aps	Sub	Gls	Aps	Sub	Gls	Aps	Sub	Gls
1963-64	7												7		

ETHERINGTON, Matthew
Winger   *Truro, 14 August 1981*

Etherington left his mark on Posh history before joining Spurs, along with team-mate Simon Davies, in a combined £1.2 million fee in January 2000. A winger who can ghost past defenders and cross accurately, Matthew became Posh's youngest ever player when debuting under Barry Fry at Brentford in May 1997. At 15, Etherington was still a pupil at Deacons School and required a letter from his headmaster granting him permission to play. Matthew starred in the youth team of 1997-98 and saw more senior action later in the season. He signed professional forms in August 1998, turned down a move to Newcastle and also rejected an offer to have Eric Hall as his agent. He scored his first League goal in the club record 9-1 League win at Barnet – making him Posh's youngest ever goalscorer – before earning England Under-18 caps. 'Mushy' crowned his season in the England Under-20s' World Cup in Nigeria, and became the first 17-year-old named in a PFA representative side. After spending a week training at Manchester United with team-mate Davies in August 1999, Matthew returned to London Road in sparkling form, scoring against Leyton Orient and Darlington. Following his move to White Hart Lane, Matthew made his Premiership debut as a sub alongside Davies in Spurs' visit to Anfield in April 2000, before lining up from the start at champions Manchester United. Matthew has found subsequent appearances hard to come by, but he gained experience on loan at First Division Bradford during 2001-02.

Season	League			FA Cup			League Cup			Other			Total		
	Aps	Sub	Gls	Aps	Sub	Gls	Aps	Sub	Gls	Aps	Sub	Gls	Aps	Sub	Gls
1996-97	1												1		
1997-98	2												2		
1998-99	21	8	3		1			1		2			23	10	3
1999-00	19		3	2			1						22		3
Total	43	8	6	2	1		1	1		2			48	10	6

EUSTACE, Peter
Midfielder   *Stocksbridge, 31 July 1944*

A gritty Yorkshireman, former England Under-23 cap Eustace spent his final professional season with Posh in the mid-1970s. Signed by Noel Cantwell to replace Freddie Hill, Eustace had top-flight experience with Sheffield Wednesday and West Ham. After starting out at Hillsborough and playing in the 1966 FA Cup final, he joined West Ham for £90,000 in January 1970 as replacement for Martin Peters. He never settled in London and returned for a second spell with the Owls after being loaned to Rotherham. His Posh debut was against Walsall on the opening day of 1975-76 and he remained a permanent fixture until his release at the end of the season. After coaching at Sunderland, he returned to Wednesday as assistant manager to Howard Wilkinson in 1984. Following a later spell in charge at Leyton Orient, Peter quit football to run a pub in Sheffield. He also scouted for West Ham.

Season	League			FA Cup			League Cup			Other			Total		
	Aps	Sub	Gls	Aps	Sub	Gls	Aps	Sub	Gls	Aps	Sub	Gls	Aps	Sub	Gls
1975-76	42	1	5	5			5						52	1	5

FAIRBROTHER, John
Centre-forward   *Cricklewood, 12 February 1941*

Fairbrother had the grim task of taking over the No 9 shirt from Derek Dougan. After starting with Watford, Fairbrother spent two years with Gloucester before Gordon Clark signed him in May 1965. John netted twice in the 4-0 League Cup quarter-final win over First Division leaders Burnley in November 1965, but saved his best form for 1966-67, when he top-scored with 23 League and Cup goals. He led the scoring again the following season until his £7,000 sale to Northampton in February 1968. John hit 56 League goals in 140 games for the Cobblers, and 35 in two seasons with Mansfield, before finishing his League days at Torquay in 1973-74. He spent many years in non-League football, serving Bath, Barnet – for whom he played in a 1977 FA Cup-tie against Posh – Hemel Hempstead, Berkhamsted, and Leverstock.

Season	League			FA Cup			League Cup			Other			Total		
	Aps	Sub	Gls	Aps	Sub	Gls	Aps	Sub	Gls	Aps	Sub	Gls	Aps	Sub	Gls
1965-66	19	2	9	1			3		2				23	2	11
1966-67	28		17	3		3	2		3				33		23
1967-68	22	1	11	3		3	1						26	1	14
Total	69	3	37	7		6	6		5				82	3	48

FARRELL, David William

Winger   *Birmingham, 11 November 1971*

A speedy winger with a liking for spectacular goals, Farrell first tasted League action with Aston Villa, who nabbed him from Redditch in 1992. He moved to Wycombe three years later, with six Premiership appearances under his belt, plus a few games for Scunthorpe on loan. At Adams Park, David hit eight goals from 60 League games in two seasons prior to joining Posh in July 1997. His bursts of speed and venomous shooting helped the team storm to the top of Division Three in 1997-98. He made less impact as Posh faded in the second half of the season, and when his indifferent form carried over into 1998-99, he temporarily lost his place. 1999-2000 brought more highs and lows, illustrated by the play-off semi-final with Barnet. Lampooned for costing his side a goal at Underhill – finishing off Andy Clarke's goalbound effort while offside – Farrell answered his critics with a second-leg hat-trick that clinched Posh's Wembley place. Confidence restored, David enjoyed his best-ever season in 2000-01, his dashing wing play and career-best goals tally attracting Second Division champions-elect Millwall and relegated Luton. But David pledged himself to Posh, signing a three-year extension to his contract in June 2001. Now in his 30s, he shows no signs of burn-out. His eight goals in 2001-02, including a special FA Cup strike against Newcastle, were an added bonus.

Season	League			FA Cup			League Cup			Other			Total		
	Aps	Sub	Gls	Aps	Sub	Gls	Aps	Sub	Gls	Aps	Sub	Gls	Aps	Sub	Gls
1997-98	40	2	6	3			4		1	4		1	51	2	8
1998-99	28	9	4	1					1	1			30	10	4
1999-00	33	2	3				2			3		3	38	2	6
2000-01	39	5	7	5	1		1	1	1				45	6	9
2001-02	35	3	6	5	2		2			1			43	3	8
Total	175	21	26	14	3		9	2	2	9		4	207	23	35

FARRELL, Sean Paul

Forward   *Watford, 28 February 1969*

Big striker Sean gained top-flight experience with Luton before netting 31 goals in 94 League games in two and a half years with Fulham. His next stop was Posh, when new boss John Still paid £120,000 for him in August 1994. Plagued by injuries, Sean struggled to justify his fee, but did better in 1995-96 when his 13 goals included a London Road hat-trick against Bognor Regis in the FA Cup. He was shut out by Barry Fry who, with a glut of forwards, sold him to Notts County in 1996-97.

Season	League			FA Cup			League Cup			Other			Total		
	Aps	Sub	Gls	Aps	Sub	Gls	Aps	Sub	Gls	Aps	Sub	Gls	Aps	Sub	Gls
1994-95	25	8	8	1			2			1			29	8	8
1995-96	20	6	9	3	1	3	1	1		2	1	1	26	9	13
1996-97	4	3	3				1	1	1				5	4	4
Total	49	17	20	4	1	3	4	2	1	3	1	1	60	21	25

FENN, Neale Michael Charles
Forward   *Edmonton, 18 January 1977*

Capped nine times at Under-21 level by the Republic of Ireland, Neale is a diminutive forward with close control. Prior to arriving on a free transfer in May 2001, Fenn spent six seasons as a professional at Spurs. Restricted to eight League sub appearances – he gained experience on loan to Leyton Orient, Norwich, Swindon and Lincoln. With Orient, Fenn stood out in their 1-0 defeat of Posh on Sky TV in February 1998. He made his Posh debut at Swindon in the opening game of 2001-02, and scored his first goal in a League Cup-tie at Swansea ten days later. He remained a first-team squad member throughout the campaign, where his considerable talent was masked by a poor goal return.

Season	League			FA Cup			League Cup			Other			Total		
	Aps	Sub	Gls	Aps	Sub	Gls	Aps	Sub	Gls	Aps	Sub	Gls	Aps	Sub	Gls
2001-02	25	11	6	6		1	1	1	1	2			34	12	8

FEUER, Anthony Ian (Ian)
Goalkeeper   *Las Vegas, 20 May 1971*

A 6ft 7in American, goalkeeper Ian Feuer served Posh on loan from West Ham near the end of 1994-95. He became the sixth keeper used that season when debuting at home to Brighton on a freezing February night. Posh won 2-1, which halted a run of 14 winless games and began a sequence of eight games unbeaten. Feuer's introduction was a big factor in the turnaround, but cash-strapped Posh let him return to Upton Park that summer. He then joined Luton for £580,000. Two years later he returned to America, but came back in 1998-99, starring in Rushden & Diamonds' FA Cup run. A free-transfer return to West Ham brought three Premiership appearances in 1999-2000. He also saw action with Derby whilst on loan from Wimbledon late in 2001.

Season	League			FA Cup			League Cup			Other			Total		
	Aps	Sub	Gls	Aps	Sub	Gls	Aps	Sub	Gls	Aps	Sub	Gls	Aps	Sub	Gls
1994-95	16												16		

FIFE, Adrian
Forward   *Peterborough, 13 September 1969*

Former St John Fisher schoolboy Adrian was a trainee when debuting at Halifax on the last day of 1986-87. The next season he made one sub appearance before being released to seek work in the music business.

Season	League			FA Cup			League Cup			Other			Total		
	Aps	Sub	Gls	Aps	Sub	Gls	Aps	Sub	Gls	Aps	Sub	Gls	Aps	Sub	Gls
1986-87	1												1		
1987-88		1												1	
Total	1	1											1	1	

FIRM, Neil John
Central Defender   Bradford, 23 January 1958

Firm was a towering, rugged player who made news for the wrong reasons when sent off on his debut at Stockport on the opening day of 1982-83. Firm had followed new manager Martin Wilkinson to Posh from Leeds, where the centre-back spent six years coming through the ranks. A mainstay in his first Posh season, he lost his place to player-manager John Wile early in 1983-84 but fought his way back. Sidelined with an Achilles injury for most of the following season, he quit professional football for a career with the Norfolk Constabulary.

Season	League			FA Cup			League Cup			Other			Total		
	Aps	Sub	Gls	Aps	Sub	Gls	Aps	Sub	Gls	Aps	Sub	Gls	Aps	Sub	Gls
1982-83	39		3	4			3						46		3
1983-84	24	1							1	1			25	2	
1984-85	8									1			9		
Total	71	1	3	4			3	1		2			80	2	3

FORAN, Mark James
Central Defender   Aldershot, 30 October 1973

Foran was an uncompromising stopper who spent nearly two years at Posh without establishing himself. Signed from Sheffield United by Mick Halsall following Gary Breen's move to Birmingham in February 1996, Foran debuted in a 2-2 home draw with Shrewsbury. He played in a further 16 League games up to 1995-96 but was bypassed by Barry Fry and in December 1997 joined Crewe. After 31 League appearances, Foran joined Bristol Rovers for £75,000 in August 2000.

Season	League			FA Cup			League Cup			Other			Total		
	Aps	Sub	Gls	Aps	Sub	Gls	Aps	Sub	Gls	Aps	Sub	Gls	Aps	Sub	Gls
1995-96	17		1							1			18		1
1996-97	2	2											2	2	
1997-98	3	1		1						1			5	1	
Total	22	3	1	1						2			25	3	1

FORBES, Steven Dualey (Steve)
Midfielder   London, 24 December 1975

A loanee from Colchester in March 1999, Forbes made one full appearance. The tall midfielder had helped Colchester to promotion from Division Three via the 1998 play-offs, having begun his League career with Millwall, who took him from Sittingbourne in 1994-95. Forbes has recently played for Stevenage, Dagenham & Redbridge, and Hendon.

Season	League			FA Cup			League Cup			Other			Total		
	Aps	Sub	Gls	Aps	Sub	Gls	Aps	Sub	Gls	Aps	Sub	Gls	Aps	Sub	Gls
1998-99	1	2											1	2	

FORINTON, Howard Lee
Forward   *Boston, 18 September 1975*

Forinton became the costliest striker in Posh history when Barry Fry paid his former club Birmingham £275,000 in September 1999 for the Boston-born striker. A prolific scorer in his early days with Oxford City and Yeovil, Howard was given few chances at St Andrews. He took a phone call from Fry while shopping in Nottingham and accepted his offer. Debuting on his 24th birthday in a 1-0 win over Cheltenham, he fired seven goals in his first 12 League games. Little was seen of Howard's goal-getting after that. A rib injury sustained at Exeter in late December curtailed his involvement in Posh's play-off push. He featured sporadically in 2000-01 but looked a pale shadow of himself. In March 2001, his loan spell with Conference title-chasers Yeovil was cut short by injury. Given an extended run with Posh during 2001-02, Howard failed to impress, and his future at London Road looks bleak.

Season	League			FA Cup			League Cup			Other			Total		
	Aps	Sub	Gls	Aps	Sub	Gls	Aps	Sub	Gls	Aps	Sub	Gls	Aps	Sub	Gls
1999-00	19	6	7	2									21	6	7
2000-01	2	6	1			2	1			2			5	8	1
2001-02	13	4	2		3								13	7	2
Total	34	16	10	2	5		1			2			39	21	10

FORSYTH, Richard Michael
Midfielder   *Dudley, 3 October 1970*

A free transfer from Blackpool in July 2000, Forsyth was Barry Fry's only summer signing in preparation for Posh's return to Division Two. A Black Country lad, Richard began his League career at Birmingham, when Fry bought him from Kidderminster for £50,000. Forsyth spent 1995-96 at St Andrews before Stoke splashed out £200,000. He made 90 League appearances for the Potters before signing for Blackpool in July 1999. Brought to Posh to replace midfield general Steve Castle, Forsyth signed a three-year contract and, despite several injuries, he made a vital contribution to a successful 2000-01 season. Scoring the winner at Oldham to earn a money-spinning FA Cup trip to Chelsea and netting a penalty in a 4-1 win over Cambridge boosted his popularity. Despite injuries in 2001-02, Richard is still an important cog.

Season	League			FA Cup			League Cup			Other			Total		
	Aps	Sub	Gls	Aps	Sub	Gls	Aps	Sub	Gls	Aps	Sub	Gls	Aps	Sub	Gls
2000-01	25	5	2	5		1	2				1		32	6	3
2001-02	30	2		4			2		1	1			37	2	1
Total	55	7	2	9		1	4		1	1	1		69	8	4

FOSTER, Colin
Central Defender   *Nottingham, 26 December 1952*

A stalwart of the Mansfield side that Peter Morris took into Division Two in 1977, Foster was reunited with him in 1979. He had played 205

League games for the Stags prior to debuting for Posh in a League Cup-tie with Charlton in August 1979. A solid stopper, Colin was ever present in his first season and played 25 League games in 1980-81 before being released. After hanging up his boots, he managed Corby, King's Lynn and Stamford before becoming a painter and decorator.

Season	League			FA Cup			League Cup			Other			Total		
	Aps	Sub	Gls	Aps	Sub	Gls	Aps	Sub	Gls	Aps	Sub	Gls	Aps	Sub	Gls
1979-80	46		2	1			6						53		2
1980-81	25		3				4						29		3
Total	71		5	1			10						82		5

FREEMAN, Neil
Goalkeeper   *Northampton, 16 February 1955*

Freeman was a Peter Morris capture following the sale of Keith Waugh to Sheffield United in September 1981. Unable to break through at his first club, Arsenal, Freeman gave good service to Grimsby, Southend, Birmingham, Walsall, and Huddersfield on loan, before joining Posh. He laid claim to the goalkeeping jersey in 1981-82 but left that summer following the arrival of David Seaman. Freeman joined his home-town club Northampton, where he ended his professional career in 1983.

Season	League			FA Cup			League Cup			Other			Total		
	Aps	Sub	Gls	Aps	Sub	Gls	Aps	Sub	Gls	Aps	Sub	Gls	Aps	Sub	Gls
1981-82	41			3									44		

FREESTONE, Trevor
Forward   *Market Bosworth, 16 February 1954*

Teenager Freestone hit the only goal on his debut against Aldershot in March 1973. After two more appearances, the Leicestershire-born lad left London Road in 1974 to try his luck abroad.

Season	League			FA Cup			League Cup			Other			Total		
	Aps	Sub	Gls	Aps	Sub	Gls	Aps	Sub	Gls	Aps	Sub	Gls	Aps	Sub	Gls
1972-73	2	1	1										2	1	1

FRENCH, Daniel John
Midfielder   *Peterborough, 25 November 1979*

The only local-born player in the current squad, Newborough-lad French signed associate schoolboy forms on his 14th birthday. At first employed in central midfield, he was switched to the right, from where his runs and crosses caused more damage. French was a member of the Under-18s who reached the semi-finals of the FA Youth Cup in 1998, scoring in the first round win over Doncaster and the quarter-final defeat of Crewe. Stepping up to reserve-team football in 1998-99, he played for the seniors as a sub several times during the following season. After spells with Boston and Bedford, Daniel's full League debut came against Walsall in April 2001. Regular first-team football eluded him during 2001-02, but at 22 time is still on French's side.

Season	League			FA Cup			League Cup			Other			Total		
	Aps	Sub	Gls	Aps	Sub	Gls	Aps	Sub	Gls	Aps	Sub	Gls	Aps	Sub	Gls
1999-00		6			1						1			7	
2000-01	1	1								1			2	2	
2001-02	1	9	1								1		1	10	1
Total	2	16	1		1					1	2		3	19	1

FUCCILLO, Pasquale (Lil)
Midfielder   *Bedford, 2 May 1956*
Although mostly remembered as Posh manager, Fuccillo served as a player in the twilight of a career that included nine years with Luton. Signed by John Wile from Southend, Lil helped Posh to the fifth round of the FA Cup in 1985-86 and missed just one League match all season. Upon his release in 1987, he played for Maltese side Valletta before finishing his career with Cambridge the following year. He returned to London Road as assistant boss to Chris Turner in 1991, and had a troubled spell as manager when Turner became club chairman a year later.

Season	League			FA Cup			League Cup			Other			Total		
	Aps	Sub	Gls	Aps	Sub	Gls	Aps	Sub	Gls	Aps	Sub	Gls	Aps	Sub	Gls
1985-86	45		3	7			2			1			55		3
1986-87	37						4						41		
Total	82		3	7			6			1			96		3

FULTON, Stephen (Steve)
Midfielder   *Greenock, 10 August 1970*
A Scottish Under-21 cap, Fulton spent most of his career in his native land. He started out at Celtic, playing 76 League games before joining Bolton in July 1993. Unsettled, he was loaned to Posh over Christmas. Fulton returned to Scotland with Falkirk shortly afterwards.

Season	League			FA Cup			League Cup			Other			Total		
	Aps	Sub	Gls	Aps	Sub	Gls	Aps	Sub	Gls	Aps	Sub	Gls	Aps	Sub	Gls
1993-94	3												3		

FURNELL, Andrew Paul
Forward   *Peterborough, 13 February 1977*
Much was expected of this local lad, whose goalscoring earned him England Youth caps. A strong forward, Furnell was 16 when debuting at home as a sub in the Division One visit of Bristol City in November 1993. In the return at Ashton Gate on the last day of the season, he scored what would be his only Posh goal. Earlier, he had missed from the spot in an FA Cup shoot-out at Spurs. He made sporadic appearances over the next two seasons before going to Rushden & Diamonds. He left Nene Park in 1998 to serve Stamford, Wisbech, and Grantham.

Season	League			FA Cup			League Cup			Other			Total		
	Aps	Sub	Gls	Aps	Sub	Gls	Aps	Sub	Gls	Aps	Sub	Gls	Aps	Sub	Gls
1993-94	5	5	1		1		1						6	6	1
1994-95	4	4											4	4	
1995-96		1			1						1			3	
Total	9	10	1		2		1				1		10	13	1

David Oldfield v Stoke, February 2001

Peter Morris

Gary Andrews

Martin O'Connor, 1996-97

Derek Payne v Crewe
August 1996

Leon McKenzie v Notts Co, October 2000

Steve Welsh

Ray Hankin scores against Torquay, September 1983

Mick Martin

David Pleat

Scott Houghton v Exeter, August 1998

Dave Syrett v Darlington
1980-81

GAGE, Wakeley Alexander John
Central Defender   *Northampton, 5 May 1958*

Discovered as a lad with Wellingborough, centre-half Gage signed in October 1979 for his home-town side, Northampton, playing 218 League games, many as skipper. He had an unhappy spell at Chester early in 1984-85 before John Wile brought him to Posh. At 6ft 4in, Gage lorded it at the heart of defence, missing only a couple of games from November 1985 to the end of 1986-87, when Noel Cantwell released him. He played for Crewe before quitting League football in 1989.

Season	League Aps	Sub	Gls	FA Cup Aps	Sub	Gls	League Cup Aps	Sub	Gls	Other Aps	Sub	Gls	Total Aps	Sub	Gls
1985-86	27									1			28		
1986-87	46	1		1			4			2			53		1
Total	73	1		1			4			3			81		1

GALLAGHER, John Christopher (Jackie)
Forward   *Wisbech, 6 April 1958*

One of only two Wisbech-born players to represent Posh, Gallagher continued his League career at London Road after failing as a teenager at Lincoln. Impressing Peter Morris during a trial period in late 1979-80, he debuted in a 2-0 home win over Bournemouth and signed a one-year contract. He scored one goal before being released in 1981. After a time in Hong Kong, he served Torquay and Wisbech before starting a second spell at Posh in August 1985. He made his mark with two goals in a 4-2 win at Preston on the opening day of 1985-86 and finished the campaign as top scorer with 15 goals. After forming a useful partnership with Steve Phillips the following season, he was transferred to Wolves, whom he helped to the Fourth Division title and the Freight Rover Trophy at Wembley in 1987-88. Jackie quit League football afterwards but carried on playing well into his 30s for Boston, King's Lynn, Grantham and Diss before enjoying FA Cup success with Wisbech in the late 1990s. In 2001-02 he helped run Wisbech reserves.

Season	League Aps	Sub	Gls	FA Cup Aps	Sub	Gls	League Cup Aps	Sub	Gls	Other Aps	Sub	Gls	Total Aps	Sub	Gls
1979-80	1												1		
1980-81	10	2	1						3				10	5	1
1985-86	40	2	12	4	1	2	2			1		1	47	3	15
1986-87	38	2	8	1			2	1		2			42	4	8
Total	89	6	21	4	2	2	4	4		3		1	100	12	24

GALLEY, John Edward
Forward   *Clowne, 7 May 1944*

John arrived on loan from Nottingham Forest in October 1974 with a goalscoring reputation forged with Rotherham and Bristol City in the 1960s. With 150 goals to his name, he added just one, in a 1-1 draw at

Crystal Palace in front of Match of the Day cameras. After returning to Forest, he reunited with John Sillett at Hereford, where he finished his League career in 1977. Nowadays Galley works for the William Guppy Paper Group and runs a hostel for Nottingham Forest apprentices.

Season	League			FA Cup			League Cup			Other			Total		
	Aps	Sub	Gls	Aps	Sub	Gls	Aps	Sub	Gls	Aps	Sub	Gls	Aps	Sub	Gls
1974-75	7		1										7		1

GARNHAM, Stuart Edward
Goalkeeper   *Selby, 30 November 1955*

Garnham was a former Wolves apprentice signed by Noel Cantwell in March 1977 as cover for Keith Waugh, following Eric Steele's move to Brighton. Garnham made two appearances for Posh, at home to Port Vale and Walsall near the end of 1976-77. His only previous League experience was on loan to Northampton in 1974-75, and he was again loaned to the Cobblers in August 1977 prior to his release from Posh.

Season	League			FA Cup			League Cup			Other			Total		
	Aps	Sub	Gls	Aps	Sub	Gls	Aps	Sub	Gls	Aps	Sub	Gls	Aps	Sub	Gls
1976-77	2												2		

GARWOOD, Colin Arthur
Forward   *Heacham, 29 June 1949*

A lively winger-cum-striker, Norfolk-born Garwood came up through the ranks. Norman Rigby gave him his debut in January 1968, aged 18, and Colin scored in a 3-3 draw at Bournemouth. Late that season his three goals in a 4-0 hiding of Northampton made him – to this day – Posh's youngest ever hat-trick scorer. His talent was used sparingly by new boss Jim Iley until 1970-71, when injury to Peter Price gave Colin his chance. His 17 League goals from 29 starts made him top scorer, and earned him a £12,000 move to Oldham in July 1971. A regular at Boundary Park, he bagged 35 goals in 93 League games and in 1974 won a Third Division champions medal before enhancing his reputation at Huddersfield, Colchester, Portsmouth, and Aldershot. His 27 League goals in 1979-80 made him top marksman in Division Four. After 157 goals in a 14-year League career, Garwood joined Boston in 1982, striking a hat-trick on his debut in the Alliance Premier League against Dagenham. Garwood also played for King's Lynn, Bourne, and Wisbech, where he was assistant boss in the early 1990s.

Season	League			FA Cup			League Cup			Other			Total		
	Aps	Sub	Gls	Aps	Sub	Gls	Aps	Sub	Gls	Aps	Sub	Gls	Aps	Sub	Gls
1967-68	7		5										7		5
1968-69	13	3	3				1						14	3	3
1969-70	9	4	5	1	3								10	7	5
1970-71	29	1	17	2		1							31	1	18
Total	58	8	30	3	3	1	1						62	11	31

GAVIN, Patrick John (Pat)

Forward   *Hammersmith, 5 June 1967*

A former postman, Gavin was plucked from the Spartan League by Gillingham in March 1989. Seven goals in 13 games in 1988-89 earned him another move to Leicester, but three games later he was loaned back to the Gills. Chris Turner paid Leicester £15,000 for the powerful striker on transfer deadline day in March 1991. Dangerous in the air, Gavin created a club record when scoring in his first five games to aid Posh's promotion push. The following season he bagged a hat-trick in a League Cup-tie with Aldershot but was soon displaced by the more mobile David Riley. In February 1993 Northampton took Gavin on a free transfer and he scored the goals that ensured their League survival on the last day of 1992-93. Gavin later moved to Wigan, before tuning out for Hayes, Farnborough and, most recently, Harrow.

Season	League			FA Cup			League Cup			Other			Total		
	Aps	Sub	Gls	Aps	Sub	Gls	Aps	Sub	Gls	Aps	Sub	Gls	Aps	Sub	Gls
1990-91	10	1	6										10	1	6
1991-92	8	3					4	1	4	2	1	1	14	5	5
1992-93		1						1			1		1	2	
Total	18	5	6				4	2	4	3	1	1	25	8	11

GENOVESE, Domenico

Forward   *Peterborough, 2 February 1961*

Failing to break through with Posh in the 1970s, Genovese was given a second chance after a decade scoring goals for Grantham, Kettering, Boston, Nuneaton and Stamford. Signed by Noel Cantwell in March 1988, the locally-born striker debuted in a home win over Exeter and scored his first goal in a 3-0 League Cup win at WBA early in 1988-89. Spending most of his time on the bench, he resumed his career with Kettering. He returned to Posh in the early 1990s as Football in the Community Officer, a duty he now performs for Kettering.

Season	League			FA Cup			League Cup			Other			Total		
	Aps	Sub	Gls	Aps	Sub	Gls	Aps	Sub	Gls	Aps	Sub	Gls	Aps	Sub	Gls
1987-88	1												1		
1988-89	7	8	1				2	1	1				9	9	2
Total	8	8	1				2	1	1				10	9	2

GIBSON, Terence Bradley (Terry)

Forward   *Walthamstow, 23 December 1962*

Gibson was a tiny striker known from his goalscoring days with Spurs and Coventry, which earned him a big-money move to Manchester United in January 1986. Failing to impress, he joined Wimbledon, with whom he won a FA Cup winners' medal in 1988. He joined Posh on a free transfer in December 1993, making a solitary League appearance in a 0-1 defeat at Barnsley before leaving for Barnet, where finished his playing career in 1996. After a spell coaching at Underhill, Terry is now assistant manager to Lawrie Sanchez at Wycombe Wanderers.

Season	League			FA Cup			League Cup			Other			Total		
	Aps	Sub	Gls	Aps	Sub	Gls	Aps	Sub	Gls	Aps	Sub	Gls	Aps	Sub	Gls
1993-94	1												1		

GILL, Matthew James
Midfielder   *Cambridge, 8 November 1980*

First appearing during Posh's final two games of 1997-98, Gill claimed a regular midfield slot the following campaign. Ankle injuries halted his progress in mid-season but he returned towards the end. Perhaps overshadowed by fellow youngsters Matthew Etherington and Simon Davies, Gill found opportunities hard to come by in 1999-2000, though he did score his first League goal in a 2-3 home defeat by Swansea. He proved his versatility in 2000-01 by deputising for right-back Dean Hooper until Gill himself was struck down by a knee injury. Sidelined for almost a year, Gill returned to action in February 2002 and made the right-back position his own. He doubled his goals haul with long-range strikes at Bournemouth and Reading. Still only 21, Matthew will be looking to develop his skills and passing ability during 2002-03.

Season	League			FA Cup			League Cup			Other			Total		
	Aps	Sub	Gls	Aps	Sub	Gls	Aps	Sub	Gls	Aps	Sub	Gls	Aps	Sub	Gls
1997-98	2												2		
1998-99	22	4					2				1		24	5	
1999-00	7	13	1	1						1	2		9	15	1
2000-01	11	6	1	3						1			15	6	1
2001-02	11	1	2										11	1	2
Total	53	24	4	4			2			2	3		61	27	4

GODDEN, Anthony Leonard (Tony)
Goalkeeper   *Gillingham, 2 August 1955*

A rising star of Ron Atkinson's talented WBA side of the late 1970s, Godden played 267 League games between 1975 and 1986 before moving on to Chelsea and Birmingham. Capable of spectacular saves, he also had loan spells at Walsall, Luton and Bury prior to joining Posh in July 1989. Tony debuted against newcomers Maidstone on the opening day of 1989-90 and appeared 30 times before retiring at the end of the season, after which he kept goal for Wivenhoe before moving into management with Warboys, March Town, King's Lynn, Bury Town and Wisbech. He has since returned to Posh as goalkeeping coach.

Season	League			FA Cup			League Cup			Other			Total		
	Aps	Sub	Gls	Aps	Sub	Gls	Aps	Sub	Gls	Aps	Sub	Gls	Aps	Sub	Gls
1989-90	24			2			2			2			30		

GOLDSMITH, Craig Stephen William
Winger   *Peterborough, 27 August 1963*

Signed by Mick Jones from Stamford-based Mirrlees in August 1988, local lad Goldsmith enjoyed a promising first season before fading. As a schoolboy, Craig wanted to become a professional table tennis player. He reached the semi-finals of the national championships at 15, but never fulfilled his dream and worked as a plasterer and as a van driver before joining Posh. He debuted as a sub in the 1-4 home defeat by Scarborough in September 1988, and scored his first goal in a League Cup-tie with Leeds later that month. Further goals in League victories over Stockport and Burnley helped Craig keep his place, providing width on the left flank with his willingness to run at defenders. He found himself out of favour under Mark Lawrenson the following season, which led to a £20,000 move to Carlisle in December 1989. After adding a further 30 League appearances, he returned to local soccer.

Season	League			FA Cup			League Cup			Other			Total		
	Aps	Sub	Gls	Aps	Sub	Gls	Aps	Sub	Gls	Aps	Sub	Gls	Aps	Sub	Gls
1988-89	34	6	6	4			2		1	2			42	6	7
1989-90	5	1					2		1			1	7	2	
Total	39	7	6	4			4		1	2		1	49	8	7

GOODING, Michael Charles (Mick)
Midfielder   *Newcastle, 12 April 1959*

Although spending just one full season with Posh, midfield dynamo Gooding made an impact. Described by Noel Cantwell as the best midfielder in Division Four upon signing from Rotherham in August 1987, the inspirational Geordie set about repaying his £25,000 fee. He scored the winner on his debut against Carlisle in the opening game of 1987-88, but his goals were a bonus, compared to his tireless running and grit. When netting three times against Newport at London Road, Mick recorded the first Posh hat-trick in nearly six years. After picking up the Player of the Season award, Mick began 1988-89 in the same vein before being sold to Wolves for £85,000. He won a Third Division champions medal in his first season at Molineux and gained more honours after moving to Reading, where he was appointed joint player-manager with Jimmy Quinn. Mick was still going strong in his 40s, playing for, and being assistant manager, at Southend in 1999-2000.

Season	League			FA Cup			League Cup			Other			Total		
	Aps	Sub	Gls	Aps	Sub	Gls	Aps	Sub	Gls	Aps	Sub	Gls	Aps	Sub	Gls
1987-88	44		18	1		2	6		2	4		2	55		24
1988-89	3		3				2						5		3
Total	47		21	1		2	8		2	4		2	60		27

GORDON, Dale Andrew

Winger   *Great Yarmouth, 9 January 1967*

Norfolk-born Gordon began with Norwich, where his dazzling wing play earned him England Under-21 caps and a £1.2 million move to Glasgow Rangers in 1991. He won two Scottish Premier League titles before spending an injury-ridden two years with West Ham. He was loaned to Posh in March 1995 as part of his rehabilitation, first appearing in a 1-1 home draw with table-topping Birmingham. A loan spell at Millwall in 1996 preceded a stay at Bournemouth, where he also did some coaching. He dropped out of professional soccer a year later, joining Great Yarmouth and, later, Gorleston, both as player-manager.

Season	League			FA Cup			League Cup			Other			Total		
	Aps	Sub	Gls	Aps	Sub	Gls	Aps	Sub	Gls	Aps	Sub	Gls	Aps	Sub	Gls
1994-95	6		1										6		1

GOULD, John Barrie (Barrie)

Forward/Wing-half   *Ammanford, 18 January 1944*

Gould signed in July 1965 after failing to break through at Arsenal and Chelsea. He started 1965-66 as a striker alongside Johnny Byrne, but struggled to find goals and was dropped midway through the season. Although reinstated in midfield in the closing weeks, he made just one appearance in 1966-67 before leaving London Road on a free transfer.

Season	League			FA Cup			League Cup			Other			Total		
	Aps	Sub	Gls	Aps	Sub	Gls	Aps	Sub	Gls	Aps	Sub	Gls	Aps	Sub	Gls
1965-66	18		3	1			2						21		3
1966-67							1						1		
Total	18		3	1			3						22		3

GRAHAM, Gerald Wilson (Gerry)

Wing-half   *Aspatria, 31 January 1941*

Signed from Blackpool in July 1960 to boost Jimmy Hagan's squad as League football beckoned, Graham was for four seasons on the fringes of the team. He played just one League game during Posh's debut season and added only a handful of outings before joining Mansfield in June 1964. He later had spells with Worcester and Workington.

Season	League			FA Cup			League Cup			Other			Total		
	Aps	Sub	Gls	Aps	Sub	Gls	Aps	Sub	Gls	Aps	Sub	Gls	Aps	Sub	Gls
1960-61	1						1						2		
1961-62	6												6		
1962-63	7						1						8		
1963-64	3		1										3		1
Total	17		1				2						19		1

GRAHAM, Milton Mackay

Midfielder *Tottenham, 2 November 1962*

London-born Graham caught the eye aged 21 at Bournemouth, scoring in their shock FA Cup win over Manchester United in 1984. Milton made 73 League appearances for the Cherries, scoring twelve goals, before in August 1985 he joined Chester, where he matured into a renowned midfielder. It took a club record £72,000 to bring him to Posh for 1989-90. He debuted in a 1-0 win over newcomers Maidstone on the opening day and bagged his first goal in a 1-1 home draw with Gillingham in October. He was on target a week later, too, hitting a ballistic winner in a seven-goal epic with leaders Exeter. Sadly, a knee injury sustained in an FA Cup-tie at Swansea prematurely ended his professional career. He re-surfaced in local football with Spalding and Holbeach, and, after helping Stamford to consecutive United Counties League titles, he moved on to Yaxley. Milton now manages local out-fit Pearl, and builds boats for a company based in Oundle, Northants.

Season	League			FA Cup			League Cup			Other			Total		
	Aps	Sub	Gls	Aps	Sub	Gls	Aps	Sub	Gls	Aps	Sub	Gls	Aps	Sub	Gls
1989-90	10	4	2	2	1		2			1			15	5	2

GRAZIOLI, Guiliano Stefano Luigi

Forward *Marylebone, 23 March 1975*

Signed from Wembley in October 1995, 'Graz' did not really launch himself until 1998-99, when his purple patch was crowned by a record-breaking five League goals in the 9-1 away win at Barnet. The Italian striker found the net a further ten times to finish as leading goalscorer – reward for his persistence. Former manager John Still's final signing, Grazioli spent his first three seasons kicking his heels or injured. He showed what he could do during loan spells with Yeovil, Enfield and Stevenage, where he achieved FA Cup fame in 1998, scoring the goals that defeated Swindon and took Newcastle to a replay. Despite his late flowering with Posh, Grazioli refused Barry Fry's new terms in June 1999 and moved to First Division Swindon, managed by former team-mate Jimmy Quinn. Injuries restricted him to a handful of games as the Robins were relegated. He had better luck in 2000-01 but was sent off in a County Ground clash with Posh on the opening day of 2001-02.

Season	League			FA Cup			League Cup			Other			Total		
	Aps	Sub	Gls	Aps	Sub	Gls	Aps	Sub	Gls	Aps	Sub	Gls	Aps	Sub	Gls
1995-96	2	1	1										2	1	1
1996-97		4			3	1		2						9	1
1998-99	21	13	15				1				2		22	15	15
Total	23	18	16		3	1	1	2			2		24	25	17

GREEN, Francis James
Forward   *Derby, 25 April 1980*

Green is a willing, pacy striker, capable of operating through the middle or out wide. Signed from Ilkeston in March 1998, Francis scored on his full debut in Posh's 1-3 defeat at Torquay the following month. He was overlooked for all but the closing weeks of the following season. Green began 1999-2000 by coming off the bench to score Posh's winner against Hartlepool on the opening day. He also came close in the play-off final against Darlington after coming on for Andy Clarke. 2000-01 proved to be Green's best season to date. Three early goals saw him head Posh's scoring chart, and despite losing his place in mid-season he was again amongst the goals as Posh finished twelfth in Division Two. He was back on the fringes during 2001-02.

Season	League			FA Cup			League Cup			Other			Total		
	Aps	Sub	Gls	Aps	Sub	Gls	Aps	Sub	Gls	Aps	Sub	Gls	Aps	Sub	Gls
1997-98	2	2	1										2	2	1
1998-99	3	4	1										3	4	1
1999-00	8	12	1	1				1		1	2		10	15	1
2000-01	18	14	6	2			2			2		1	24	14	7
2001-02	12	11	3	2			1	1			1	1	15	13	4
Total	43	43	12	5			3	2		3	3	2	54	48	14

GREEN, William (Bill)
Central Defender   *Newcastle, 22 December 1950*

John Barnwell smashed Posh's transfer record when paying West Ham £60,000 for Bill Green in July 1978. The towering central defender made 35 First Division appearances for the Hammers after starting his career with Hartlepool and Carlisle, whom he captained to the top flight in 1974. Green failed the hard task of replacing Chris Turner, and his one season with Posh ended with relegation to Division Four. He recaptured his better form after signing for Chesterfield in June 1979, appearing in 160 League games in four years. A final move took him to Doncaster, whom he helped climb to Division Three in 1983-84.

Season	League			FA Cup			League Cup			Other			Total		
	Aps	Sub	Gls	Aps	Sub	Gls	Aps	Sub	Gls	Aps	Sub	Gls	Aps	Sub	Gls
1978-79	30						8						38		

GREENMAN, Christopher James (Chris)
Defender   *Bristol, 22 December 1968*

A lightweight but confident defender, Greenman tasted Premiership action with Coventry before signing on a free transfer in March 1993. He debuted in a 0-0 home draw with Watford and showed neat skills as Posh settled into Division One. He struggled thereafter, however, and was released following relegation in 1994. He joined Bromsgrove, then Worcester City, where he was quickly made club captain.

Season	League			FA Cup			League Cup			Other			Total		
	Aps	Sub	Gls	Aps	Sub	Gls	Aps	Sub	Gls	Aps	Sub	Gls	Aps	Sub	Gls
1992-93	8	1											8	1	
1993-94	24	1		2			3						29	1	
Total	32	2		2			3						37	2	

GREGORY, David Harry

Midfielder/Forward   Peterborough, 6 October 1951

David Gregory's rise from park football to Posh star made the local lad a huge favourite in the 1970s. Having been twice rejected on account of his size, Gregory was working as a mechanic while playing football for Peterborough Rovers and Chatteris Town when Noel Cantwell offered him a one-year contract in May 1973. David was not about to let his chance slip. Pitched in as a half-time substitute in a pre-season home friendly with Plymouth, Gregory took the ball from the kick-off, dribbled through the Argyle defence, dummied the keeper, then calmly scored. Despite this, he was held back in Posh's Fourth Division title success of 1973-74, but an injury to John Cozens early in the following campaign gave David his chance. With his electrifying speed and penchant for spectacular goals, Gregory starred in the run to round five of the FA Cup and ended the season as top scorer. He top-scored again in 1975-76, when his 17 goals included a hat-trick in a 4-2 victory over Grimsby and a solo effort against Wrexham. He was also voted into the PFA select side that season. Although his match-winning qualities were subdued during 1976-77, his £55,000 transfer to Stoke that summer was a record receipt. A change of management saw his departure from Stoke after just 23 League games and three goals, whereupon he was loaned to Blackburn before becoming Bury's record signing. He then helped Portsmouth get out of Division Four in 1980 before joining Wrexham two years later. David hit 31 goals in 153 League games for the Robins, for whom he also appeared in the Cup-Winners' Cup, prior to ending his League career back with Posh in 1986-87. He spent three years at King's Lynn before joining Spalding and Holbeach, where he currently lives and works as a self-employed ceramic tiler.

Season	League			FA Cup			League Cup			Other			Total		
	Aps	Sub	Gls	Aps	Sub	Gls	Aps	Sub	Gls	Aps	Sub	Gls	Aps	Sub	Gls
1973-74	3	9					1						3	10	
1974-75	35	6	9	8		5							43	6	14
1975-76	46		14	5		1	5		2				56		17
1976-77	41	2	9		1		5						46	3	9
1986-87	16	15	8	1			2	1		2		1	21	16	9
Total	141	32	40	14	1	6	12	2	2	2		1	169	35	49

GREGORY, David Spencer

Midfielder   Colchester, 23 January 1970

Right-sided midfielder Gregory signed in July 1995 from Ipswich, where he had come through the ranks to exceed 50 appearances. A free transfer by John Still, he was given few opportunities before joining his hometown club, Colchester, early in 1996. He scored the 1998 play-off winner against Torquay that took the U's into Division Two.

Season	League			FA Cup			League Cup			Other			Total		
	Aps	Sub	Gls	Aps	Sub	Gls	Aps	Sub	Gls	Aps	Sub	Gls	Aps	Sub	Gls
1995-96	3			1			1			2			4	3	

GREGORY, Neil Richard

Forward   *Zambia, 7 October 1972*

Neil is the younger brother of David Gregory, though they were born oceans apart. Like his brother, Neil was a product of Ipswich's youth policy. Arriving at London Road on loan in November 1997, he scored on his debut in a table-topping clash at Notts County. He made three more scoreless appearances before returning to Portman Road. A move to Colchester saw the brothers reunited but Neil's time at Layer Road was brief and he now plays for Canvey Island.

Season	League			FA Cup			League Cup			Other			Total		
	Aps	Sub	Gls	Aps	Sub	Gls	Aps	Sub	Gls	Aps	Sub	Gls	Aps	Sub	Gls
1997-98	2	1	1							1			3	1	1

GRIEMINK, Bart

Goalkeeper   *Oss, Holland, 29 March 1972*

A giant Dutch Under-21 cap, goalkeeper Bart arrived in October 1996 after becoming redundant at Birmingham, where he was signed by Barry Fry from Dutch side AWK. Griemink found it tough in his early Posh career, but he recovered from on-field mishaps to give some fine displays while belting the ball the length of the pitch. He was forced aside for all of 1997-98 by the excellent Mark Tyler, but regained a first-team slot on occasions during 1998-99. His early clangers returned to haunt him when deputising for flu-victim Tyler against Rotherham on Boxing Day 1999, as he contributed to Posh's 0-5 thrashing. Bart was on loan to First Division Swindon when Tyler's shoulder injury provided him with another opportunity to redeem himself. He kept four clean sheets in 13 games to help Posh's promotion push, but stepped down for the play-offs. Bart signed for Swindon soon afterwards and by the end of 2001-02 had made 70 Second Division appearances.

Season	League			FA Cup			League Cup			Other			Total		
	Aps	Sub	Gls	Aps	Sub	Gls	Aps	Sub	Gls	Aps	Sub	Gls	Aps	Sub	Gls
1996-97	27			4						4			35		
1998-99	17						1						18		
1999-00	14												14		
Total	58			4			1			4			67		

GRIFFITHS, Carl Brian
Forward   *Oswestry, 15 July 1971*

An impish Welsh Under-21 cap, Griffiths became Posh's record buy when Mick Halsall took him from Portsmouth for £225,000 on transfer deadline day in 1996. Griffiths started out with Shrewsbury, where his 27 League goals in 1992-93 led to a £500,000 move to Manchester City. Opportunities were few at Maine Road and he netted four goals in 18 League games before joining Pompey. He scored within two minutes of his Posh debut at home to Walsall, but added just one more League goal before signing for Leyton Orient for £50,000 in March 1997. After missing out on the 2001 play-off final, Carl left to try his luck at Luton.

Season	League			FA Cup			League Cup			Other			Total		
	Aps	Sub	Gls	Aps	Sub	Gls	Aps	Sub	Gls	Aps	Sub	Gls	Aps	Sub	Gls
1995-96	4		1										4		1
1996-97	2	10	1	1	1	1	2	1			1		3	14	3
Total	6	10	2	1	1	1	2	1			1		7	14	4

GUNN, Brynley Charles (Bryn)
Defender   *Kettering, 21 August 1958*

Bryn Gunn arrived in August 1986 with the pedigree of eleven years at Nottingham Forest, with whom he won the European Cup in 1980. A versatile and experienced defender, he started at left-back with Posh but enjoyed most success in the centre of defence alongside Paul Price. Bryn weighed in with important goals as Posh's regular penalty taker. Ever present during 1987-88 and 1988-89, it was a surprise when Mick Jones released him to Chesterfield on a free transfer in July 1989. Gunn spent three years at Saltergate before moving into the semi-professional ranks with Corby in 1992 and Arnold Town four years later.

Season	League			FA Cup			League Cup			Other			Total		
	Aps	Sub	Gls	Aps	Sub	Gls	Aps	Sub	Gls	Aps	Sub	Gls	Aps	Sub	Gls
1986-87	38	1	7	1			4			2			45	1	7
1987-88	46			2			6		1	4			58		1
1988-89	46		7	4			4		1	2			56		8
Total	130	1	14	7			14		2	8			159	1	16

GUY, Alan
Midfielder/Forward   *Jarrow, 8 September 1957*

Arriving from Newcastle, Alan Guy made an instant impact when netting twice on his debut in a 2-0 win over John Toshack's high-flying Swansea in March 1979. Although a midfielder by trade, Guy's explosive start saw him continue up front during his early Posh career, but when goals became elusive he dropped deeper in 1979-80. He featured in 34 League games that season but was released a year later owing to the emergence of local youngsters Micky Gynn and Trevor Quow.

Season	League			FA Cup			League Cup			Other			Total		
	Aps	Sub	Gls	Aps	Sub	Gls	Aps	Sub	Gls	Aps	Sub	Gls	Aps	Sub	Gls
1978-79	13	2	4										13	2	4
1979-80	1	3		1									2	3	
1980-81	28	6					3	2	1				31	8	1
Total	42	11	4	1			3	2	1				46	13	5

GYNN, Michael (Micky)

Midfielder   *Peterborough, 19 August 1961*

Micky Gynn was one of the finest home-grown players ever to wear a Posh shirt. A huge favourite, Gynn's close control and mazy dribbling earned him an unprecedented three consecutive Player of the Season awards in the early 1980s. The pint-sized midfielder went on to spend a decade playing at the highest level with Coventry. Born at Thorpe Hall, Peterborough, Gynn started playing football at St Marks Junior School in Gladstone Street, where his classmates included another future Posh star, Trevor Quow. Moving to nearby Whittlesey as an 11-year-old, Gynn was offered an apprenticeship with Posh upon leaving school in 1977 and helped the Under-18s reach the quarter-finals of the FA Youth Cup the following year. He was pitched into the first team as Peter Morris's side slipped towards relegation in 1978-79. Still only 18, he was used sparingly the following season, but earned a regular place in 1980-81 after starring in the run to round five of the FA Cup. Fans responded to his direct running and hard tackling with the first of his three awards. He was ever present in 1981-82 as Posh narrowly missed promotion. 1982-83 proved to be Micky's last season at London Road, his 21 goals taking him to Coventry for £60,000 in August 1983. He made almost 300 appearances for the Sky Blues, enjoying his finest hour in May 1987 when helping them lift the FA Cup by beating Spurs in extra-time. After ten years service, Gynn had a spell with Stoke in 1993-94 before injury terminated his full-time career. He played for Hednesford and Kettering, and latterly King's Lynn, Stamford, Corby and Warboys Town, whilst working as a postman in Coventry.

Season	League			FA Cup			League Cup			Other			Total		
	Aps	Sub	Gls	Aps	Sub	Gls	Aps	Sub	Gls	Aps	Sub	Gls	Aps	Sub	Gls
1978-79	9	2	2										9	2	2
1979-80	26	1	1				6						32	1	1
1980-81	28	1	7	6									34	1	7
1981-82	46		6	3			2						51		6
1982-83	43		17	4		3	4		1				51		21
Total	152	4	33	13		3	12		1				177	4	37

Martin Pike v Hereford, January 1985

Andy Rogers (right)
v Wrexham, April 1977

Brian McGorry, 1994-95

Norman Rigby   John Wile signs Les Lawrence, 1986

Francis Green v Swansea, August 2000

Errington Kelly
v Leeds, FA Cup
January 1986

Gary Kimble, 1991-92

Mark Tyler

Gregor Rioch

HACKETT, Gary Stuart
Midfielder   *Stourbridge, 11 October 1962*

Lil Fuccillo signed left-sided Hackett from WBA in September 1993 for £40,000. He had served Stoke, Aberdeen and Shrewsbury, who signed him aged 21 from Bromsgrove in 1983. He debuted for Posh in a 1-2 Division One home loss to Grimsby, but he is remembered for his solo League Cup goal at Blackpool in November 1993. After one season he joined Chester in September 1994 on a free transfer, and a year later went to Halesowen. He is now assistant boss at Bromsgrove Rovers.

Season	League			FA Cup			League Cup			Other			Total		
	Aps	Sub	Gls	Aps	Sub	Gls	Aps	Sub	Gls	Aps	Sub	Gls	Aps	Sub	Gls
1993-94	18	4	1				5		1			1	23	5	2

HAILS, William (Billy)
Outside-right   *Nettlesworth, 19 February 1935*

A star of Posh's all-conquering Midland League side of the late 1950s, Durham-born Hails was a diminutive right-winger who signed from Lincoln in 1955 and marked his arrival with a hat-trick in a 5-1 victory over Mansfield's reserves. After helping Posh to five Midland League titles, he played in every match in 1960-61, scoring 21 League goals, as Jimmy Hagan's side won the Fourth Division at the first attempt. Billy was part of arguably Posh's finest ever forward line, along with Terry Bly, Dennis Emery, Peter McNamee and Ray Smith. In addition to his goals, Hails would speed down the right flank, beat his man and deliver pin-point crosses, many of which were converted by Bly. The wing wizard closed the door on seven years service in October 1962 when joining Northampton, whom he helped become Third Division champions that season. He spent one more season with the Cobblers, then saw out his League career at Luton. Spells with Nuneaton and Rugby followed before Jim Iley brought Hails back as trainer in the late 1960s. Billy had a short time as Posh manager following John Barnwell's resignation in 1978, before spending many years as Watford physio.

Season	League			FA Cup			League Cup			Other			Total		
	Aps	Sub	Gls	Aps	Sub	Gls	Aps	Sub	Gls	Aps	Sub	Gls	Aps	Sub	Gls
1960-61	46		21	5		2	1		1				52		24
1961-62	37		6	6		1	1		1				44		8
1962-63	11		1										11		1
Total	94		28	11		3	2		2				107		33

HALEY, Grant
Right-back   *Bristol, 20 September 1979*

Grant Haley was born in his grandmother's bed at their Bristol home as the ambulance was late. A product of Posh's youth policy, diminutive full-back Haley shone in the reserves in 1999-2000. Nicknamed 'Sugar', Grant was a surprise first-team call-up against Southend in

October 1999 as Dean Hooper was suspended. Grant's assured display was rewarded by Barry Fry with a five-year contract. Haley's progress stuttered, and after spending much of 2000-01 helping Bedford into the Ryman Premier League, he joined the non-Leaguers in June 2001.

Season	League			FA Cup			League Cup			Other			Total		
	Aps	Sub	Gls	Aps	Sub	Gls	Aps	Sub	Gls	Aps	Sub	Gls	Aps	Sub	Gls
1999-00	1												1		

HALL, James Leonard (Jim)
Forward   *Northampton, 2 March 1945*

Whenever football conversation turns to Posh's best ever striker, Jim Hall's name is always mentioned. Strong, unpretentious and brave, Hall belonged to an earlier mould. Imperious in the air, he also possessed a neat touch and a sweet left foot, attributes that helped net him 137 Posh goals, a record that looks unbeatable. Born in Northampton, Hall signed professional forms for his hometown club in 1963, but after making only 56 League appearances in over four years, he transferred to London Road in December 1967 in a player-plus-cash deal that saw Johnny Byrne depart. It was the start of an eight-year love affair between the Posh faithful and 'Big Jim'. He bagged 13 goals in 22 League games in half a season, while in 1968-69 he became the first Posh player to hit 20 League goals in a season since Derek Dougan five years earlier. In 1969-70, four of his 24 League goals came in the then club record League 8-1 defeat of Oldham. Having formed a telepathic partnership with Peter Price, Jim developed an equal understanding with John Cozens during Posh's Fourth Division title-winning season of 1973-74. Although less prolific than in the past, 'Big Jim' enjoyed another four-goal haul in a 5-1 win over Doncaster, taking him to eight Posh hat-tricks overall. When he returned to Northampton in May 1975, he had scored a record 122 League goals. Before retiring, he was loaned to Cambridge, where 15 goals from 24 League games helped Ron Atkinson's side win the Fourth Division in 1977. Jim became a teacher in Northampton, then worked for Social Services for 20 years. Pensioned off following surgery on his legs and ankles – a legacy of his football career – Jim lives in Scratby near Great Yarmouth.

Season	League			FA Cup			League Cup			Other			Total		
	Aps	Sub	Gls	Aps	Sub	Gls	Aps	Sub	Gls	Aps	Sub	Gls	Aps	Sub	Gls
1967-68	20	2	13										20	2	13
1968-69	46		20	1			5		4				52		24
1969-70	41	1	24	4		3	2						47	1	27
1970-71	39		10	2		1	1						42		11
1971-72	41		16	3		4							44		20
1972-73	46		21	4		2	1						51		23
1973-74	40		13	4		1	2						46		14
1974-75	25	1	5	1	1		1						27	2	5
Total	298	4	122	19	1	11	12		4				329	5	137

HALSALL, Michael (Mick)

Midfielder   *Bootle, 21 July 1961*

One of Posh's finest captains, Mick Halsall was a fierce competitor whose grit and and will to win epitomised Posh's never-say-die spirit under Chris Turner. Signed from Grimsby in 1987 for a £25,000 fee raised by Posh fans, the former Liverpool, Birmingham and Carlisle player made the first of over 300 appearances in a home win over Carlisle on the opening day of 1987-88. Playing alongside fellow new-boy Mick Gooding, Halsall soon became a firm favourite. He missed only five League games in his first two seasons before skippering Posh through their most successful years. In 1989-90 he played every match and top-scored, and a year later helped the side to promotion from the old Fourth Division. Mick was instrumental in Posh's second promotion the following year, scoring a vital goal in the first leg of their play-off semi-final with Huddersfield, then skippering the side to glory at Wembley in May 1992. An inspiration to those around him, he made up for any lack of finesse with his energy, passion and zeal. Mick made 25 First Division appearances in 1992-93 before an Achilles injury sustained in a 2-3 home defeat by Wolves sidelined him for ten months. By the time he returned in December 1993, Posh had sunk to the foot of Division One, but he could inspire no recovery, suffering a setback after just two appearances that ultimately forced his retirement. He remained at London Road as assistant to new boss John Still in 1994-95, before being handed the reins following Still's dismissal in October 1995. A popular choice for the job amongst the fans, Mick lasted only seven months before returning to a coaching role following Barry Fry's ill-fated purchase of the club. Relieved of his duties as a cost-cutting measure by Fry, Mick teamed up with Still as assistant manager at Barnet before taking up a position as youth-team coach at Walsall.

Season	League			FA Cup			League Cup			Other			Total		
	Aps	Sub	Gls	Aps	Sub	Gls	Aps	Sub	Gls	Aps	Sub	Gls	Aps	Sub	Gls
1987-88	45		4	2			6		1	3			56		5
1988-89	42		1	4		1	4			2			52		2
1989-90	46		11	3			2		1	2			53		12
1990-91	45		5	5		2	4			2			56		7
1991-92	45		5	3		1	8		1	11		2	67		9
1992-93	25		2	3			2		1	1			31		3
1993-94		1					1						1	1	
Total	248	1	28	20		4	27		4	21		2	316	1	38

HAMPTON, Ivan Keith

Full-back   *Heanor, 15 October 1942*

Born in Nottinghamshire, full-back Hampton started as a pro at Notts County where he made 141 League appearances before joining Halifax in July 1967, playing 59 League games before he joined Posh two years later. He debuted in a 0-0 Fourth Division encounter at Port Vale on the first day of 1969-70. He was given only a few subsequent first-team opportunities before Jim Iley released him at the end of the season.

Season	League			FA Cup			League Cup			Other			Total		
	Aps	Sub	Gls	Aps	Sub	Gls	Aps	Sub	Gls	Aps	Sub	Gls	Aps	Sub	Gls
1969-70	3	1					2						5	1	

HANKIN, Raymond (Ray)
Forward *Wallsend, 2 February 1956*

Ray Hankin was a gifted striker whose short Posh career was marred by disciplinary ructions. A former England Under-23 cap, big Ray burst onto the First Division scene as a teenager with Burnley in the 1970s, hitting 37 goals in 112 League games to earn himself a £200,000 move to Leeds in September 1976. His career peaked in 1977-78 when he scored 20 League goals in just 33 games to help take Leeds back into Europe after a five-year absence. But in the early 1980s, Ray faded during spells with Vancouver Whitecaps and Middlesbrough, enabling John Wile to land him for a nominal fee in September 1983. After scoring twice on his Posh debut in a 5-0 home crushing of Torquay, he netted again four days later when Crystal Palace were dumped from the League Cup. Posh fans marvelled at Hankin's subtle skills, heading power and determination, but the honeymoon was short-lived. Ray's aggression irked referees and by the end of his first season he had been dismissed four times, straining Wile's patience. A groin injury sidelined Hankin for the first half of 1984-85, and within weeks of his return he was out of London Road following yet another sending off in a home match with Port Vale. His contract was terminated, whereupon Ray joined Tommy Docherty's struggling Wolves but, after ten appearances in the famous Old Gold, Hankin quit professional football – aged just 29. He later returned to the professional game with Darlington, firstly as a coach, before trying his hand as manager in 1992. These days he is Football in the Community officer at Newcastle.

Season	League			FA Cup			League Cup			Other			Total		
	Aps	Sub	Gls	Aps	Sub	Gls	Aps	Sub	Gls	Aps	Sub	Gls	Aps	Sub	Gls
1983-84	25	2	7				3		1				28	2	8
1984-85	6		1							2			8		1
Total	31	2	8				3		1	2			36	2	9

HANLON, Richard Kenneth (Ritchie)
Midfielder *Kenton, 26 May 1978*

Former Chelsea apprentice Hanlon came from Rushden & Diamonds in a player-plus-cash deal that saw Miguel De Souza move to Nene Park. Ritchie spent two years at Stamford Bridge without playing a first-team match but made a couple of League appearances during a season (1996-97) with Southend. He also had a year with Welling prior to joining Rushden for £20,000 in 1998. He debuted for Posh as a sub in a 3-1 home win over Scarborough in December 1998, and opened his goalscoring account with a late equaliser against Hull a month later. Unable to claim a regular place, Hanlon spent part of 1999-2000 back on loan to Welling, where he netted 14 goals from midfield. Recalled to Posh, he played a minor role in the club's promotion push. His winning goal on the last day condemned Chester to the Conference, but he was on the bench for the play-offs, coming on in the semi-final second-leg victory over Barnet and the final against Darlington. Although not the most gifted player, it was testimony to Ritchie's dedication that he appeared in over half of Posh's Second Division matches in 2000-01. Ritchie joined newcomers Rushden & Diamonds in September 2001.

Season	League			FA Cup			League Cup			Other			Total		
	Aps	Sub	Gls	Aps	Sub	Gls	Aps	Sub	Gls	Aps	Sub	Gls	Aps	Sub	Gls
1998-99		4	1							1			1	4	1
1999-00	9	7	1							1	2		10	9	1
2000-01	21	5	1		1		1	1		2			24	7	1
2001-02		1												1	
Total	30	17	3		1		1	1		4	2		35	21	3

HANN, Matthew
Forward   *Saffron Walden, 6 September 1980*

A pacy, all-action striker, Hann was called up from the youth team in 1998-99 for an Auto Windscreens Shield tie at Bournemouth. One of several youngsters tipped for stardom, he also made a few substitute appearances. Frustrated in the reserves, Matthew left for pastures new and after a loan spell with Stamford, he now plays for Cambridge City.

Season	League			FA Cup			League Cup			Other			Total		
	Aps	Sub	Gls	Aps	Sub	Gls	Aps	Sub	Gls	Aps	Sub	Gls	Aps	Sub	Gls
1998-99		4								1			1	4	

HARLE, David
Midfielder   *Denaby, 15 August 1963*

A former England Youth cap, Yorkshireman Harle began his nomadic football career with Doncaster in the early 1980s. He joined Exeter in 1982 but a year later returned to star in Billy Bremner's Rovers that won promotion to Division Three. Spells with Leeds, Bristol City and Scunthorpe followed before his free transfer to Posh in March 1989. After appearing in a handful of games, he was omitted by Mick Jones at the start of 1989-90. Recalled by new manager Mark Lawrenson for the visit of Fourth Division pacesetters Exeter, Harle scored in Posh's 4-3 win. He left the club in March 1990 for a third spell with Doncaster.

Season	League			FA Cup			League Cup			Other			Total		
	Aps	Sub	Gls	Aps	Sub	Gls	Aps	Sub	Gls	Aps	Sub	Gls	Aps	Sub	Gls
1989-90	7												7		
1990-91	14	1	2							2	1	1	16	2	3
Total	21	1	2							2	1	1	23	2	3

HAWKES, Kenneth Kilby (Ken)
> *Left-back*   *Shotton Colliery, 6 May 1933*

Jimmy Hagan signed Hawkes from Luton for £2,000 in June 1961. Left-back Ken had exceeded 100 games for the Hatters, among them the 1959 FA Cup final defeat by Nottingham Forest, but injuries restricted him to just one game for Posh. He suffered a broken arm, cracked ribs and had a cartilage removed, all within ten months. Released on a free transfer to Bedford in June 1962, he served St Neots as player-coach while working as a sales representative for a wholesale food company.

Season	League			FA Cup			League Cup			Other			Total		
	Aps	Sub	Gls	Aps	Sub	Gls	Aps	Sub	Gls	Aps	Sub	Gls	Aps	Sub	Gls
1961-62	1												1		

HEALD, Greg James
> *Central Defender*   *Enfield, 26 September 1971*

One of John Still's many non-League buys, Heald cost £35,000 when joining from Enfield in July 1994. Indifferent early displays suggested he might struggle in the Second Division but by the end of his first season he looked a sound investment. A reliable stopper, liked by fans for his commitment, he appeared in over 100 League games until reuniting with former boss Still at Barnet in August 1997.

Season	League			FA Cup			League Cup			Other			Total		
	Aps	Sub	Gls	Aps	Sub	Gls	Aps	Sub	Gls	Aps	Sub	Gls	Aps	Sub	Gls
1994-95	27	2					1			3		1	31	2	1
1995-96	40		4	3			3			5			51		4
1996-97	34	2	2	5	1		4			3		1	46	3	3
Total	101	4	6	8	1		8			11		2	128	5	8

HEATH, Donald (Don)
> *Winger*   *Stockton, 26 December 1944*

Heath was a utility player signed from Oldham in July 1972, near the end of Jim Iley's time in charge. Don started out at Middlesbrough in 1962, but it was only after joining Norwich two years later that he made his League debut. After three seasons with the Canaries, making 82 League appearances, he signed for Swindon Town for £10,000 in September 1967. He won the League Cup with the Robins in their 1969 extra-time victory over Arsenal at Wembley, and a year later helped them lift the Anglo-Italian Cup in Naples. Heath spent one season in Posh colours, as a right-sided forward, and missed just two matches in 1972-73. Although he retained his place after Iley's dismissal, new boss

Noel Cantwell released him on a free transfer in the summer of 1973. Heath returned to his native north-east, where he had two years with Hartlepool, before playing for Gateshead and Crook Town. Hanging up his boots in 1976, he scouted for Sunderland, Cardiff, Portsmouth and Swansea, while earning a living as a materials controller for ICI.

Season	League Aps	Sub	Gls	FA Cup Aps	Sub	Gls	League Cup Aps	Sub	Gls	Other Aps	Sub	Gls	Total Aps	Sub	Gls
1972-73	43	1	4	4			1						48	1	5

HEELEY, David Mark (Mark)
Winger   *Peterborough, 8 September 1959*

Stanground-lad Heeley became Posh's youngest ever player when he came on as a 16-year-old sub for Tommy Robson against Shrewsbury in May 1976. The teenager was undaunted, displaying the confidence, even arrogance, that might have been expected of Robson, when nut-megging an opponent within minutes of taking the field. Heeley's talent blossomed the following campaign, with his pace and ability to cross to either the near or far post. He could also score, his first goal, against Portsmouth, being followed by two more against Swindon and Lincoln. After such heroics, Heeley expected to have a big part in John Barnwell's plans in 1977-78, but refused to play when named only as sub for the opening match against Portsmouth, an act for which he was disciplined and suspended. With his career hanging by a thread, and Mark stating that he had lost interest in football and was considering college, he was thrown a shock lifeline. In September, Arsenal took him on loan. A staggering £50,000 transfer – rising to £100,000 depending on appearances – saw Heeley lining up alongside Liam Brady and Alan Hudson in the Gunners' midfield. His Arsenal adventure lasted a further two seasons, but after making only 15 League appearances in that time, scoring one goal, he returned to the lower leagues with Northampton. After 92 League games for the Cobblers in a more defensive role, he quit the professional game in 1983, aged just 23! He served Stamford and Buckingham of the United Counties League and in 1985 started pre-season training with John Wile's Posh squad, but was gone within days.

Season	League Aps	Sub	Gls	FA Cup Aps	Sub	Gls	League Cup Aps	Sub	Gls	Other Aps	Sub	Gls	Total Aps	Sub	Gls
1975-76		1												1	
1976-77	12	4	3										12	4	3
Total	12	5	3										12	5	3

HELLAWELL, Michael Stephen (Mike)
Outside-right   *Keighley, 30 June 1938*

Hellawell was one of four ex-England internationals who served short, unspectacular spells with Posh in the 1960s. Signed on a free transfer from Huddersfield in December 1968, he made his League debut with QPR in 1955, before moving on to Birmingham and Sunderland. His two England caps were earned in 1962 while with Birmingham, with whom he won the League Cup the following year. His Posh debut came against Halifax and was memorable for being the last game to be abandoned at London Road. Snow and ice made the pitch unplayable after 45 goalless minutes. Mike's 'official' debut came in a 1-2 defeat at Southend on Boxing Day. After making a further eight appearances for Posh, he left the club for non-League Bromsgrove Rovers in 1969.

Season	League			FA Cup			League Cup			Other			Total		
	Aps	Sub	Gls	Aps	Sub	Gls	Aps	Sub	Gls	Aps	Sub	Gls	Aps	Sub	Gls
1968-69	9												9		

HENRY, Liburd Algernon
Forward   *Dominica, 29 August 1967*

This well-travelled, West Indian-born striker gained League experience with Watford, Halifax, Maidstone and Gillingham prior to joining Posh on a free transfer in August 1994. Although signed as a squad player, he received an early call-up following an injury to Paul Moran. Quick and strong, Liburd took his chance and showed moments of promise, hitting ten goals in 22 games prior to Christmas. He struggled thereafter, and on losing his place was freed by John Still in 1995. Liburd joined numerous minor clubs, including Woking, Dagenham & Redbridge, Borehamwood, Erith & Belvedere, and Dover Athletic.

Season	League			FA Cup			League Cup			Other			Total		
	Aps	Sub	Gls	Aps	Sub	Gls	Aps	Sub	Gls	Aps	Sub	Gls	Aps	Sub	Gls
1994-95	22	10	7	2		1			1	2		2	26	11	10

HEPPOLETTE, Richard Alfred William (Ricky)
Midfielder   *India, 8 April 1949*

A £30,000 capture from Chesterfield in the 1979 close season, experienced midfielder Heppolette proved a costly purchase as injury forced his retirement after just one season. Indian-born Ricky began his career at Preston, for whom he made 154 League appearances between 1967 and 1972, winning a Third Division champions medal in 1970-71. He spent four years at Leyton Orient, then shorter stints at Crystal Palace and Chesterfield in the late 1970s. Appointed captain at London Road, he debuted in a 3-1 League Cup win over Charlton in August 1979, but played only a few more games before retiring. He remained in the Peterborough area and owns a party shop in the Rivergate Centre.

Season	League			FA Cup			League Cup			Other			Total		
	Aps	Sub	Gls	Aps	Sub	Gls	Aps	Sub	Gls	Aps	Sub	Gls	Aps	Sub	Gls
1979-80	5						3						8		

HERBERT, Edward (Eddie)
Goalkeeper   *Peterborough, 9 October 1968*

Mark Lawrenson spotted Eddie playing for Peterborough League side Deeping Rangers and offered the tall, blond goalkeeper a one-year contract. A former tree surgeon, Herbert appeared in both legs of a League Cup first-round tie with Fulham early in 1990-91, but tasted senior action just once more, in a Leyland Daf Trophy tie at Wrexham before being released. He has since played for Wisbech and Spalding.

Season	League			FA Cup			League Cup			Other			Total		
	Aps	Sub	Gls	Aps	Sub	Gls	Aps	Sub	Gls	Aps	Sub	Gls	Aps	Sub	Gls
1990-91							2			1			3		

HILL, Frederick (Freddie)
Midfielder   *Sheffield, 17 January 1940*

Hill was a former England cap whose £5,000 signing from Manchester City in August 1973 was testimony to Noel Cantwell's ability to attract big-name players. An expert passer, the cultured playmaker had also served Bolton and Halifax during a distinguished career spanning 15 years. It was while at Bolton that Bill Shankly dubbed Hill the 'best midfielder in the country' but a big-money move to Liverpool in 1964 collapsed when a medical divulged high blood pressure. Posh fans would never have suspected, as Hill helped steer Cantwell's side to the Fourth Division title in 1973-74, his vision and subtle skills complementing the aggression of Paul Walker and energy of Bert Murray. Freddie was ever present and scored the all-important goal at home to Darlington that confirmed Posh's return to Division Three. Although never prolific, Hill's goals were generally memorable, such as his volley against Northampton in November 1973, and a trademark free-kick against Division Three leaders Blackburn a year later. Freddie treated London Road to his array of skills until the summer of 1975, when he was released to play Second Division football in Sweden. When he later returned to England he tried managing Oswestry Town.

Season	League			FA Cup			League Cup			Other			Total		
	Aps	Sub	Gls	Aps	Sub	Gls	Aps	Sub	Gls	Aps	Sub	Gls	Aps	Sub	Gls
1973-74	46		6	4		1	2						52		7
1974-75	27	2	1	6	1		1						34	3	1
Total	73	2	7	10	1	1	3						86	3	8

HILL, Paul James
Defender   *Nottingham, 28 January 1973*

Paul began as a Posh trainee in July 1989. Turning professional a year later, he made one first team appearance, standing in for the injured Noel Luke in a 0-2 defeat at Hartlepool, before being released in 1991. He helped Raunds Town and Stamford to the United Counties League title, and more recently graced the Dr Martens League with Wisbech.

Season	League			FA Cup			League Cup			Other			Total		
	Aps	Sub	Gls	Aps	Sub	Gls	Aps	Sub	Gls	Aps	Sub	Gls	Aps	Sub	Gls
1990-91	1												1		

HINDLEY, Peter
Defender   *Worksop, 19 May 1944*

Former England Under-23 cap Hindley was a strongly built right-back who came to the fore in the 1960s at Nottingham Forest, with whom he spent nearly 13 years and made 366 League appearances. He was a stalwart of the side that finished runners-up to Manchester United in 1967. He added a further 33 Leagues games with Coventry before Noel Cantwell signed him in July 1976. Hindley exceeded 100 League appearances for Posh in three seasons. He excelled in 1977-78, when John Barnwell's side came close to promotion, in large part due to a mean defence that conceded only 33 League goals. Peter's only Posh goal helped secure a 3-1 win over Northampton in March 1977. Known for his love of dogs, Hindley owned and raced a pair of grey-hounds, which he sometimes exercised on the track around the pitch. He once caused consternation by allowing them to swim in the team's communal bath. Hindley retired following Posh's relegation in 1978-79 but remained local, living in Bretton as a painter and decorator.

Season	League			FA Cup			League Cup			Other			Total		
	Aps	Sub	Gls	Aps	Sub	Gls	Aps	Sub	Gls	Aps	Sub	Gls	Aps	Sub	Gls
1976-77	42		1	2			5						49		1
1977-78	40			3			3						46		
1978-79	30			1			3						34		
Total	112		1	6			11						129		1

HINE, Mark
Midfielder   *Middlesbrough, 18 May 1964*

A hard-working midfielder, Hine started out with Whitby before turning professional with Grimsby in October 1983. Struggling to get into their team, he switched to Darlington in 1986. He appeared in over 150 games, helping the Quakers to regain League status. Mark Lawrenson signed him for a small fee in January 1990. Hine's Posh debut came in a 1-2 defeat at Wrexham and he kept his place until joining Scunthorpe in March 1991. He returned to non-League with Gateshead a year later and earned two caps for the England semi-professional side.

Season	League			FA Cup			League Cup			Other			Total		
	Aps	Sub	Gls	Aps	Sub	Gls	Aps	Sub	Gls	Aps	Sub	Gls	Aps	Sub	Gls
1989-90	22		4							1			23		4
1990-91	33		3	5			3			2			43		3
Total	55		7	5			3			3			66		7

HODGSON, Gordon Henry

Midfielder   *Newcastle, 13 October 1952, Died April 1999*

A former England Youth cap, Gordon started out with Newcastle but moved to Mansfield for first-team football, having made nine League appearances for the Magpies. He captained the Stags from Division four into Division Two in three seasons in the 1970s. After a spell with Oxford, he rejoined former Stags' manager Peter Morris when signing for Posh for £10,000 in August 1980, and debuted in a 1-1 draw at Lincoln on the opening day of 1980-81. Gordon, comfortable in possession, anchored midfield as Morris's side launched promotion bids in 1981 and 1982. In the summer of 1982 Hodgson quit professional football for a career with the Cambridgeshire Constabulary, though he turned out for King's Lynn and March Town. Detective Constable Hodgson died of a heart attack on Thorpe Wood golf course aged 46.

Season	League			FA Cup			League Cup			Other			Total		
	Aps	Sub	Gls	Aps	Sub	Gls	Aps	Sub	Gls	Aps	Sub	Gls	Aps	Sub	Gls
1980-81	44		2	6			2						52		2
1981-82	38	1	3	2			1						41	1	3
Total	82	1	5	8			3						93	1	5

HODSON, Stuart William

Defender   *Peterborough, 5 November 1950*

In November 1974 Noel Cantwell offered local lad Hodson a contract after the stocky Chatteris Town defender had impressed during a three-month trial. Stuart debuted later that month when handed the No 2 shirt at home to Port Vale. Although never a regular, Hodson stayed for nearly three years as understudy to Cantwell's defensive stars. He was released at the end of 1976-77, whereupon he returned to local non-League soccer with March, Stamford and Bourne.

Season	League			FA Cup			League Cup			Other			Total		
	Aps	Sub	Gls	Aps	Sub	Gls	Aps	Sub	Gls	Aps	Sub	Gls	Aps	Sub	Gls
1974-75	11	7											11	7	
1975-76	11	1						1					11	2	
1976-77	2	2					2	1					4	3	
Total	24	10					2	2					26	12	

HOGG, Anthony Raymond (Ray)

Full-back   *Lowick, 11 December 1929*

Northumberland-born right-back Hogg was plucked from his local club, Berwick Rangers, by Aston Villa in 1955. He played 21 League games in three seasons, then joined Mansfield. After making a further eleven League appearances, his next port of call was Posh in June 1960. Signed by Jimmy Hagan as cover for Ellis Stafford, Hogg languished in the reserves, stepping up just twice prior to his release in March 1961. Ray returned to Birmingham to work in a betting office near to Villa Park, and after 30 years as a bookie he is now retired in Berwick.

Season	League			FA Cup			League Cup			Other			Total		
	Aps	Sub	Gls	Aps	Sub	Gls	Aps	Sub	Gls	Aps	Sub	Gls	Aps	Sub	Gls
1960-61	2												2		

HOLLIDAY, Edwin (Eddie)

Outside-left   Barnsley, 7 June 1937

Capped three times by England after making his mark in the late 1950s alongside Brian Clough at Middlesbrough, Eddie Holliday was a tall left-winger who wound up his career with Posh in 1969. After leaving Boro in March 1962 he spent three years at Sheffield Wednesday prior to returning to Ayresome Park in June 1965. He also had spells with Hereford and Workington before Jim Iley secured him on a free transfer. Posh never saw the best of Eddie, and he hung up his boots after breaking a leg in a Fourth Division clash at Exeter in November 1969.

Season	League			FA Cup			League Cup			Other			Total		
	Aps	Sub	Gls	Aps	Sub	Gls	Aps	Sub	Gls	Aps	Sub	Gls	Aps	Sub	Gls
1969-70	12	4	1	1			1						14	4	1

HOLLOW, Michael John (Mike)

Full-back   Nazeing, 5 September 1943

Having been admired by several clubs while with Bishops Stortford, Hollow signed for First Division Leyton Orient in August 1962, but was unable to establish himself and came to Posh after making only 34 League appearances in three years. He scored on his debut as Posh kicked off 1965-66 with a 1-0 home win over Gillingham, but he soon lost his place. He made a few appearances before the end of the season, mainly at right-back, before joining Cambridge City in May 1966.

Season	League			FA Cup			League Cup			Other			Total		
	Aps	Sub	Gls	Aps	Sub	Gls	Aps	Sub	Gls	Aps	Sub	Gls	Aps	Sub	Gls
1965-66	14		1				1						15		1

HOLMAN, Harold William (Harry)

Forward   Exeter, 16 November 1957

Holman was one of several strikers tried during 1978-79 in a bid to end Posh's goal famine. A former England Schoolboy cap, he arrived just before Christmas 1978 having gained experience with his home-town club Exeter, where he bagged nine goals in 52 League games. Despite scoring in his third game for Posh, which earned Billy Hails' strugglers a point at Mansfield, Harry made his last appearance against his former club Exeter before turning his back on professional football.

Season	League			FA Cup			League Cup			Other			Total		
	Aps	Sub	Gls	Aps	Sub	Gls	Aps	Sub	Gls	Aps	Sub	Gls	Aps	Sub	Gls
1978-79	9		1										9		1

HOLMES, James Paul (Jimmy)
Defender   *Dublin, 11 November 1953*

A veteran left-back known to John Wile from their days at Vancouver Whitecaps, Jimmy signed for Posh in November 1983. Capped 30 times by the Republic of Ireland while with Coventry and Spurs in the 1970s, Holmes also served Leicester, Brentford and Torquay. A regular in the Posh defence during 1983-84, he gradually took a back seat as Wile appointed him team coach for the following season. One of his last appearances, in September 1985, saw him used as an emergency goalkeeper following John Turner's dismissal against Northampton. Jimmy probably regretted donning the gloves, as his ineptitude contributed to a record 0-5 home drubbing. After leaving Posh in 1986, Jimmy joined Nuneaton and briefly managed Hitchin and Bedworth before starting a career with the West Midlands police force.

Season	League Aps	Sub	Gls	FA Cup Aps	Sub	Gls	League Cup Aps	Sub	Gls	Other Aps	Sub	Gls	Total Aps	Sub	Gls
1983-84	20	1	2							1			21	1	2
1984-85	13		1	2			2			2			19		1
1985-86	15		4	2			2						19		4
Total	48	1	7	4			4			3			59	1	7

HOOPER, Dean Raymond
Right-back   *Harefield, 13 April 1971*

Dean joined Posh for a second time in August 1998 after a loan spell three years earlier was curtailed through injury. He had started out with Marlow, Yeading, Chalfont St Peter and Hayes, where bright performances earned him a contract with Swindon in March 1995. A loan spell at Posh in December 1995 was going well until a knee injury forced his return to the County Ground. Released by Robins boss Steve McMahon, Dean turned out for Hayes, Stevenage, and Kingstonian, where his all-action displays earned him England semi-professional honours. Barry Fry gave him another chance, and Dean emerged from his first full season at London Road with credit. Quick, strong and competitive, he established himself at right-back, combining his fierce tackling with subtle skills and surging forward runs. A succession of injuries put paid to his involvement in Posh's promotion campaign of 1999-2000 but Dean returned to the fray the following season and even improved his poor disciplinary record until sent off in the penultimate game at former club Swindon. 2001-02 proved frustrating for Dean, who lost his place and opted for a loan to Dagenham & Redbridge.

Season	League Aps	Sub	Gls	FA Cup Aps	Sub	Gls	League Cup Aps	Sub	Gls	Other Aps	Sub	Gls	Total Aps	Sub	Gls
1995-96	4												4		
1998-99	36	2	2		1		2			1			39	3	2
1999-00	28	1		2			2			1			33	1	

2000-01	28	5		3	1	2	2		35	6
2001-02	7	6		2	2		1		10	8
Total	103	14	2	7	4	6	5		121	18	2

HOPKINS, Oliver Thomas (Ollie)
Centre-half   *South Kirby, 15 November 1935*

Yorkshireman Hopkins had the job of replacing Norman Rigby at the heart of Posh's defence in the early 1960s. Big Ollie entered the League scene with Barnsley in 1957, scoring ten goals in 50 appearances before joining Posh in July 1961. After sharing defensive duties with Rigby in his first season, Ollie produced his best form in 1962-63 as linchpin of the Posh defence, appearing in 41 League matches. Frank Rankmore's arrival in 1963 saw Hopkins replaced as centre-half, but he continued for two more years, mainly at right-back. Having played under three different Posh managers in four years, he joined Chelmsford in 1965.

Season	League			FA Cup			League Cup			Other			Total		
	Aps	Sub	Gls	Aps	Sub	Gls	Aps	Sub	Gls	Aps	Sub	Gls	Aps	Sub	Gls
1961-62	26			5									31		
1962-63	41			3			1						45		
1963-64	22												22		
1964-65	15						1						16		
Total	104			8			2						114		

HOROBIN, Roy
Inside-forward   *Brownhills, 10 March 1935*

Signed by Jimmy Hagan for £5,000 from Notts County in June 1962, Horobin's two years with Posh showed his creative skills and a good goals ratio. He debuted in a 3-3 draw with Bournemouth on the opening day of 1962-63 and kept his place despite Hagan's sacking. In July 1964 Horobin joined Crystal Palace, making four League appearances.

Season	League			FA Cup			League Cup			Other			Total		
	Aps	Sub	Gls	Aps	Sub	Gls	Aps	Sub	Gls	Aps	Sub	Gls	Aps	Sub	Gls
1962-63	40		12	3									43		12
1963-64	40		8	2			1						43		8
Total	80		20	5			1						86		20

HOUGHTON, Scott Aaron
Winger   *Hitchin, 22 October 1971*

This former England Youth winger signed for £60,000 from Walsall shortly after Barry Fry's arrival in 1996. Originally with Spurs, where he made 14 first-team appearances from the subs' bench, Scott had loan spells at Ipswich, Cambridge, Gillingham and Charlton before arriving at the Bescot Stadium via a short spell with Luton. With Posh he took the eye with some neat touchline runs and spectacular goals, and was one of the few to emerge from relegation in 1996-97 with any credit. Injuries cost him his place on the left wing to young Matthew

Etherington in 1998-99. Houghton's thirst for first-team football led to a reluctant transfer request. He joined Third Division rivals Southend before Christmas 1998 and a further move in October 2000 took him to Leyton Orient, for whom he scored in their Third Division play-off final defeat by Blackpool at the Millennium Stadium. Released in February 2002, Scott spent a month at Halifax, then joined Stevenage.

Season	League			FA Cup			League Cup			Other			Total		
	Aps	Sub	Gls	Aps	Sub	Gls	Aps	Sub	Gls	Aps	Sub	Gls	Aps	Sub	Gls
1996-97	26	6	8	5		1	2	2				1	33	9	9
1997-98	24	6	4	2			3			1		1	30	6	5
1998-99	7	1	1				1						8	1	1
Total	57	13	13	7		1	6	2		1	1	1	71	16	15

HOWARTH, Lee
Central Defender   *Bolton, 3 January 1968*

A reliable centre-half, Howarth was signed from Chorley in August 1991 by Chris Turner. Best remembered for his goal-line clearance in the 1992 Wembley play-off final against Stockport, moments before Ken Charlery hit Posh's winner, Lee played most of his games during the club's two years in Division One. He joined Mansfield for £15,000 in August 1994, then served Barnet, Stevenage, Boston and Kettering.

Season	League			FA Cup			League Cup			Other			Total		
	Aps	Sub	Gls	Aps	Sub	Gls	Aps	Sub	Gls	Aps	Sub	Gls	Aps	Sub	Gls
1991-92	6	1								2	2	1	8	3	1
1992-93	26	4		2			4			1			33	4	
1993-94	24	1		1			4						29	1	
Total	56	6		3			8			3	2	1	70	8	1

HUDSON, George Anthony
Centre-forward   *Manchester, 14 March 1937*

One of the most skilful centre-forwards in Posh history, barrel-chested Hudson brought style and panache during the club's early years in the Football League. Catching Jimmy Hagan's eye with a hat-trick against Posh for ailing Accrington in 1960-61, Hudson signed for £6,000 in October 1961. He scored on his debut in a 3-2 win at Newport and scored regularly alongside Terry Bly, before coming into his own following Bly's departure to Coventry in 1962. George hit 26 goals from only 36 games in 1962-63 before suddenly leaving London Road in April. George was also Coventry-bound, Jimmy Hill signing him to replace Bly. After firing a hat-trick on his Sky Blues debut, Hudson scored 62 League goals in 113 games before joining Northampton in March 1966. His final move took him north to Tranmere, where he ended his League career in 1969. Today, George is based in his home city of Manchester, where he works for the *Daily Mirror* newspaper.

Season	League			FA Cup			League Cup			Other			Total		
	Aps	Sub	Gls	Aps	Sub	Gls	Aps	Sub	Gls	Aps	Sub	Gls	Aps	Sub	Gls
1961-62	33		16	6		7							39		23
1962-63	32		22	3		3	1		1				36		26
Total	65		38	9		10	1		1				75		49

HUGHES, Lyndon James
Midfielder/Full-back   Smethwick, 16 September 1950

A well-built former England Schoolboys cap, Lyndon Hughes spent three seasons with Posh during the late 1970s. He began at WBA, playing over 100 games for the Baggies in seven years before joining Posh on a free transfer in July 1975. After missing just four games in his first season, he was less prominent in 1976-77, but showed his versatility when replacing Jeff Lee at left-back in February 1978. He linked up with Lee again a few months later when joining Kettering, where he spent two seasons before retiring in 1980. Since then, Lyndon has been employed as business development manager for the Thresher Group.

Season	League			FA Cup			League Cup			Other			Total		
	Aps	Sub	Gls	Aps	Sub	Gls	Aps	Sub	Gls	Aps	Sub	Gls	Aps	Sub	Gls
1975-76	42		4	5		1	5						52		5
1976-77	10	2											10	2	
1977-78	23		1	2			1						26		1
Total	75	2	5	7		1	6						88	2	6

HUXFORD, Richard John
Full-back   Scunthorpe, 25 July 1969

A defender who joined Barry Fry's Barnet in August 1992, Huxford also served Millwall and Birmingham on loan before joining Bradford City in 1994. The Bantams loaned him to Posh in October 1996 and he debuted in a 4-3 win at Preston. Three months later Richard joined Burnley. He later played for Dunfermline and Alloa.

Season	League			FA Cup			League Cup			Other			Total		
	Aps	Sub	Gls	Aps	Sub	Gls	Aps	Sub	Gls	Aps	Sub	Gls	Aps	Sub	Gls
1996-97	7												7		

ILEY, James (Jim)
Wing-half   South Kirby, 15 December 1935

Posh's first player-manager in League football, Iley arrived in January 1969 with nearly 500 League appearances to his credit from his time with Sheffield United, Tottenham, Nottingham Forest and Newcastle. Dominant in midfield, dangerous from dead-ball situations, Jim played regularly until 1970, after which time he picked himself only in emergencies. His last game, as sub, was in August 1972, just before his sacking as manager, when Posh fell to a then club-record 2-8 defeat at Chester. Iley also created unwelcome history: in August 1969 his dismissal at Port Vale made him Posh's first player expelled in the

Football League. After he left London Road, Jim managed Barnsley, Blackburn Rovers, Bury and Exeter City.

Season	League			FA Cup			League Cup			Other			Total		
	Aps	Sub	Gls	Aps	Sub	Gls	Aps	Sub	Gls	Aps	Sub	Gls	Aps	Sub	Gls
1968-69	22		1										22		1
1969-70	33	2	3	3			2		1				38	2	4
1970-71	8	1		2			1						11	1	
1971-72	1												1		
1972-73		1											1		
Total	64	4	4	5			3		1				72	4	5

IMLACH, Michael Thomas (Mike)
Full-back   *Croydon, 19 September 1962*

A former Everton apprentice, blond defender Imlach followed new boss Martin Wilkinson to Posh from Leeds in August 1982. He made sporadic appearances during 1982-83 before settling as left-back during the following season. He moved to Tranmere in 1984-85 but played just four League games before quitting to work on a North Sea oil rig.

Season	League			FA Cup			League Cup			Other			Total		
	Aps	Sub	Gls	Aps	Sub	Gls	Aps	Sub	Gls	Aps	Sub	Gls	Aps	Sub	Gls
1982-83	8	2					2		1				10	2	1
1983-84	29	3	1	1			4			1			35	3	1
Total	37	5	1	1			6		1	1			45	5	2

INGRAM, Godfrey Patrick
Forward   *Luton, 25 October 1959*

A teenage star with Luton in the late 1970s, Ingram then headed for America, appearing for St Louis Storm and San Jose Earthquakes in 1981-82. The former England Youth cap signed for Cardiff in a club record £200,000 deal the following summer. He played eleven League games for the Bluebirds before crossing the Atlantic for a ten-year stay. He returned to England in August 1992 and trialled at London Road following Posh's promotion to the new First Division. Debuting as a sub in a League Cup-tie at Barnet, Godfrey saw senior action in two more games, but Chris Turner opted against offering him a contract.

Season	League			FA Cup			League Cup			Other			Total		
	Aps	Sub	Gls	Aps	Sub	Gls	Aps	Sub	Gls	Aps	Sub	Gls	Aps	Sub	Gls
1992-93		1						1			1			1	2	

INMAN, Niall Edward
Midfielder   *Wakefield, 6 February 1978*

A neat passer, young Irishman Niall showed promise when selected for first-team duty. Progressing through the ranks, he debuted at Oxford on the final day of 1995-96. Whilst further opportunities were scarce, Niall made his mark internationally, winning several caps for the Republic of Ireland Under-21s. He also gained experience on loan to Stevenage in 1997-98 where, alongside team-mate Giuliano Grazioli, he participated in their FA Cup battles with Newcastle. Niall spent part of 1999-2000 on loan to Doncaster and much of the following season helping Kettering in their futile fight against relegation from the Conference. In the summer of 2001 Niall's quest for first-team football saw him join Dover. He has since moved on to Kettering.

Season	League			FA Cup			League Cup			Other			Total		
	Aps	Sub	Gls	Aps	Sub	Gls	Aps	Sub	Gls	Aps	Sub	Gls	Aps	Sub	Gls
1995-96	1												1		
1996-97		3			1			1					1	4	
1997-98	4		1										4		1
1998-99	1	2	1					1					1	3	1
1999-00		1						1						2	
Total	6	6	2		1			1	2				7	9	2

IORFA, Dominic
Forward   *Lagos, 1 October 1968*

An enigmatic Nigerian international whose performances mixed the sublime with the ridiculous, Dominic Iorfa rarely failed to entertain. Blessed with pace, Iorfa first appeared for Posh in October 1992, when he was employed as an effective substitute. The following season he was more involved and for a short while provided Posh's greatest goalscoring threat. A free spirit, 'Dom' showed glimpses of the ability that prompted QPR to part with £145,000 to sign him from Belgian side Antwerp in 1990. He scored memorable goals but disappointed as often as he delighted a frustrated and bemused London Road crowd. He left for Southend in August 1994, scoring on his Shrimpers debut, then falling victim to injury. Popular wherever he goes, 'Dom' later played for Falkirk, apparently thinking the Scottish town was a Greek island. More recently, Dom has turned out for Irish side Waterford, Aylesbury United and Billericay Town of the Ryman League.

Season	League			FA Cup			League Cup			Other			Total		
	Aps	Sub	Gls	Aps	Sub	Gls	Aps	Sub	Gls	Aps	Sub	Gls	Aps	Sub	Gls
1992-93	3	23	1	1	1								4	24	1
1993-94	24	10	8	1	1		2	1		1		1	28	12	9
Total	27	33	9	2	2		2	1		1		1	32	36	10

IPPOLITTO, Mario
Forward   *Peterborough, 16 April 1964*

One of the first youngsters to be given a chance with Posh through the Youth Opportunities Scheme, local lad Ippolitto hit the headlines after stepping up following Robbie Cooke's departure in February 1983. After scoring on his debut in a 3-0 home win over Tranmere, his dream start continued when he struck twice at Halifax three days later. Mario made a further six League appearances that season and was given a professional contract. The good times came to an end, and his career stalled under John Wile in 1983-84. Restricted to just one sub appearance that season, he later joined King's Lynn and Cambridge City.

Season	League			FA Cup			League Cup			Other			Total		
	Aps	Sub	Gls	Aps	Sub	Gls	Aps	Sub	Gls	Aps	Sub	Gls	Aps	Sub	Gls
1982-83	8		3										8		3
1983-84								1						1	
Total	8		3					1					8	1	3

Adam Drury (right) v Swansea, August 2000

Pat Sharkey

Ronnie Robinson

David Gregory, 1976-77

Kevin Russell
shields the ball, 1990-91

Peter Hindley (left), 1976-77

Keith Waugh   Bobby Smith

JACKSON, Brian Harvill

Right wing-half   *Walton-On-Thames, 1 April 1933*

An industrious competitor, Jackson arrived in July 1962 with 300-plus League appearances under his belt. Having failed to progress as an amateur at Arsenal, he tried his luck with Leyton Orient before joining Liverpool in November 1951 for £7,000, a then sizeable sum for an 18-year-old. He played 124 League games in seven years at Anfield, then added 162 appearances with Port Vale. He waited three months for his Posh debut in a 3-2 win at Watford, following Billy Hails' move to Northampton. Brian became a regular until the end of 1963-64. He soon left for Lincoln, where he finished his professional career in 1966.

Season	League			FA Cup			League Cup			Other			Total		
	Aps	Sub	Gls	Aps	Sub	Gls	Aps	Sub	Gls	Aps	Sub	Gls	Aps	Sub	Gls
1962-63	22		2	3									25		2
1963-64	25		2				1						26		2
Total	47		4	3			1						51		4

JEFFRIES, Derrick

Central Defender   *Manchester, 22 March 1951*

Signed on loan by Noel Cantwell in October 1976, Jeffries appeared in seven League games and two FA Cup-ties – including the defeat by Northwich Victoria – before returning to Crystal Palace. He had begun at Manchester City in 1968, blossoming under Malcolm Allison. He was later loaned to Millwall, before joining Chester, retiring in 1981.

Season	League			FA Cup			League Cup			Other			Total		
	Aps	Sub	Gls	Aps	Sub	Gls	Aps	Sub	Gls	Aps	Sub	Gls	Aps	Sub	Gls
1976-77	7			2									9		

JELLEYMAN, Gareth Anthony

Left-back   *Holywell, 14 November 1980*

Emerging from Posh's Academy, Jelleyman was introduced in August 1999 in a friendly with Spurs. The young full-back was already in the Welsh Under-21s, alongside team-mate Simon Davies (the pair had been regulars in the Under-18s). In his League debut in January 2000 against Northampton, Jelleyman was lucky to stay on when, booked in the first half, he committed a rash foul in the dying moments of Posh's 1-0 win. Thereafter Gareth's career prospered. He featured in all three play-off matches, with many voting him Man of the Match at Wembley against Darlington. Much was expected from Gareth in Division Two but his progress has been hampered by injury.

Season	League			FA Cup			League Cup			Other			Total		
	Aps	Sub	Gls	Aps	Sub	Gls	Aps	Sub	Gls	Aps	Sub	Gls	Aps	Sub	Gls
1999-00	14	6			1					3	1		17	8	
2000-01	6	2		1	1					2			9	3	

| 2001-02 | 6 | 4 | | 1 | | | | | | 2 | | | 9 | 4 |
| Total | 26 | 12 | | 2 | 2 | | | | | 7 | 1 | | 35 | 15 |

JEPSON, Ronald Francis (Ronnie)
  Forward   Audley, 12 May 1963

An old-fashioned centre-forward, Jepson was a Posh favourite while on loan from Port Vale from January 1990. Although big and strong, Ronnie showed neat skills and used the ball intelligently. After helping Posh climb the Fourth Division table, he was allowed to return to Vale Park before the end of the season. He managed only a handful of subsequent appearances for Vale but went on to give fine service to Preston, Exeter, Huddersfield, Bury, Oldham and Burnley.

Season	League			FA Cup			League Cup			Other			Total		
	Aps	Sub	Gls	Aps	Sub	Gls	Aps	Sub	Gls	Aps	Sub	Gls	Aps	Sub	Gls
1989-90	18		5										18		5

JOHNSON, David Nicholas Conrad
  Winger/Forward   Gloucester, 26 December 1963

Watford boss Graham Taylor plucked Johnson from non-League Redhill in March 1982. After a few First Division starts, he joined Posh on a free transfer in August 1984. Lean and athletic, David produced flashes of brilliance in his first season – such as his goal at home to Hereford – but lacked consistency. He was mostly overlooked in 1985-86, and after his release played for King's Lynn and Cambridge City.

Season	League			FA Cup			League Cup			Other			Total		
	Aps	Sub	Gls	Aps	Sub	Gls	Aps	Sub	Gls	Aps	Sub	Gls	Aps	Sub	Gls
1984-85	26	4	4	1			2						29	4	4
1985-86	2	3								1		1	3	3	1
Total	28	7	4	1			2			1		1	32	7	5

JOHNSON, Peter
  Right-back   Rotherham, 31 July 1931

Tall full-back Johnson began with his home-town club Rotherham, from where he was snapped up by Sheffield Wednesday in December 1957. He spent over seven years at Hillsborough, during which the Owls lifted the old Second Division title in 1959 before finishing League runners-up to Spurs in 1961. Gordon Clark persuaded him to finish his playing days with Posh, and 34-year-old Johnson debuted on the opening day of 1965-66. A regular in the side that reached the League Cup semi-finals, Peter was retained for the following season, sharing right-back duties with Ron Cooper and Peter Thompson.

Season	League			FA Cup			League Cup			Other			Total		
	Aps	Sub	Gls	Aps	Sub	Gls	Aps	Sub	Gls	Aps	Sub	Gls	Aps	Sub	Gls
1965-66	22		1	1			5						28		1
1966-67	20			3			1						24		
Total	42		1	4			6						52		1

JOHNSON, Peter Edward

Left-back   *Harrogate, 5 October 1958*

An experienced, tenacious left-back, Johnson began his long career with Middlesbrough in 1976. After an unsuccessful £60,000 move to Newcastle in 1980, he had nomadic spells with Bristol City, Doncaster, Darlington and Whitby. He returned to League soccer with Crewe and Exeter before settling at Southend, where he made 126 League appearances in three years. After leaving Roots Hall for Gillingham in 1989, he came to Posh on non-contract terms in October 1991. He stayed only two months but helped Chris Turner's side record League Cup victories over Newcastle and Liverpool. Johnson was not offered full-time terms and played his last game for Posh in the League Cup quarter-final clash against another of his former clubs, Middlesbrough.

Season	League			FA Cup			League Cup			Other			Total		
	Aps	Sub	Gls	Aps	Sub	Gls	Aps	Sub	Gls	Aps	Sub	Gls	Aps	Sub	Gls
1991-92	11			3			3						17		

JONES, Michael (Mick)

Central Defender   *Sunderland, 24 March 1947*

A solid, consistent centre-back, Jones began as an apprentice with Derby in 1964. Unable to break through, he moved on to Notts County, where he made 102 League appearances and helped the Magpies win Division Four in 1971 with a record points haul. Mick arrived at Posh on the eve of 1973-74 and debuted in the first-day win over Mansfield. He and Chris Turner formed a mean defence that anchored the side's title success. Jones missed just one League game that season, but the rest of his time with Posh was marred by injury. He left in 1976 to be player-boss at Kettering, but after managing Mansfield and Halifax he returned to Peterborough for a turbulent year as Posh boss in 1988-89. Mick has also been assistant manager to Notts County and Plymouth.

Season	League			FA Cup			League Cup			Other			Total		
	Aps	Sub	Gls	Aps	Sub	Gls	Aps	Sub	Gls	Aps	Sub	Gls	Aps	Sub	Gls
1973-74	45		3	4			2		1				51		4
1974-75	15	1		1			1						17	1	
1975-76	22	5	1	2	1	1	2						26	6	2
Total	82	6	4	7	1	1	5		1				94	7	6

JOSEPH, Marc Ellis

Defender   *Leicester, 10 November 1976*

Joseph joined Posh in 2001 from Cambridge where he rose through the ranks and signed professional forms in May 1995. He notched up 153 League appearances for the U's and also went on loan to Premiership Coventry during 1995-96 (without playing). Industrious Marc missed just two League games for Posh during 2001-02. Used mainly as centre-back, he was equally at home at full-back. His goals in consecutive home games against Bournemouth and Bristol City were his first in over six years of professional football. He was denied a winning goal against Cambridge at the Abbey in December by a linesman's flag.

Season	League			FA Cup			League Cup			Other			Total		
	Aps	Sub	Gls	Aps	Sub	Gls	Aps	Sub	Gls	Aps	Sub	Gls	Aps	Sub	Gls
2001-02	44		2	5			2			2			53		2

KEELEY, John Henry

Goalkeeper   *Plaistow, 27 July 1961*

A well-travelled keeper, Keeley endured a torrid time under John Still. Londoner Keeley had amassed 250 League appearances in a career that began with Southend in 1979. After a time with Chelmsford, he resumed his full-time career with Brighton, who sold him to Oldham four years later for a hefty £240,000. He played only two League games for the Latics and was loaned to Oxford, Reading and Chester. Spells at Colchester and Stockport followed before he joined Posh on a free transfer in January 1995. He never won over the fans – whom he later claimed to be the worst he had ever known – and walked out after conceding ten goals in three games. In March 1995 he rejoined Chelmsford before having spells with Canvey Island and Worthing.

Season	League			FA Cup			League Cup			Other			Total		
	Aps	Sub	Gls	Aps	Sub	Gls	Aps	Sub	Gls	Aps	Sub	Gls	Aps	Sub	Gls
1994-95	3												3		

KELLOCK, William (Billy)

Midfielder   *Glasgow, 7 February 1954*

Glasgow-born Kellock made his entry in League football with Welsh side Cardiff, after being rejected as a lad by Aston Villa. He played 35 League games for the Bluebirds between 1971 and 1973 before serving Norwich and Millwall. He then spent four seasons with Kettering before Peter Morris tempted him back to League Football in August 1979. Billy proved to be a revelation in the Fourth Division, combining aggressive tackling with subtle skills and fearsome shooting. After finishing 1979-80 as top scorer he was voted the best player in the Fourth Division by the *Sunday People*. Billy became the perfect foil for striker Robbie Cooke for two seasons, captaining Peter Morris's side that missed promotion two years in a row. Big-money moves were often predicted for Billy but when he did move on – bemoaning Posh's lack of ambition – First Division Luton paid just £30,000 for a natural leader who had hit nearly 50 goals in three seasons. His stay at Kenilworth Road was brief and in March 1983 he joined Wolves, whom he helped to promotion to the top flight. After making three First Division starts he rejoined former boss Morris at Southend, ending his League career with Port Vale and Halifax. He returned to Kettering in 1987 and was later head of marketing at the Barnsdale Country Club, Leicestershire.

Season	League			FA Cup			League Cup			Other			Total		
	Aps	Sub	Gls	Aps	Sub	Gls	Aps	Sub	Gls	Aps	Sub	Gls	Aps	Sub	Gls
1979-80	45		19	1		1	6		3				52		23
1980-81	46		13	6			4		1				56		14
1981-82	43		11	3			2						48		11
Total	134		43	10		1	12		4				156		48

KELLY, Anthony Gerald (Tony)

Midfielder   *Prescot, 1 October 1964*

A nomadic veteran, Kelly was released by Bolton in 1994 and signed for Posh on a free transfer in December. He became a cult after scoring with a freakish 40-yard free-kick on his home debut against Brentford. Tony showed good vision and fine passing skills but was blighted by injuries and a constant weight problem. He became a fringe player as the season wore on, and was released to Wigan before joining Barrow.

Season	League			FA Cup			League Cup			Other			Total		
	Aps	Sub	Gls	Aps	Sub	Gls	Aps	Sub	Gls	Aps	Sub	Gls	Aps	Sub	Gls
1994-95	12	1	2										12	1	2

KELLY, Errington Edison

Forward   *St Vincent, 8 April 1958*

John Wile claimed Kelly was the fastest player he had ever seen. The West Indian-born striker also showed an eye for goal while on loan from Coventry in March 1984. Seven goals in eleven games made him an instant hit and he signed permanent forms that summer. He was top scorer in 1984-85 when his tally included both goals in an FA Cup defeat of Cambridge. Falling out with Wile, he struggled the following season, prompting his departure in 1986 to try his luck in Sweden. Within six months he was back with Posh under new manager Noel Cantwell, who used Kelly's pace to good effect in a wide position.

Season	League			FA Cup			League Cup			Other			Total		
	Aps	Sub	Gls	Aps	Sub	Gls	Aps	Sub	Gls	Aps	Sub	Gls	Aps	Sub	Gls
1983-84	11		7										11		7
1984-85	33	7	11	2		2	2		1	1			38	7	14
1985-86	15	6	4	5	1	1		1		1		1	21	8	6
1986-87	26	2	4										26	2	4
1987-88	10	8	2	1	1		2	1	1	1	1		14	11	3
Total	95	23	28	8	2	3	4	2	2	3	1	1	110	28	34

KERR, John Joseph

Forward   *Vancouver, 6 March 1965*

Though born in Canada, Kerr is a USA international, winning 17 caps between 1984 and 1995. With a BA in political science, John came to England in 1986 and played for Harrow Borough before Portsmouth signed him the following year. During Pompey's 0-0 draw at Watford he created League history by becoming the first ever substitute to be subbed. He made four First Division appearances for Pompey in 1987-

88 and was loaned to Posh midway through the season. Although he showed polished skills and a turn of pace, Kerr returned to America to play for Washington Stars. By the time of his return to Millwall in 1992, he had served five clubs in five countries. Wycombe, of the Conference, French Third Division side Boulogne-Sur-Mer, Northern Irish club Linfield, Hamilton Steelers of Canada, and American team San Diego Sockers all benefited from Kerr's trusty right boot and explosive pace. After eight League goals in 43 games for Millwall, Kerr went back to America in 1995 to play for Dallas Burn, New England Revolution and Boston Bulldogs, the latter as player-coach. He retired from playing in 1999 to be head soccer coach at Harvard University.

Season	League			FA Cup			League Cup			Other			Total		
	Aps	Sub	Gls	Aps	Sub	Gls	Aps	Sub	Gls	Aps	Sub	Gls	Aps	Sub	Gls
1987-88	10		1									1	11		1

KEVAN, Derek Tennyson
Inside-forward   *Ripon, 6 March 1935*

Big Yorkshireman Derek Kevan signed in 1966 with a wealth of experience and over 200 League goals. After starting out with Bradford in the early 1950s, Kevan's career took off after a move to WBA, where his goalscoring earned him 14 England caps between 1957 and 1961. Twice on target in the 1958 World Cup finals in Sweden, Derek also scored goals for Chelsea, Manchester City and Crystal Palace prior to joining Posh, for whom he scored within four minutes of his debut in a 5-2 win at Exeter in March 1966. He added just one more goal before moving on to Luton in December 1966. Kevan hit four goals in eleven games for the Hatters, then joined Stockport before ending his career at Macclesfield, Boston and Stourbridge. Now based in Birmingham, Kevan was last known to be working as a drier for a sign company.

Season	League			FA Cup			League Cup			Other			Total		
	Aps	Sub	Gls	Aps	Sub	Gls	Aps	Sub	Gls	Aps	Sub	Gls	Aps	Sub	Gls
1965-66	13		2										13		2
1966-67	3	1											3	1	
Total	16	1	2										16	1	2

KIMBLE, Alan Frank
Defender   *Poole, 6 August 1966*

Experienced left-back Kimble was loaned from Wimbledon following Tom Williams' transfer to Birmingham in March 2002. The twin of former Posh winger Gary, Alan arrived with over 500 League games to his credit, 215 of them during nine years with the Dons. Kimble began, alongside Garry, at Charlton in 1984 before joining Cambridge two years later, via a loan stint at Exeter. He appeared in 299 League games for a U's side that climbed the divisions under John Beck. After Joe

Kinnear paid £175,000 for Alan in July 1993, Kimble impressed with strong tackling and an accurate left foot, which Dons fans referred to as 'the wand'. Posh, however, saw little evidence of Alan's magic as injury restricted him to just three appearances.

Season	League			FA Cup			League Cup			Other			Total		
	Aps	Sub	Gls	Aps	Sub	Gls	Aps	Sub	Gls	Aps	Sub	Gls	Aps	Sub	Gls
2001-02	3												3		

KIMBLE, Gary Leslie
Winger   *Poole, 6 August 1966*

Though spending just one season with Posh, left-winger Gary Kimble left an indelible mark. His goal against Liverpool in a League Cup fourth-round tie in December 1991 sealed the club's finest-ever cup victory. Well-travelled Gary started his career at Charlton with twin brother Alan, before exceeding 150 League games during spells at Cambridge, Doncaster, Fulham and Gillingham. Chris Turner signed him on a free transfer in July 1991. He was a regular until Bobby Barnes' arrival left him in the cold. Released soon after Posh's play-off success in May 1992 – in which he did not play – Kimble joined Dagenham & Redbridge before appearing for Welling, Sittingbourne and Chelmsford. In 1999-2000 Kimble returned to Dagenham. After a stay at Braintree he was last sighted at Bishop's Stortford.

Season	League			FA Cup			League Cup			Other			Total		
	Aps	Sub	Gls	Aps	Sub	Gls	Aps	Sub	Gls	Aps	Sub	Gls	Aps	Sub	Gls
1991-92	30		4	3			8		2	3			44		6

KIRKHAM, John Kenneth
Wing-half   *Wednesbury, 13 May 1941*

West Midlander Kirkham played 100 League games for Wolves in the early 1960s. The former England Under-23 cap spent nearly two years with Posh after being signed by Gordon Clark in November 1965. John debuted in a 1-4 defeat at Millwall and played in both legs of the club's League Cup semi-final with WBA. The tall, rangy wing-half never established himself, and after a solitary appearance at the start of 1967-68, he moved on to Exeter, then signed for part-timers Horwich RMI.

Season	League			FA Cup			League Cup			Other			Total		
	Aps	Sub	Gls	Aps	Sub	Gls	Aps	Sub	Gls	Aps	Sub	Gls	Aps	Sub	Gls
1965-66	18		1	1			2						21		1
1966-67	27		1	4			1						32		1
1967-68	1												1		
Total	46		2	5			3						54		2

KLUG, Bryan Paul

Midfielder   *Coventry, 8 October 1960*

John Wile signed former Ipswich apprentice Klug on a free transfer from Chesterfield in August 1984. Operating in central midfield, the former England Youth cap missed only a few games in 1984-85 but was not retained. He later played for the Sudbury Town side that lost an FA Vase final replay against Tamworth played at London Road in 1989. Bryan returned to his first club, Ipswich, as a coach in 1990.

Season	League			FA Cup			League Cup			Other			Total		
	Aps	Sub	Gls	Aps	Sub	Gls	Aps	Sub	Gls	Aps	Sub	Gls	Aps	Sub	Gls
1984-85	39		2	2			2			1			44		2

KNIGHT, Zatayah (Zat)

Defender   *Solihull, 2 June 1980*

A 6ft 7in defender, Knight was loaned in February 2000 from Fulham. After debuting in a 1-2 defeat at Cheltenham, Zat displayed neat skills and an obvious aerial threat before returning to Craven Cottage. He was marginalised by new boss Jean Tigana in 2000-01 – his three first-team outings being restricted to early rounds of the League Cup – before gaining a Premiership debut early in the following season.

Season	League			FA Cup			League Cup			Other			Total		
	Aps	Sub	Gls	Aps	Sub	Gls	Aps	Sub	Gls	Aps	Sub	Gls	Aps	Sub	Gls
1999-00	8												8		

KOOGI, Anders Bo

Midfielder   *Aarhus, 8 September 1979*

Danish Anders Koogi joined Posh in his early teens and signed as a professional at 17. A fine prospect, he represented Denmark at schoolboy and youth levels. He anchored midfield in Posh's Under-18 team that reached the last four of the FA Youth Cup in 1998, and his efforts for the reserves in 1998-99 earned him a late-season call-up to the full squad. He came off the bench in a 3-0 home win over Leyton Orient in May 1999 and created Posh's third goal. He was a sub again in a 1-2 defeat at Plymouth at the start of the following season, but then faded. A loan to Cambridge City preceded his release in May 2000.

Season	League			FA Cup			League Cup			Other			Total		
	Aps	Sub	Gls	Aps	Sub	Gls	Aps	Sub	Gls	Aps	Sub	Gls	Aps	Sub	Gls
1998-99		1												1	
1999-00		1												1	
Total		2												2	

KOWALSKI, Andrew Michael (Andy)

Midfielder   *Mansfield, 26 February 1953*

Mansfield-born Kowalski was spotted by Stags' rivals Chesterfield playing for Alfreton in 1973. He made 365 League appearances in ten seasons with the Spireites and also served two years at Billy Bremner's Doncaster prior to joining Posh in 1985. A resolute competitor, he held a regular place in midfield and captained Posh to the fifth round of the FA Cup in 1986. Kowalski returned to Chesterfield at the end of the season, then had spells with Boston, Gainsborough, and Matlock before becoming sales manager for a financial services company.

Season	League			FA Cup			League Cup			Other			Total		
	Aps	Sub	Gls	Aps	Sub	Gls	Aps	Sub	Gls	Aps	Sub	Gls	Aps	Sub	Gls
1985-86	35		3	7		1	2						44		4

KRYSZYNSKI, Zbigniew (Detzi)
Midfielder   *West Germany, 14 October 1961*

An experienced midfielder, Kryszynski played for Lech Gdansk and German sides FC08 Hamburg and Saarbrucken before signing for Wimbledon in December 1988. Detzi appeared over 70 times in the top flight for the Dons before his trial with Posh early in 1994. He did well on his debut in the 1-1 draw with Spurs in the FA Cup, and in three First Division games, but after two months he moved to Oxford City. Detzi then tried his luck with Bobby Gould at Coventry before playing for St Albans, Hayes, Crawley, Chertsey, Kingstonian, and Hampton.

Season	League			FA Cup			League Cup			Other			Total		
	Aps	Sub	Gls	Aps	Sub	Gls	Aps	Sub	Gls	Aps	Sub	Gls	Aps	Sub	Gls
1993-94	2	1		2									4	1	

KWIATKOWSKI, Richard (Dick)
Full-back/Midfielder   *Peterborough, 7 April 1948*

A commentator's nightmare, Kwiatkowski was born in Peterborough to a Polish father and German mother. He progressed through the ranks, debuted in 1967-68, and remained for five seasons in a variety of midfield and defensive roles. His best run was in 1970-71 when he played in 28 League and Cup games. Released in 1972, he signed for local non-Leaguers Stamford, whom he helped to Wembley in the FA Vase finals of 1976 and 1980, en route to establishing the club's appearance record. Moving to Holbeach, Dick came back to London Road in 1982 with the Tigers side that switched their 'home' FA Cup-tie with Wrexham. After managing Bourne Town in the mid-1980s, he quit football and now lives in a village outside Lincoln as a bank manager.

Season	League			FA Cup			League Cup			Other			Total		
	Aps	Sub	Gls	Aps	Sub	Gls	Aps	Sub	Gls	Aps	Sub	Gls	Aps	Sub	Gls
1967-68	6	1											6	1	
1968-69		1												1	
1969-70	17	5		1									18	5	
1970-71	23	4					1						24	4	
1971-72	3												3		
Total	49	11		1			1						51	11	

LA RONDE, Everald
Right-back　　　　　　　*West Ham, 24 January 1963*

This stocky, former West Ham right-back spent two months on loan from Bournemouth during 1984-85. After debuting in a 1-1 home draw with Hereford in January 1985, he played a further seven League games for John Wile's side before returning to Dean Court. He later dropped into non-League, first with Dagenham, then Wealdstone.

Season	League			FA Cup			League Cup			Other			Total		
	Aps	Sub	Gls	Aps	Sub	Gls	Aps	Sub	Gls	Aps	Sub	Gls	Aps	Sub	Gls
1984-85	8												8		

LAMBERT, Michael Arnold (Mick)
Winger　　　　　　　*Balsham, 20 May 1950*

Peter Morris paid his former club Ipswich £40,000 for this winger in July 1979. A veteran of over 200 First Division games, Cambridgeshire-born Lambert had spent a decade at Portman Road, but in two seasons with Posh he showed little. He debuted in a 3-1 League Cup home win over Charlton in August 1979 before losing form and fitness.

Season	League			FA Cup			League Cup			Other			Total		
	Aps	Sub	Gls	Aps	Sub	Gls	Aps	Sub	Gls	Aps	Sub	Gls	Aps	Sub	Gls
1979-80	12	4	2				3						15	4	2
1980-81	3	2						1					3	3	
Total	15	6	2				3	1					18	7	2

LANGAN, David Francis
Right-back　　　　　　　*Dublin, 15 February 1957*

Seeking a replacement for departing right-back Alan Paris, Mick Jones bought experienced 31-year-old David Langan from Bournemouth for £25,000 in August 1988. A veteran of over 350 League games and 25 appearances for the Republic of Ireland, Langan began his illustrious career at Derby in the 1970s. Birmingham paid a club record £350,000 for his services in 1980. After four seasons' top-flight action he rejoined former Blues boss Jim Smith at Oxford, winning a Second Division champions medal in 1985 and a League Cup winners medal a year later. Langan was loaned to Leicester before signing for Bournemouth. David's days with Posh were curtailed by a back injury that forced his retirement from football after just one season. In that time he set a new club record, albeit unwanted, when he became the first Posh substitute to be subbed, at home to Hartlepool in March 1989. He remained local, drove a delivery van, and then worked in the security industry.

Season	League			FA Cup			League Cup			Other			Total		
	Aps	Sub	Gls	Aps	Sub	Gls	Aps	Sub	Gls	Aps	Sub	Gls	Aps	Sub	Gls
1988-89	18	1		1			3			1			23	1	

LAWRENCE, Leslie Oliver (Les)

Forward   *Wolverhampton, 18 May 1957*

A nomad with Shrewsbury, Torquay (five years), Port Vale, Aldershot, Rochdale and Burnley, Lawrence was a powerful forward signed from Turf Moor by John Wile for £10,000. Les debuted on the first day of 1986-87, scoring in a 2-0 win over Southend, but a ruptured Achilles tendon cost him most of the campaign. Recovering after three operations to reclaim a spot under new boss Noel Cantwell at the start of the next season, Lawrence joined Cambridge early in 1988. He later played for Kettering, Aylesbury, Corby, and Bourne, and managed Spalding.

Season	League			FA Cup			League Cup			Other			Total		
	Aps	Sub	Gls	Aps	Sub	Gls	Aps	Sub	Gls	Aps	Sub	Gls	Aps	Sub	Gls
1986-87	12		4	1			3						16		4
1987-88	16	5	4	2		1	4	1	1	1			23	5	6
Total	28	5	8	3		1	7	1	1	1			39	5	10

LE BIHAN, Neil Ernest

Midfielder   *Croydon, 14 March 1976*

A former Spurs trainee, Le Bihan played under three managers in three years with Posh without convincing any of them. Signed by John Still in July 1994, the teenage midfielder made no headway for twelve months, but tasted action several times under Mick Halsall in 1995-96. Best remembered for scoring direct from a corner-kick in an FA Cup win over Wrexham that season, Neil was released by Barry Fry near the end of the following season, joining Dover and then Crawley.

Season	League			FA Cup			League Cup			Other			Total		
	Aps	Sub	Gls	Aps	Sub	Gls	Aps	Sub	Gls	Aps	Sub	Gls	Aps	Sub	Gls
1994-95	3	1											3	1	
1995-96	16	9		2	1	2	2	1	1	3	1		23	12	3
1996-97	2									2	1		4	1	
Total	21	10		2	1	2	2	1	1	5	2		30	14	3

LEE, Jason Benedict

Forward   *Forest Gate, 9 May 1971*

Released by Charlton as a youngster, Lee made his full League debut with Lincoln in the early 1990s. 21 goals in 93 League games caught the attention of Barry Fry, then with First Division Southend. After joining the Shrimpers for £150,000 in August 1993 Jason's strength and aerial prowess led to a £200,000 transfer to Nottingham Forest eight months later. He gained Premiership experience at the City Ground, where he courted publicity with his pineapple hairstyle. After loans to Charlton and Grimsby, Jason spent two seasons at Watford before Fry rescued him from an unhappy stay at Chesterfield. Initially on loan, Lee netted crucial goals to help Posh's late promotion push, his introduction producing a more direct style. After rejecting an unexpected offer of international football with the Cayman Islands, Jason signed a three-year Posh contract in March 2000. Having helped steer Posh into the Third Division play-offs, Jason scored in the semi-final first leg at Barnet, but sustained a knee injury that denied him his place in the Wembley final. Further frustration followed in 2000-01 as Jason struggled for fitness. Often relegated to the bench, he proved his worth as a foil for smaller strikers Andy Clarke and Leon McKenzie whilst also weighing in with several goals. Jason's injury jinx cost him the whole of 2001-02.

Season	League			FA Cup			League Cup			Other			Total		
	Aps	Sub	Gls	Aps	Sub	Gls	Aps	Sub	Gls	Aps	Sub	Gls	Aps	Sub	Gls
1999-00	23		6							2		1	25		7
2000-01	14	16	8	4		1						1	18	17	9
Total	37	16	14	4		1				2	1	1	43	17	16

LEE, Jeffrey Wreathall (Jeff)
Left-back   *Countesthorpe, 3 October 1945*

Left-back Lee was a vital cog in Posh's 1974 Fourth Division title win, missing just one game after signing from Halifax for £6,000 the previous summer. Jeff had made 240 League appearances in eight years at the Shay, earning a reputation as a keen, aggressive competitor, qualities that served him well for nearly five years with Posh. His level of performance rarely dropped, and he weighed in with crucial goals as penalty-taker. He was still holding down his place when, in February 1978, he joined former team-mate Mick Jones at Kettering, for whom he played in the 1979 FA Trophy final at Wembley. After serving as Jones's number two at Mansfield, Lee worked in insurance before becoming assistant manager at Rochdale and Hull in the early 1990s.

Season	League			FA Cup			League Cup			Other			Total		
	Aps	Sub	Gls	Aps	Sub	Gls	Aps	Sub	Gls	Aps	Sub	Gls	Aps	Sub	Gls
1973-74	45		4	3			2		1				50		5
1974-75	31		4	7			1						39		4
1975-76	30	1		3			4						37	1	
1976-77	38	1	4	1			4		1				43	1	5
1977-78	26			5			5						36		
Total	170	2	12	19			16		2				205	2	14

LEGG, Andrew (Andy)
Midfielder   *Neath, 28 July 1966*

Welsh cap Legg was reputed to possess the longest throw in football. His arrival in October 1998 prompted a typical response from Barry Fry who – when asked how far Legg could throw the ball – claimed all he needed was to find someone who could head it! Besides his throws, Legg also displayed neat control and fine passing during his loan spell from Reading. Although he had played in midfield for his earlier clubs – Swansea, Notts County and Birmingham – he operated mainly at left-back for Posh. Efforts to sign Andy on a permanent basis came to nothing when he opted for a move to Third Division rivals Cardiff.

Season	League			FA Cup			League Cup			Other			Total		
	Aps	Sub	Gls	Aps	Sub	Gls	Aps	Sub	Gls	Aps	Sub	Gls	Aps	Sub	Gls
1998-99	5												5		

LEWIS, Alan Trevor
Left-back   *Oxford, 19 August 1954*

Arriving on loan from Derby in March 1974, full-back Lewis played ten games during the Fourth Division championship run in, his last being the title showdown at home to Gillingham. Noel Cantwell opted against a firm signing, so Lewis spent a season with Brighton before having five years with Reading, where he clocked up 151 League games prior to leaving full-time football for Witney Town. No longer in football, Lewis is a building maintenance contractor in Reading.

Season	League			FA Cup			League Cup			Other			Total		
	Aps	Sub	Gls	Aps	Sub	Gls	Aps	Sub	Gls	Aps	Sub	Gls	Aps	Sub	Gls
1973-74	10		1										10		1

LEWIS, Neil Anthony
Left-back   *Wolverhampton, 28 June 1974*

A gifted left-back, Lewis joined in July 1997 from Leicester in a £60,000 deal. He had risen through the ranks at Filbert Street and made 67 League appearances, some in the Premiership. After impressing with Posh, a return to the big time seemed a formality for a pacy full-back who delighted the home crowd with his willingness to break forward. Big-money moves to Arsenal or Rangers were in the offing when things started to go wrong. With Barry Fry's early season table-toppers tumbling down the Third Division, Lewis lost form and confidence. His forays up the pitch increased, to the detriment of his defensive duties, and he was dropped in favour of an emerging Adam Drury. At the end of 1997-98, after just one season with Posh, Lewis shocked everyone by announcing his decision to quit football. He was just 23.

Season	League			FA Cup			League Cup			Other			Total		
	Aps	Sub	Gls	Aps	Sub	Gls	Aps	Sub	Gls	Aps	Sub	Gls	Aps	Sub	Gls
1997-98	31	3		3			4			1			38	4	

LIMBER, Nicholas (Nick)
Defender   *Doncaster, 23 January 1974*

Yorkshireman Limber played two First Division games on loan from Manchester City in October 1992. After a 0-0 draw with Brentford at home, the stocky defender featured in a 2-0 win at Leicester, screened live by Central Television. Limber had begun his career with home-town club Doncaster, then making a £75,000 move to Maine Road.

Unable to break through, he returned to Doncaster in March 1994 but made only ten League appearances before a back injury caused him to drop out of the League when signing for Weymouth in August 1995. He has subsequently seen action with Gainsborough and Frickley.

Season	League			FA Cup			League Cup			Other			Total		
	Aps	Sub	Gls	Aps	Sub	Gls	Aps	Sub	Gls	Aps	Sub	Gls	Aps	Sub	Gls
1992-93	2												2		

LINNELL, John Lovell Leonard

Wing-half   *Holcot, 2 January 1944*

Hailing from near Northampton, powerful wing-half Linnell was on the Cobblers' books as a lad but made his senior debut with Posh in a League Cup-tie against Northampton in August 1967. An England Youth cap, he went on to appear 28 times for Posh, scoring one goal – a 30-yarder in a 5-1 victory over Watford. He left in 1968 for Banbury, then had four years at Wellingborough before finishing his playing days with Long Buckby. He has worked in the family gravedigging business, as he did in his days with Posh, stopping off en route to his Northampton home after training to fill up a grave dug by his father.

Season	League			FA Cup			League Cup			Other			Total		
	Aps	Sub	Gls	Aps	Sub	Gls	Aps	Sub	Gls	Aps	Sub	Gls	Aps	Sub	Gls
1967-68	24	2	1	1			1						26	2	1

LINTON, Desmond Martin (Des)

Right-back   *Birmingham, 5 September 1971*

Groomed at Leicester, with whom he made eleven League appearances, tough-tackling defender Linton joined Luton in October 1991. He played 83 League games for the Hatters, among them an FA Cup Wembley semi-final in 1994, before joining Posh on transfer deadline day three years later. Quick for a tall man, Des liked to carry the ball on long runs upfield, although his final pass was sometimes awry. Though strong and reliable, he never established himself, and after sharing the No 2 shirt with Chris McMenamin in 1997-98, he played second fiddle the following season to Dean Hooper. After two years with Posh, Des was loaned to Swindon in March 1999 and left on a free transfer two months later. He has since played for Cambridge City.

Season	League			FA Cup			League Cup			Other			Total		
	Aps	Sub	Gls	Aps	Sub	Gls	Aps	Sub	Gls	Aps	Sub	Gls	Aps	Sub	Gls
1996-97	8												8		
1997-98	25	5		2	1		2			2			31	6	
1998-99	8			1									9		
Total	41	5		3	1		2			2			48	6	

LINTON, Ivor
Midfielder   *West Bromwich, 20 November 1959*

Aston Villa gave Linton his break and the midfielder played 30-odd games when Villa won the League and the European Cup. He was brought to Posh on a free transfer in August 1982 by Martin Wilkinson and Ivor debuted in a 1-1 draw at Stockport in the curtain raiser. He was never a regular and, given fewer opportunities after John Wile took charge, Ivor moved on in December 1983. He played four League games for First Division Birmingham, then quit the professional game.

Season	League			FA Cup			League Cup			Other			Total		
	Aps	Sub	Gls	Aps	Sub	Gls	Aps	Sub	Gls	Aps	Sub	Gls	Aps	Sub	Gls
1982-83	21	3	3				3						24	3	3
1983-84	3						2						5		
Total	24	3	3				5						29	3	3

LLEWELLYN, David John (Dave)
Forward   *Cardiff, 9 August 1949*

Llewellyn was a tall front-runner who arrived on a free transfer from West Ham in August 1973. A Wales Under-23 cap, Llewellyn had played just six First Division games in seven years. Even with Posh, he found first-team opportunities hard to come by, largely due to the form of John Cozens and Jim Hall, although he contributed three goals as Posh won the Fourth Division title. His best run came in January 1974 when he played six consecutive matches, including the FA Cup-tie with Leeds, filling in for the injured Paul Walker. After starting 1974-75 on loan to Mansfield, he returned for a few more games prior to being released. Dave still lives locally, managing a local gymnasium and acting as bench coach to Peterborough Pirates ice-hockey team.

Season	League			FA Cup			League Cup			Other			Total		
	Aps	Sub	Gls	Aps	Sub	Gls	Aps	Sub	Gls	Aps	Sub	Gls	Aps	Sub	Gls
1973-74	8	1	3	2									10	1	3
1974-75	3	1		2		1							5	1	1
Total	11	2	3	4		1							15	2	4

LONGHURST, David John (Dave)
Forward   *Northampton, 15 January 1965, Died September 1990*

Lean striker Longhurst spent two fruitless years at Brian Clough's Nottingham Forest before kick-starting his League career with Halifax in 1985. He hit 24 goals in 85 League games, which earned him a transfer to his hometown club, Northampton, in July 1987. He found goals harder to come by at the County Ground and joined Mick Jones's Posh in October 1988 for £55,000 – the club's costliest signing for a decade. Noted for his neat control and ability to lead the line, Dave's best Posh performance came in an FA Cup-tie at Gillingham when he bagged a hat-trick in a 3-3 draw. Though popular with fans, he left midway through 1989-90 for York, where he collapsed and died during a game against Lincoln in September 1990. Today, the Dave Longhurst Stand at Bootham Crescent is a fitting memorial to a much-missed figure.

Season	League			FA Cup			League Cup			Other			Total		
	Aps	Sub	Gls	Aps	Sub	Gls	Aps	Sub	Gls	Aps	Sub	Gls	Aps	Sub	Gls
1988-89	37		7	4		3	1			2		1	44		11
1989-90	14	7		1	1		2			2			19	8	
Total	51	7	7	5	1	3	3			4		1	63	8	11

LORMOR, Anthony (Tony)
Forward   *Ashington, 29 October 1970*

This strong, aggressive goalscorer arrived from Lincoln in July 1994. Signed by John Still on a free transfer, he began his career at Newcastle where he mustered three League goals in eight games before joining the Imps for £25,000 in 1990. He scored 30 goals in 100 League appearances but was given few opportunities to repeat that ratio at Posh. In December 1994 he was released to Chesterfield, where he proved to be a revelation. From his debut, the Spireites completed 21 games unbeaten, and he netted in their 2-0 Wembley play-off win over Bury that sealed promotion to Division Two. He moved to Preston soon afterwards, then joined Mansfield in 1998, before settling at Hartlepool.

Season	League			FA Cup			League Cup			Other			Total		
	Aps	Sub	Gls	Aps	Sub	Gls	Aps	Sub	Gls	Aps	Sub	Gls	Aps	Sub	Gls
1994-95	2	3		1						1	1		4	4	

LOWTHER, Shaun
Right-back   *North Shields, 24 January 1962*

A Canadian international, full-back Lowther made little impact with Posh, starting only three matches during a trial in 1984-85. Born in the north-east of England, he had emigrated to Canada with his family in 1978 after being released as a schoolboy by Sunderland. Over the next few years he played with Edmonton Drillers of the North American Soccer League, League of Ireland side UCD, and Manchester United, where he spent 1979-80 in their youth team. It was in Canada where he found most success. He spent four years with Vancouver Whitecaps from 1980, and broke into the national side. He returned to England again in 1985 and, after a spell with Blyth Spartans, accepted an offer of a trial by former Vancouver team-mate John Wile. He helped Posh to a 1-0 home win over Torquay and played in both legs of a Freight-Rover Trophy tie with Cambridge before opting to return to Canada. He played for Vancouver 86ers, Winnipeg Fury and Hamilton Steelers before becoming a coach. Shaun is still involved in soccer as part-owner of semi-professional Okanagan Predators in British Columbia.

Season	League			FA Cup			League Cup			Other			Total		
	Aps	Sub	Gls	Aps	Sub	Gls	Aps	Sub	Gls	Aps	Sub	Gls	Aps	Sub	Gls
1984-85	1									2			3		

LUKE, Noel Emmanuel
Winger/Right-back   *Birmingham, 28 December 1964*

Noel 'Doris' Luke was one of Posh's most loyal servants. A veteran of nearly 350 appearances, stretching over seven seasons and three divisions, Noel signed in August 1986 from Mansfield, for whom he had played 50 League games following his teen-aged release from WBA. Signed as a winger by Noel Cantwell, Luke spent two seasons on the flanks before converting into an attacking right-back near the end of 1988-89. A wholehearted performer, Noel enjoyed a rapport with the fans, who admired his work-rate and sorties up the wing. A survivor of the dark days of the late 1980s, Noel played a key role in Posh's meteoric rise under Chris Turner, helping the club to its finest hour at Wembley in 1992. Supporters were upset by his release in March 1993. He had a spell with Boston and later served Holbeach, Corby, King's Lynn and Raunds Town, and was briefly landlord of the Posh pub.

Season	League			FA Cup			League Cup			Other			Total		
	Aps	Sub	Gls	Aps	Sub	Gls	Aps	Sub	Gls	Aps	Sub	Gls	Aps	Sub	Gls
1986-87	30		10				2		1	1		1	33	1	11
1987-88	43		7	2			6			4		1	55		8
1988-89	45		3	4			4			1			54		3
1989-90	43		5	3			1			3		1	50		6
1990-91	45		2	5			4			2		1	56		3
1991-92	42	1		3			8			8			61	1	
1992-93	22	6		1	2		3			1			27	8	
Total	270	7	27	18	2		28		1	20	1	3	336	10	31

LYTTLE, Gerard Francis
Full-back   *Belfast, 22 November, 1977*

Regarded as a fine prospect by Barry Fry, young Ulsterman Gerard Lyttle came from Celtic in 1998. He had spent five years rising through the ranks at Parkhead and was capped by Northern Ireland at Under-21 level. He featured once in first-team action for Posh – coming on for Dean Hooper in a League Cup-tie with Reading in August 1998 – before being released.

Season	League			FA Cup			League Cup			Other			Total		
	Aps	Sub	Gls	Aps	Sub	Gls	Aps	Sub	Gls	Aps	Sub	Gls	Aps	Sub	Gls
1998-99								1						1	

Billy Kellock v Doncaster, 1980-81

Peter Thompson

Andy Edwards

Jack Carmichael with his Player of the Year awards 1975-76

David Langan

John Turley

Gary Breen (centre) v Hull, September 1994

Zeke Rowe

McANEARNEY, Thomas (Tom)
Wing-half   *Dundee, 6 January 1933*

A veteran of over 350 League games for Sheffield Wednesday, Scot McAnearney arrived at London Road in November 1965. He debuted in a 0-3 loss at Grimsby, but in his next outing helped Gordon Clark's side account for First Division leaders Burnley, 4-0 in the League Cup. That win earned a two-legged semi-final against WBA, and Tom played in both before joining Aldershot a few months later. He played 106 League games for the Shots, and had two spells as manager.

Season	League			FA Cup			League Cup			Other			Total		
	Aps	Sub	Gls	Aps	Sub	Gls	Aps	Sub	Gls	Aps	Sub	Gls	Aps	Sub	Gls
1965-66	12			1			3						16		

McCLURE, Doug Hugh
Full-back   *Islington, 6 September 1964*

Following his early release by QPR, McClure had spells with Exeter, Torquay and Wimbledon before trying his luck in Finland. Within a few months he was back home, having a spell as a non-contract player with Posh in October 1985. Although a full-back by trade, John Wile played him in midfield, due to the absence through injury of Andy Kowalski. Doug made four appearances for Posh, including the club-record 0-7 defeat at Tranmere, before joining Crewe in January 1986.

Season	League			FA Cup			League Cup			Other			Total		
	Aps	Sub	Gls	Aps	Sub	Gls	Aps	Sub	Gls	Aps	Sub	Gls	Aps	Sub	Gls
1985-86	4												4		

McCORMICK, David
Forward   *Southwark, 29 December 1951*

Cantwell claimed to have found 'another David Gregory' after discovering lanky forward McCormick at Biggleswade. After impressing on trial, McCormick debuted in the opening game of 1975-76, a 0-0 home draw with Walsall remembered for a female streaker at half-time. He was not offered professional terms and was soon released.

Season	League			FA Cup			League Cup			Other			Total		
	Aps	Sub	Gls	Aps	Sub	Gls	Aps	Sub	Gls	Aps	Sub	Gls	Aps	Sub	Gls
1975-76	1												1		

McDONALD, David Hugh
Right-back   *Dublin, 2 January 1971*

A Republic of Ireland Under-21 cap, McDonald served his apprenticeship at Spurs, playing twice in the Premiership before joining Posh on a free transfer in August 1993. He laboured in a struggling side destined for relegation from Division One and was sent off twice against Birmingham for fouls on winger Ted McMinn. On transfer deadline day 1994 he joined Third Division Barnet, where he played 100 games.

Season	League			FA Cup			League Cup			Other			Total		
	Aps	Sub	Gls	Aps	Sub	Gls	Aps	Sub	Gls	Aps	Sub	Gls	Aps	Sub	Gls
1993-94	28	1		2			4			1			35	1	

MacDONALD, Gary
Central Defender   Iselone (W Germany), 25 October 1979

Born in Germany, as his father worked for the RAF, Gary moved to England when a few months old. Signed as central defensive cover from Havant & Waterlooville in February 2001, Gary had a four-day trial and hit the winning goal in a reserve match against Colchester. A three-and-a-half-year contract resulted for the left-footed defender, who had been three years at Portsmouth before joining Havant, whom he captained during his 18-month stay. MacDonald debuted for Posh in a 1-1 draw with Rotherham on the final day of 2000-01, but was then set back by injury. He scored the goal in a 1-0 win over Cambridge.

Season	League			FA Cup			League Cup			Other			Total		
	Aps	Sub	Gls	Aps	Sub	Gls	Aps	Sub	Gls	Aps	Sub	Gls	Aps	Sub	Gls
2000-01	1												1		
2001-02	7	1	1	1			2						10	1	1
Total	8	1	1	1			2						11	1	1

McELHINNEY, Gerard (Gerry)
Central Defender   Derry, 19 September 1956

Northern Ireland international Gerry McElhinney arrived in August 1988 to replace Paul Price. As a lad, Gerry was an Ulster Senior boxing champion, and was also selected for a National Gaelic Football final by Derry, and it was easy to see why. A no-nonsense defender, he made his mark in English soccer with Bolton, Rochdale and Plymouth prior to joining Posh, and quickly formed an experienced defensive barrier with fellow veteran Keith Oakes. Never subtle or graceful, big Gerry was fiercely competitive, which earned him cult status on the terraces. He was at his best alongside David Robinson in 1989-90, while the following season – his last as a player – he helped Posh win promotion. Gerry stayed for one more season as Youth Team manager in 1991-92.

Season	League			FA Cup			League Cup			Other			Total		
	Aps	Sub	Gls	Aps	Sub	Gls	Aps	Sub	Gls	Aps	Sub	Gls	Aps	Sub	Gls
1988-89	33		1	4			4			1			42		1
1989-90	34			3						1			38		
1990-91	20			5			4			2			31		
Total	87		1	12			8			4			111		1

McEWAN, William Johnston McGowan (Billy)
Midfielder   Wishaw, 20 June 1951

This tough-tackling Scot started with Hibs, where he topped 100 first-team games, played in Europe and gained Scotland Under-23 honours. His energy earned a transfer to Second Division Blackpool in May

1973, then Brian Clough's Brighton in February 1974, then Chesterfield nine months later. He spent a couple of years at Saltergate before joining Mansfield, with whom he won the Third Division under Peter Morris in 1977. John Barnwell paid £17,500 for McEwan's energy and experience in November 1977. After debuting in a 1-0 home win over Plymouth, he anchored midfield when Posh just missed promotion to Division Two. In 1979, following relegation, Billy joined Rotherham, with whom he won a second Third Division title in 1981. He later managed Sheffield United and Rotherham, and coached Derby.

Season	League			FA Cup			League Cup			Other			Total		
	Aps	Sub	Gls	Aps	Sub	Gls	Aps	Sub	Gls	Aps	Sub	Gls	Aps	Sub	Gls
1977-78	29		1	5									34		1
1978-79	33	1	2	1			8						42	1	2
Total	62	1	3	6			8						76	1	3

McGEE, Paul
Winger   *Dublin, 17 May 1968*

Capped four times for the Republic of Ireland Under-21s, this diminutive winger was loaned from Wimbledon in March 1993. With Posh battling against the drop, McGee found it hard to demonstrate his Premiership pedigree. He debuted in a 1-3 home defeat by Sunderland and played a few more times, but never on the winning side. Released shortly afterwards by the Dons, McGee joined Linfield in Belfast.

Season	League			FA Cup			League Cup			Other			Total		
	Aps	Sub	Gls	Aps	Sub	Gls	Aps	Sub	Gls	Aps	Sub	Gls	Aps	Sub	Gls
1993-94	5	1											5	1	

McGLASHAN, John
Midfielder   *Dundee, 3 June 1967*

Lil Fuccillo equalled Posh's club record transfer when paying Millwall £100,000 for this rugged Scot in January 1993. The midfielder, formerly with Montrose, had few opportunities at The Den and was loaned to Cambridge and Fulham before joining Posh. He set up winning goals in his first two games, 1-0 at home to Southend and 3-2 at Derby. John kept his place for the rest of 1992-93, replacing the injured Mick Halsall, and stayed in contention throughout the relegation battle in 1993-94. He joined Rotherham in November 1994 on a free transfer.

Season	League			FA Cup			League Cup			Other			Total		
	Aps	Sub	Gls	Aps	Sub	Gls	Aps	Sub	Gls	Aps	Sub	Gls	Aps	Sub	Gls
1992-93	18												18		
1993-94	26	2	3	1			4	1	1	2		1	33	3	5
Total	44	2	3	1			4	1	1	2		1	51	3	5

McGLEISH, Scott
Forward   *Camden Town, 10 February 1974*

A lively little striker signed from Charlton by John Still, Londoner McGleish had few opportunities, despite scoring regularly on loan to Colchester and Cambridge. A free transfer arrival in July 1995, Scott spent most of his time in the reserves or on the bench, and left for Leyton Orient in November 1996. He later rejoined Still in a £80,000 move to Barnet in October 1997, and joined Colchester in January 2001.

Season	League			FA Cup			League Cup			Other			Total		
	Aps	Sub	Gls	Aps	Sub	Gls	Aps	Sub	Gls	Aps	Sub	Gls	Aps	Sub	Gls
1995-96	3	9			1			1		3	1	2	6	12	2
1996-97		1												1	
Total	3	10			1			1		3	1	2	6	13	2

McGORRY, Brian Paul
Midfielder   *Liverpool, 16 April 1970*

Nicknamed 'Baywatch' because of his former job as a Weymouth life-guard, blond McGorry was a busy midfielder who cost £60,000 from Bournemouth in February 1994. He debuted in a 1-0 home win over Middlesbrough and featured regularly until relegation was confirmed. He spent another season with Posh before joining Wycombe on a free transfer in 1995. He played for Hereford – demoted from the League in 1997 – Cardiff, Torquay, Telford, Southport, Woking, and Chester.

Season	League			FA Cup			League Cup			Other			Total		
	Aps	Sub	Gls	Aps	Sub	Gls	Aps	Sub	Gls	Aps	Sub	Gls	Aps	Sub	Gls
1993-94	14	4	3										14	4	3
1994-95	30	4	3	2			2			2			34	6	3
Total	44	8	6	2			2			2			48	10	6

McINERNEY, Ian
Forward   *Limerick, 1 September 1972*

An Irish-born front runner, McInerney progressed through the youth and reserve teams before signing as a professional in 1991. Debuting as a sub in a 1-0 win over Preston on the opening day of 1991-92, he registered his only Posh goal when hitting the winner at Hull a week later. Unable to claim a regular place, he was released at the end of the campaign and played locally for Corby, Raunds Town and Stamford.

Season	League			FA Cup			League Cup			Other			Total		
	Aps	Sub	Gls	Aps	Sub	Gls	Aps	Sub	Gls	Aps	Sub	Gls	Aps	Sub	Gls
1991-92	3	7	1					1		1	1		4	9	1

McKEEVER, Mark Anthony
Winger   *Derry, 16 November 1978*

Irish youngster McKeever played a few games before being signed by Sheffield Wednesday in a joint £1 million deal, along with youth-team colleague David Billington. Having starred for Posh's Under-18s in 1995-96, the spike-haired winger debuted as a sub in a Second Division game at home to York in September 1996, and first started a game two weeks later on the left wing against Southampton in the League Cup. After his move to Hillsborough on transfer deadline day in 1997, Mark was loaned to Bristol Rovers and Reading before making his Premiership debut against Chelsea in April 1999. Further opportunities were few, prompting a free-transfer move to Bristol Rovers in March 2001.

Season	League			FA Cup			League Cup			Other			Total		
	Aps	Sub	Gls	Aps	Sub	Gls	Aps	Sub	Gls	Aps	Sub	Gls	Aps	Sub	Gls
1996-97	2	1					1						3	1	

McKENZIE, Leon Mark
Forward   *Croydon, 17 May 1978*

A member of a famous boxing family, Leon McKenzie joined Crystal Palace as a trainee in 1994, graduating to the first team in 1995-96. Not featuring under Terry Venables early in 1998-99, Leon was loaned to Posh, where his goalscoring made him popular. After scoring twice on his debut in a 3-1 success at Cardiff in August, he was injured while netting at home to Exeter, prompting his return to Selhurst Park after just four matches. With Posh reeling from the departure of Jimmy Quinn, Leon returned for a further two months in October. Although slightly built, his pace, trickery and strength terrorised Third Division defenders. He played eleven games in his second spell, scoring six goals, including the winner at home to Cambridge. Fans demanded his signature but Posh could not even meet Palace's reduced asking price. Leon made 25 First Division appearances for the Eagles in 1999-2000, scoring four goals, before finally signing for Posh in October 2000. He finished 2000-01 as leading scorer, a feat he repeated the next season when, despite several injuries, he met his personal 20-goal target. Signed for a cut-price £25,000, Leon is the current Posh darling.

Season	League			FA Cup			League Cup			Other			Total		
	Aps	Sub	Gls	Aps	Sub	Gls	Aps	Sub	Gls	Aps	Sub	Gls	Aps	Sub	Gls
1998-99	14		8							1		1	15		9
2000-01	30		13	3	1								33	1	13
2001-02	28	2	18	3		1	1			1		1	33	2	20
Total	72	2	39	6	1	1	1			2		2	81	3	42

McLACHLAN, Dugald
Midfielder   *Falkirk, 10 September 1953*

Failing to break through at Preston, this tiny midfielder's only League experience was on loan to Halifax in 1972-73. Signed by Noel Cantwell in July 1973, the red-haired Scot played once in Posh's Fourth Division title-winning campaign. Released in 1974, he joined Burton Albion.

Season	League			FA Cup			League Cup			Other			Total		
	Aps	Sub	Gls	Aps	Sub	Gls	Aps	Sub	Gls	Aps	Sub	Gls	Aps	Sub	Gls
1973-74	1												1		

McLAUGHLIN, James Christopher (Jimmy)

Winger   *Derry, 22 December 1940*

A left-sided winger with an eye for goal, McLaughlin was a Northern Ireland cap with a knack of scoring against Posh for Shrewsbury and Swansea in the early 1960s. He signed towards the end of 1966-67 and, in his third game, netted twice in a 2-2 draw at Reading. Jimmy never settled though, and rejoined Shrewsbury in September 1967. A hit with fans at Gay Meadow, he stayed five years, taking his Shrews goal-tally to 77 from 297 League games. In November 1972 he rejoined Swansea where he ended his playing days before managing in Ireland.

Season	League			FA Cup			League Cup			Other			Total		
	Aps	Sub	Gls	Aps	Sub	Gls	Aps	Sub	Gls	Aps	Sub	Gls	Aps	Sub	Gls
1966-67	8		2										8		2

McMANUS, Charles Eric (Eric)

Goalkeeper   *Limavady, 14 November 1950*

McManus was a well-travelled keeper who began his League career with Coventry in the late 1960s, but came to notice after joining Notts County in 1972. He made 229 League appearances for the Magpies, then joined Bradford City after short stops at Stoke and Lincoln. After losing his place at Valley Parade, the big Irishman spent part of 1985-86 on loan to Posh, standing in for broken-leg victim John Turner. He then returned to Valley Parade, had a short spell at Tranmere in March 1986, before finishing his career at Boston. In more recent times, Eric has been employed as youth-team coach at Walsall and Derby.

Season	League			FA Cup			League Cup			Other			Total		
	Aps	Sub	Gls	Aps	Sub	Gls	Aps	Sub	Gls	Aps	Sub	Gls	Aps	Sub	Gls
1985-86	18												18		

McMENAMIN, Christopher (Chris)

Full-back   *Donegal, 27 December 1973*

A confident Irish defender, Chris arrived on a free transfer from Coventry in August 1997. He debuted in a 5-0 win at Doncaster, then earned a run in the side in the autumn. After sharing the right-back slot with Des Linton thereafter, Chris was frozen out following Dean Hooper's arrival in 1998, prompting his release in March 1999. He has subsequently turned out for Borehamwood and St Albans.

Season	League			FA Cup			League Cup			Other			Total		
	Aps	Sub	Gls	Aps	Sub	Gls	Aps	Sub	Gls	Aps	Sub	Gls	Aps	Sub	Gls
1997-98	25	3		2			2			3			32	3	
1998-99	4	1											4	1	
Total	29	4		2			2			3			36	4	

McNAMEE, Peter

Outside-left   *Glasgow, 20 March 1935*

McNamee first played for Posh aged 20 in 1955 and chalked up over 100 games prior to the club joining the Football League in 1960. George Swindin had signed the Glasgow-born winger, giving him his debut in a 1-0 Midland League win at King's Lynn. It was not until 1957-58 that Peter established himself, whereupon he figured in three title-winning sides and several famous FA Cup-ties. Noted for his control, dribbling, and left-footed crosses, he missed just two matches in 1960-61 as Posh lifted the Fourth Division title. McNamee continued his magic for four more seasons, maintaining his respectable goalscoring ratio. To this day, only Jim Hall, Tommy Robson, Terry Bly and Peter Price have outscored him in the League. Peter saved his most important strike for the FA Cup when, in his last full season, his goal knocked out Arsenal in 1965. Later that year, his ten years service earned a testimonial against St Mirren, who presented him with a gold watch. McNamee ended his association with Posh early the following season. After a stay at King's Lynn he returned to the League with Notts County. He played three games for the Magpies before retiring from professional soccer in 1966, when orthodox wingers were becoming extinct. He said later that he knew his time was up the day he was asked to 'tackle back', claiming never to have made a tackle in his life. Peter stayed many years with March Town, whom he also managed in the 1970s.

Season	League			FA Cup			League Cup			Other			Total		
	Aps	Sub	Gls	Aps	Sub	Gls	Aps	Sub	Gls	Aps	Sub	Gls	Aps	Sub	Gls
1960-61	44		16	5		3	1						50		19
1961-62	25		9	1		1							26		10
1962-63	45		13	3		1	1						49		14
1963-64	42		11				1		1				43		12
1964-65	31		9	8		2							39		11
1965-66	5		2										5		2
Total	192		60	17		7	3		1				212		68

McVAY, David Reid (Dave)

Defender   *Workington, 5 March 1955*

Skilful, versatile McVay came to notice in midfield with Notts County in the 1970s, making 113 League appearances before Peter Morris paid £25,000 to sign him in July 1979. He performed various defensive roles during his first season before settling at right-back in 1980-81, when he was a regular in the side that reached round five of the FA Cup. That summer he joined Lincoln on a free transfer and a year later trialled with Boston before returning to Nottingham to take up journalism.

Season	League			FA Cup			League Cup			Other			Total		
	Aps	Sub	Gls	Aps	Sub	Gls	Aps	Sub	Gls	Aps	Sub	Gls	Aps	Sub	Gls
1979-80	23	2					3						26	2	
1980-81	24		1	6			4						34		1
Total	47	2	1	6			7						60	2	1

MADRICK, Carl James

Forward   *Bolton, 20 September 1968*

Striker Carl began at home-town club Bolton, for whom he scored one goal in eight League games in 1987-88. Mick Jones signed him on a free transfer in September 1988, but Carl spent most of his time on the subs' bench. Five of his nine appearances came whilst wearing the No 12 shirt and he was an unused substitute on a further 18 occasions.

Season	League			FA Cup			League Cup			Other			Total		
	Aps	Sub	Gls	Aps	Sub	Gls	Aps	Sub	Gls	Aps	Sub	Gls	Aps	Sub	Gls
1988-89	3	5					1						4	5	

MALOY, Kenneth Frederick (Ken)

Outside-left   *Edmonton, 16 September 1940*

After scoring eleven League goals in 62 games in five years with Plymouth, balding forward Ken Maloy signed in July 1964. He was kept out of the side by the excellent form of veteran Peter McNamee and was released to Aldershot a year later. Ken did better with the Shots, hitting twelve goals in 52 League games before retiring in 1967.

Season	League			FA Cup			League Cup			Other			Total		
	Aps	Sub	Gls	Aps	Sub	Gls	Aps	Sub	Gls	Aps	Sub	Gls	Aps	Sub	Gls
1964-65	6		1										6		1

MANUEL, William Albert James (Billy)

Midfielder   *Hackney, 28 June 1969*

A fiery midfielder, former Spurs apprentice Manuel tasted action with Gillingham and Brentford – with whom he won the Third Division in 1992 – before joining Posh on a non-contract basis in September 1994. In five weeks he failed to make the team and signed for Cambridge. Returning to Posh on a free transfer in February 1995, Billy's arrival coincided with a winning run. He stayed a while the following season, then rejoined Gillingham in 1996, before linking up with former Posh-mates at Barnet. More recently, Billy played for Folkestone Invicta.

Season	League			FA Cup			League Cup			Other			Total		
	Aps	Sub	Gls	Aps	Sub	Gls	Aps	Sub	Gls	Aps	Sub	Gls	Aps	Sub	Gls
1994-95	14		1										14		1
1995-96	13		1	1	1		4		3	2			20	1	4
Total	27		2	1	1		4		3	2			34	1	5

MARTIN, Jae Andrew

Winger   *Hampstead, 5 February 1976*

Acquired for a small fee from Lincoln in 1998, Jae Martin had served under Barry Fry at Southend and Birmingham. He made just four substitute appearances in 1998-99 before going on loan to Grantham. He played a few games the following season and scored his first goal in a

4-2 home win over Darlington, before signing for Welling. Jae spent 2000-01 with Woking but has since moved on to Moor Green.

Season	League			FA Cup			League Cup			Other			Total		
	Aps	Sub	Gls	Aps	Sub	Gls	Aps	Sub	Gls	Aps	Sub	Gls	Aps	Sub	Gls
1998-99		4												4	
1999-00	7	8	1				1	1		1			9	9	1
Total	7	12	1				1	1		1			9	13	1

MARTIN, Michael Paul (Mick)
Midfielder   *Dublin, 9 July 1951*

Capped 51 times by the Republic of Ireland, Dublin-born Martin joined Manchester United from Irish side Bohemians in 1972. He made 40 League appearances for the Red Devils before starring in Ron Atkinson's talented WBA side of the late 1970s. After 89 League appearances for the Baggies, he added a further 147 games following a £100,000 move to Newcastle. He then turned out for Vancouver Whitecaps and Cardiff prior to joining Posh on a weekly contract in January 1985. Mick's form mirrored that of John Wile's struggling team. A move to Rotherham in the summer proved equally short-lived, but after switching to Preston he played another 35 League games before calling it a day. He became a coach at Celtic before leaving football to run a sports trophy shop near Newcastle's Metro Centre, called Zico's, in reference to the nickname he acquired during his playing days at St James' Park. Mick also works as a radio host.

Season	League			FA Cup			League Cup			Other			Total		
	Aps	Sub	Gls	Aps	Sub	Gls	Aps	Sub	Gls	Aps	Sub	Gls	Aps	Sub	Gls
1984-85	13									1			14		

MARTINDALE, Gary
Forward   *Liverpool, 26 June 1971*

Having been scared off by Bolton's £100,000 price tag on Martindale in 1994, Posh got their man on a free transfer a year later following the Lancashire club's promotion to the Premiership. The ex-Burscough player had failed to make the first team at Burnden Park, but was thrust into Posh's starting eleven for the 1995-96 curtain raiser at home to Brighton. Gary netted in Posh's 3-1 win. A hard-working striker with good technique, he improved as the season progressed and was sold to Second Division rivals Notts County for £175,000 in March 1996. At the time he was Posh's top scorer with 18 goals in League and Cup, including a hat-trick in a 3-2 victory at Hull. He subsequently scored the goals that took County to a Wembley play-off final, prior to joining Rotherham in 1998 via a loan spell with Mansfield. He was unable to command in place in the Millers side that won promotion to Division Two in 1999-2000 and joined Telford, initially on loan.

Season	League			FA Cup			League Cup			Other			Total		
	Aps	Sub	Gls	Aps	Sub	Gls	Aps	Sub	Gls	Aps	Sub	Gls	Aps	Sub	Gls
1995-96	26	5	15	4			4		1	4		2	38	5	18

MASON, John Francis
Centre-forward   *Coventry, 23 January 1943*

A close-season signing from Alvechurch in 1966, bustling Mason found the net regularly until breaking his leg. In and out during 1966-67, 'Stingray' hit seven goals in five matches during the run-in to help Gordon Clark's team avoid the drop to Division Four. They took his season's tally to 15, second only to John Fairbrother, and the former Altrincham striker grabbed three more the following season before breaking his leg in a reserve game at Leicester. He never recovered full fitness and was released in 1968, joining the ex-Posh fraternity in South African soccer – Johnny Byrne, Ron Barnes and John Kirkham.

Season	League			FA Cup			League Cup			Other			Total		
	Aps	Sub	Gls	Aps	Sub	Gls	Aps	Sub	Gls	Aps	Sub	Gls	Aps	Sub	Gls
1966-67	27		15	3			1						31		15
1967-68	10		3										10		3
Total	37		18	3			1						41		18

MASSEY, Stephen (Steve)
Forward   *Denton, 28 March 1958*

Peter Morris took this free-transfer in August 1981 from Bournemouth, where the blond striker – who had come to notice as a teenager with Stockport in the 1970s – had hit 19 League goals in 97 games. He made little impact with Posh, staying six months then joining Northampton. His best Posh game was on 4 November 1981 when he scored twice in a 7-1 win over Aldershot. He shone for the Cobblers, netting 21 League goals in 1982-83 before moving to Hull, Cambridge, and Wrexham. He retired from League football in 1988 to run holiday camps in Cornwall.

Season	League			FA Cup			League Cup			Other			Total		
	Aps	Sub	Gls	Aps	Sub	Gls	Aps	Sub	Gls	Aps	Sub	Gls	Aps	Sub	Gls
1981-82	13	5	3	1	1								14	6	3

MAYNARD, Michael Clements (Mike)
Left-back   *Guyana, 7 January 1947*

The first black player to represent Posh in the Football League, left-back Maynard arrived in July 1967 after failing to emerge at Crystal Palace. He waited four months for his Posh debut, coming on as a sub in a 2-3 November defeat at Gillingham. He kept his place for the next three games but was released at the end of 1967-68.

Season	League			FA Cup			League Cup			Other			Total		
	Aps	Sub	Gls	Aps	Sub	Gls	Aps	Sub	Gls	Aps	Sub	Gls	Aps	Sub	Gls
1967-68	2	1		1									3	1	

MERCER, Stephen Jack (Steve)
Defender   *Barking, 1 May 1965*

An East London lad previously with Cambridge on a non-contract basis, Mercer joined Posh in September 1982 but did not debut until April, when he stood in for Neil Firm in a 4-3 home win over Swindon. He played twice more before drifting into non-League football.

Season	League			FA Cup			League Cup			Other			Total		
	Aps	Sub	Gls	Aps	Sub	Gls	Aps	Sub	Gls	Aps	Sub	Gls	Aps	Sub	Gls
1982-83	3												3		

MEREDITH, Thomas James Anthony (Tom)
Midfielder   *Enfield, 27 October 1977*

A Londoner of Irish descent, Meredith signed professional forms in July 1996 after starting as a trainee two years earlier. He debuted as a sub in a 1-2 defeat at Crewe in the penultimate game of 1995-96, then started in the final match at Oxford. He did not feature in 1996-97 and was released into non-League soccer with Stevenage and St Albans.

Season	League			FA Cup			League Cup			Other			Total		
	Aps	Sub	Gls	Aps	Sub	Gls	Aps	Sub	Gls	Aps	Sub	Gls	Aps	Sub	Gls
1995-96	1	1											1	1	

MERRICK, Alan Ronald
Right-back   *Birmingham, 20 June 1950*

An England Youth cap, Merrick joined WBA as an apprentice in August 1967. He spent nine years at the Hawthorns, in which time he made 139 League appearances, mostly in the First Division, and many alongside John Wile. Noel Cantwell got him on loan early in 1975-76 – Alan's last season in League football – and he made six appearances at right-back before returning to WBA. He later coached in Minnesota, but has since returned to England and now lives in Huntingdon.

Season	League			FA Cup			League Cup			Other			Total		
	Aps	Sub	Gls	Aps	Sub	Gls	Aps	Sub	Gls	Aps	Sub	Gls	Aps	Sub	Gls
1975-76	5						1						6		

METCHICK, David John (Dave)
Inside-forward   *Bakewell, 14 August 1943*

Although born in Derbyshire, it was with Fulham and Leyton Orient that skilful inside-forward Metchick made his mark during the 1960s. Rising through the ranks at Craven Cottage, he played 47 League games, scoring nine goals, before joining Orient in December 1964. A former England youth cap, he added 15 goals from 75 League games for the O's, then joined Posh in March 1967. He helped his new club finish strongly to stave off relegation to Division Four, and remained for 1967-68 before signing for QPR in August 1968. After just three sub appearances in two years, he had a spell in Arsenal's reserves during their 'double' season, 1970-71, before trying his luck in America with Atlanta Chiefs. He returned to England in September 1973, spent two years with Brentford, then quit to became a London taxi driver.

Season	League			FA Cup			League Cup			Other			Total		
	Aps	Sub	Gls	Aps	Sub	Gls	Aps	Sub	Gls	Aps	Sub	Gls	Aps	Sub	Gls
1966-67	14		2										14		2
1967-68	24		4	2			1						27		4
Total	38		6	2			1						41		6

MILLINGTON, Anthony Horace (Tony)
   Goalkeeper   *Hawarden, 5 June 1943*

Posh's most capped player, Millington represented Wales eight times whilst with the club. He first saw League action with WBA in the early 1960s before moving to Crystal Palace, from where Gordon Clark signed him for £15,000 in March 1966 in a deal that also landed Derek Kevan. An entertainer as well as a capable goalkeeper, Tony was a big hit with Posh fans in his three seasons with the club. His best season was 1967-68 when he was ever present. He was sold a year later for just £5,000 to Swansea, where he played 178 League games and continued his international career, retiring with 21 caps in 1974. Now confined to a wheelchair, he runs the Wrexham disabled supporters club.

Season	League			FA Cup			League Cup			Other			Total		
	Aps	Sub	Gls	Aps	Sub	Gls	Aps	Sub	Gls	Aps	Sub	Gls	Aps	Sub	Gls
1966-67	33			4									37		
1967-68	46			3			1						50		
1968-69	39			1			5						45		
Total	118			8			6						132		

MOORE, Martin Terence
   Winger   *Middlesbrough, 10 January 1966*

Moore quit his job on a Teesside shipyard for professional football with Posh in January 1990. Signed by Mark Lawrenson from Stockton, the left-winger debuted in a 0-2 defeat at Hartlepool in February 1990, but he found opportunities few and was released in the summer.

Season	League			FA Cup			League Cup			Other			Total		
	Aps	Sub	Gls	Aps	Sub	Gls	Aps	Sub	Gls	Aps	Sub	Gls	Aps	Sub	Gls
1989-90	6	1											6	1	

MORAN, Paul
   Winger   *Enfield, 22 May 1968*

Once considered to have a great future, slender winger Moran joined Posh on a free transfer from Tottenham in July 1994. He made almost 50 appearances for Spurs in nine years and was loaned to Portsmouth, Leicester, Newcastle, and Southend. Posh fans never got to see the best of him on account of injuries. Released in 1995, Paul dropped into non-League with home-town club Enfield, playing in the FA Cup against Posh the following year. During 1999-2000 he joined Kingsbury.

Season	League			FA Cup			League Cup			Other			Total		
	Aps	Sub	Gls	Aps	Sub	Gls	Aps	Sub	Gls	Aps	Sub	Gls	Aps	Sub	Gls
1994-95	5	2		1			2			1			9	2	

MORGAN, Darren Joseph

Midfielder   *Camberwell, 5 November 1967*

One of a League record six signings made by Chris Turner on transfer-deadline day in March 1991, Welsh Youth cap Morgan was a loanee from Millwall. Although unlucky with injuries, he impressed with his tenacity and was in the side that clinched promotion to Division Three at Chesterfield on the last day of 1990-91. Posh were unable to tempt him with a contract, and Morgan joined Bradford City in August 1991.

Season	League			FA Cup			League Cup			Other			Total		
	Aps	Sub	Gls	Aps	Sub	Gls	Aps	Sub	Gls	Aps	Sub	Gls	Aps	Sub	Gls
1990-91	5												5		

MORRIS, Peter John

Midfielder   *New Houghton, 8 November 1943*

Manager between 1979 and 1982, Morris donned a Posh shirt when injuries forced him out of retirement for one game in October 1979. His experience helped Posh to a 0-0 draw at Rochdale in what was the 615th League game of a playing career that began at Mansfield, whom he skippered as a teenager in the early 1960s. Morris played 287 League games for the Stags before transferring to Ipswich in 1967 and recording a further 220 appearances. After two seasons with Norwich in the mid-1970s, he returned to Mansfield as player-manager in 1976. He was later assistant to Bill McGarry at Newcastle before his three-year stint with Posh. Since then Peter has managed Crewe, Kettering, Boston, Northampton and King's Lynn, whilst living in Peterborough.

Season	League			FA Cup			League Cup			Other			Total		
	Aps	Sub	Gls	Aps	Sub	Gls	Aps	Sub	Gls	Aps	Sub	Gls	Aps	Sub	Gls
1979-80	1												1		

MORRISON, David Ellison

Winger   *Waltham Forest, 30 November 1974*

A skilful but inconsistent left-winger, Morrison was given his chance in League football by John Still, who signed him from Chelmsford in 1994 for £25,000 – a record fee received by the non-League club. After showing promise early in 1994-95, with his mazy runs and spectacular goals, he faded badly. In March 1997 Barry Fry sold him for a nominal fee to Leyton Orient. In 2000-01 David was loaned to Dover Athletic.

Season	League			FA Cup			League Cup			Other			Total		
	Aps	Sub	Gls	Aps	Sub	Gls	Aps	Sub	Gls	Aps	Sub	Gls	Aps	Sub	Gls
1994-95	34	8	8			1	1		1	2			37	9	9
1995-96	21	3	2	2			3	1		2	1		28	5	2
1996-97	4	7	2	3	2					2	1		9	10	2
Total	59	18	12	5	3		4	1	1	6	2		74	24	13

MORROW, Stephen Joseph (Steve)
Defender/Midfielder   Belfast, 2 July 1970

A utility player loaned from QPR, following Adam Drury's sale to
Norwich in March 2001, Morrow's career began at Arsenal, where he
won caps for Northern Ireland and a Cup-Winners' Cup medal under
George Graham in the early 1990s. He is best remembered for the 1993
Coca-Cola Cup final when, having scored the winner against Sheffield
Wednesday, he broke an arm in the post-match celebrations when top-
pling from the shoulders of Tony Adams. Whilst his team-mates collected their medals, Morrow departed on a stretcher under an oxygen
mask. Though never a Highbury regular, he played 62 League games
before joining QPR in March 1997. Known to Barry Fry when loaned
to Barnet from Arsenal, Morrow now plays in the United States.

Season	League			FA Cup			League Cup			Other			Total		
	Aps	Sub	Gls	Aps	Sub	Gls	Aps	Sub	Gls	Aps	Sub	Gls	Aps	Sub	Gls
2000-01	11												11		

MORTON, Alan
Inside-forward   Peterborough, 6 March 1942

Local lad Alan Morton was a Posh apprentice before Arsenal snapped
him up in 1959. In October 1961 he found himself back, having failed
to break through at Highbury. He debuted in a Third Division game at
Hull and had a few games the following season before leaving for
Wisbech. He returned to the League in July 1963 with Lincoln, hitting
20 League goals in 58 games before switching to Chesterfield in 1965.

Season	League			FA Cup			League Cup			Other			Total		
	Aps	Sub	Gls	Aps	Sub	Gls	Aps	Sub	Gls	Aps	Sub	Gls	Aps	Sub	Gls
1961-62	1												1		
1962-63	6		2				1						7		2
Total	7		2				1						8		2

MOSS, Ernest (Ernie)
Forward   Chesterfield, 19 October 1949

Big Ernie was one of the most successful lower-division target men of
his age. A late starter, he was working in a bank and scoring goals for
amateurs Chesterfield Tube Works when Spireites' manager Jimmy
McGuigan signed him in October 1968. Moss bagged 20 League goals
to help Chesterfield to the Fourth Division title in 1969-70. Ernie continued banging them in, and when Noel Cantwell paid a club-record

£25,000 to land the burly striker in January 1976, many felt he had got a bargain. Regrettably, Ernie failed to settle and lasted less than a year with Posh. He debuted in a 3-0 home win over Chester, and opened his scoring account with both goals in a 2-0 defeat of Preston a week later. He hit his 100th League goal later that season, but after struggling early the next was sold to Mansfield for £20,000 in December 1976. He returned to Chesterfield in 1979, then had spells with Port Vale, Lincoln and Doncaster before having a third stint at Saltergate in 1984 (becoming the club's record scorer with 161 League goals). Moss continued at Stockport, Scarborough and Rochdale before retiring in 1988 from League soccer with 244 goals in 749 League games – not bad for a late starter. He turned out for Kettering and Matlock before quitting in 1990. After running a sports shop in Chesterfield, he managed Gainsborough and Matlock, and assisted Peter Morris at Kettering.

Season	League			FA Cup			League Cup			Other			Total		
	Aps	Sub	Gls	Aps	Sub	Gls	Aps	Sub	Gls	Aps	Sub	Gls	Aps	Sub	Gls
1975-76	21		6										21		6
1976-77	13	1	3	2		1	5		2				20	1	6
Total	34	1	9	2		1	5		2				41	1	12

MOSS, Robert Stephen (Bobby)
Winger   *Harrow, 15 February 1949*

The first ever winner of Posh's Player of the Season, in 1969-70, this tricky little winger was loved for his runs down the right touchline. London-born Moss played only a few games for his first club Fulham, but became a Posh regular after Jim Iley signed him in July 1969. Moss could create goals and score them, and was on target in Posh's record home win when stuffing Oldham 8-1 in November 1969. Bobby scored six goals in his first season and a dozen in his second. Although going off the boil thereafter, he remained with the club until a knee injury forced his retirement in 1973. He remained living in Peterborough and has worked for local engineering firm, Perkins, for the last 25 years.

Season	League			FA Cup			League Cup			Other			Total		
	Aps	Sub	Gls	Aps	Sub	Gls	Aps	Sub	Gls	Aps	Sub	Gls	Aps	Sub	Gls
1969-70	38	2	6	2			2						42	2	6
1970-71	28	5	10	1	1	2							29	6	12
1971-72	17	9	1	1	1		1						19	10	1
1972-73	3	2		1									4	2	
Total	86	18	17	5	2	2	3						94	20	19

MOULDEN, Anthony (Tony)
Inside-forward   *Farnworth, 28 August 1942*

Moulden joined Posh in unusual circumstances. He was signed by club directors in November 1962 when the manager's chair was empty following the sacking of Jimmy Hagan. Tony arrived with just a few

League games under his belt, with Bury and Rochdale. His Posh career got off to a flyer, scoring in a 3-0 home win over Bournemouth and the 3-3 draw at Coventry soon after. He enjoyed a settled run in 1963-64 but struggled the following season. The little inside-forward joined Notts County for a small fee in May 1965, playing 23 League games before finishing back in Lancashire with a second spell at Rochdale.

Season	League			FA Cup			League Cup			Other			Total		
	Aps	Sub	Gls	Aps	Sub	Gls	Aps	Sub	Gls	Aps	Sub	Gls	Aps	Sub	Gls
1962-63	14		2										14		2
1963-64	30		4	2									32		4
1964-65	18		3	1			1						20		3
Total	62		9	3			1						66		9

MOULDS, Jeremy
Defender   *Peterborough, 28 December 1967*

Joining Posh as a YTS trainee in 1984, this Yaxley lad was retained on non-contract terms and debuted in the Freight-Rover Trophy at home to Aldershot in April 1986. He never played again, although he made the subs' bench for a League Cup-tie at Norwich in 1986-87. Released later that season, Moulds played for Stamford, Wisbech, Bourne and Spalding. He still lives in Yaxley, running the family tile business.

Season	League			FA Cup			League Cup			Other			Total		
	Aps	Sub	Gls	Aps	Sub	Gls	Aps	Sub	Gls	Aps	Sub	Gls	Aps	Sub	Gls
1985-86										1			1		

MURRAY, Albert George (Bert)
Midfielder/Right-back Hoxton, 22 September 1942

Capped six times by England Under-23s, Londoner Murray brought quality to Noel Cantwell's Posh side of the 1970s. Dependable either in midfield or at right-back, Bert won a Fourth Division winners medal in 1973-74, arriving from Brighton, initially on loan, in September. He had come to notice at Chelsea, where he played 160 League games alongside the likes of Terry Venables and George Graham. After collecting a League Cup winners' medal in 1965, he left Stamford Bridge a year later, spending five seasons with Birmingham before joining Brighton in 1971. He debuted for Posh in a 1-2 League Cup defeat by Scunthorpe in September 1973 and was a regular throughout his three seasons with the club. Bert did his bit in the FA Cup runs of 1975 and 1976, in epic ties against Middlesbrough, Nottingham Forest and Manchester United. He played his 100th League game for Posh in a 1-0 win against Brighton in November 1975. By then he was operating at right-back, a position he held until retiring at the end of 1975-76. Nowadays Bert welcomes regulars to his pub, The Bull, at Market Deeping.

Season	League			FA Cup			League Cup			Other			Total		
	Aps	Sub	Gls	Aps	Sub	Gls	Aps	Sub	Gls	Aps	Sub	Gls	Aps	Sub	Gls
1973-74	42		9	4		1	1						47		10
1974-75	45			8		1	1						54		1
1975-76	36		1	5			5						46		1
Total	123		10	17		2	7						147		12

MURRAY, Daniel (Dan)

Defender   *Cambridge, 16 May 1982*

When Murray debuted in Posh's 1-1 draw at Macclesfield in March 2000 – standing in for injured Andy Edwards – Barry Fry hailed the 17-year-old centre-back as 'the best player on the pitch'. It had been a memorable week for Dan, who signed a five-year contract and also scored his first goal for the reserves. His first home appearance came the following month when an injury to Simon Rea gave him his chance in a 3-1 win over Exeter. Subsequent games have been few, although at 20 time is on his side. Coming from a footballing family – his father played for Cambridge City, Stevenage, and Kettering – Murray was voted Posh Under-18 Player of the Season in 1998-99.

Season	League			FA Cup			League Cup			Other			Total		
	Aps	Sub	Gls	Aps	Sub	Gls	Aps	Sub	Gls	Aps	Sub	Gls	Aps	Sub	Gls
1999-00	2												2		
2000-01	1	2								2			3	2	
Total	3	2								2			5	2	

Darren Morgan, 1990-91

Sean Farrell
v Wycombe, 1994-95

John Cozens

Phil Chard (left) v Wigan, May 1982

Joe Cooke (right)
v Luton, July 1979

Phil Crosby v Maidstone, August 1989

Richie Norman

Craig Goldsmith (left), 1988-89

Mick Halsall

Jimmy Holmes

David Riley (centre) v West Brom, April 1992

Tony Kelly

John Mason

NAYLOR, Stuart William
Goalkeeper   *Wetherby, 6 December 1962*

A well-travelled former England Youth international, 6ft 4in Naylor's long career included a loan spell at London Road in 1982-83. He arrived from Lincoln to replace cracked collarbone victim David Seaman and debuted in a 3-0 home win over Tranmere in February 1983. After spending 1983-84 on loan to Crewe, Naylor earned a regular place at Lincoln before joining WBA for £100,000 in February 1986. He was the Baggies' first-choice keeper for ten years, making 355 League appearances and gaining England 'B' honours prior to joining Bristol City in August 1996. Naylor was on the move again in 1999, joining Third Division Exeter, but has since teamed up with League newcomers Rushden & Diamonds after impressing in a loan spell.

Season	League			FA Cup			League Cup			Other			Total		
	Aps	Sub	Gls	Aps	Sub	Gls	Aps	Sub	Gls	Aps	Sub	Gls	Aps	Sub	Gls
1982-83	8												8		

NEAL, Ashley James
Defender   *Northampton, 16 December 1974*

Son of ex-Liverpool star Phil Neal, big defender Ashley joined Posh following his father's appointment as assistant manager. Having started as an apprentice at Anfield, Ashley tasted League action on loan to Brighton before joining Huddersfield in December 1996. Unable to break into the Terriers' team he signed for Posh in March 1997 and played four times that season. He had to wait a year for his next chance in the team and after failing to feature in 1998-99 he departed.

Season	League			FA Cup			League Cup			Other			Total		
	Aps	Sub	Gls	Aps	Sub	Gls	Aps	Sub	Gls	Aps	Sub	Gls	Aps	Sub	Gls
1996-97	4												4		
1997-98	2	2		1									2	3	
Total	6	2		1									6	3	

NEENAN, Joseph Patrick (Joe)
Goalkeeper   *Manchester, 17 March 1959*

A big, red-haired keeper, Joe Neenan arrived in July 1987 with over 300 League games to his name from his time with York, Scunthorpe and Burnley. He debuted on the opening day of 1987-88, keeping a clean sheet in a 1-0 home win over Carlisle. He became Cantwell's first-choice keeper, missing just six League matches. Dislodged from the side by Paul Crichton early the following season, Neenan was loaned to Scarborough before being released to non-League Chorley.

Season	League			FA Cup			League Cup			Other			Total		
	Aps	Sub	Gls	Aps	Sub	Gls	Aps	Sub	Gls	Aps	Sub	Gls	Aps	Sub	Gls
1987-88	40			2			5			2			49		
1988-89	15			4									19		
Total	55			2			9			2			68		

NIGHTINGALE, Mark Barry Douglas
Defender/Midfielder   Salisbury, 1 February 1957

A former England Youth cap, Nightingale joined Posh on a free transfer in July 1986 from Bournemouth, where he had made 199 League appearances in two spells. He had also spent time with Crystal Palace, Norwich and Bulova in Hong Kong. After a shaky start for Posh – being sent off during a home defeat by Crewe in September 1986 – the experienced campaigner improved to become a regular member of the side until his departure in 1988 to Kettering Town. He later had spells with King's Lynn and Wisbech before joining his former Poppies team-mate Robbie Cooke at Jewson League side Warboys Town.

Season	League			FA Cup			League Cup			Other			Total		
	Aps	Sub	Gls	Aps	Sub	Gls	Aps	Sub	Gls	Aps	Sub	Gls	Aps	Sub	Gls
1986-87	40		2	1			3			2		1	46		3
1987-88	31	7	1	2			2			4			39	7	1
Total	71	7	3	3			5			6		1	85	7	4

NIMMO, Ian Wallace
Forward   Boston, 23 January 1958

Ian Nimmo was loaned to Posh from Sheffield Wednesday in January 1977, scoring in a 3-1 home win over Grimsby. All told he made 45 League appearances for the Owls, ending his career at Doncaster where he scored 29 goals in 86 League games between 1979 and 1982.

Season	League			FA Cup			League Cup			Other			Total		
	Aps	Sub	Gls	Aps	Sub	Gls	Aps	Sub	Gls	Aps	Sub	Gls	Aps	Sub	Gls
1976-77	4		1										4		1

NIXON, Jonathan Charles (Jon)
Winger   Ilkeston, 20 January 1948

A former Derby apprentice, Jon Nixon spent five seasons with Notts County before becoming Noel Cantwell's most expensive signing at £15,000 in September 1974. A nippy winger and good crosser, Jon scored important FA Cup goals during his three years with Posh. In 1975 his goal earned a fifth-round replay with First Division Middlesbrough, and a year later he hit a third-round replay winner against Brian Clough's Nottingham Forest, which earned a trip to Manchester United. After more than 100 League games for Posh, he signed for Third Division rivals Shrewsbury in August 1977. By his own admission, he had never quite lived up to his billing, spending so much time in Cantwell's office that his name might have been written above the door. Nixon later played for Barnsley and Halifax, before joining Burton Albion in 1979. Spells in management followed, notably at Grantham and Kettering, where he assisted ex-Notts County colleague Dave Needham. Now living in West Hallam, Derbyshire, Jon works as a sales director for Barnsley-based Cambridge Online Learning.

Season	League			FA Cup			League Cup			Other			Total		
	Aps	Sub	Gls	Aps	Sub	Gls	Aps	Sub	Gls	Aps	Sub	Gls	Aps	Sub	Gls
1974-75	38	1	5	5	3	3							43	4	8
1975-76	33	2	6	5		3	5						43	2	9
1976-77	33	3	5	2									35	3	5
Total	104	6	16	12	3	6	5						121	9	22

NOBLE, Frank

Full-back   *Sheffield, 26 October 1945*

A reliable full-back, Noble started with hometown club Sheffield Wednesday, but joined Posh in July 1967 after just two Division One appearances for the Owls. Frank was a polished and consistent performer during five seasons with Posh, proving his versatility by playing left or right-back. He debuted in a League Cup-tie with Northampton in August 1967 and exceeded 200 League games for the club. Ever-present in 1969-70, he missed just two games the following season, as captain, before retiring through injury in 1973. At the time, only Brian Wright and Ollie Conmy had played more League games for Posh.

Season	League			FA Cup			League Cup			Other			Total		
	Aps	Sub	Gls	Aps	Sub	Gls	Aps	Sub	Gls	Aps	Sub	Gls	Aps	Sub	Gls
1967-68	43		1	3			1						47		1
1968-69	38	2		1			5						44	2	
1969-70	46			4			2						52		
1970-71	44			2									46		
1971-72	34						1						35		
Total	205	2	1	10			9						224	2	1

NOGAN, Kurt

Forward   *Cardiff, 9 September 1970*

A natural goalscorer, Nogan joined Posh on a free transfer from Luton in September 1992. A Welsh Under-21 international, he made just one appearance in a 0-2 Anglo-Italian Cup defeat at Wolves before signing for Brighton. He hit 41 League goals in two seasons at the Goldstone Ground, which in April 1995 led to a £250,000 move to Burnley. A move to Preston followed in March 1997 before Kurt became a transfer-deadline signing for Cardiff in March 2000.

Season	League			FA Cup			League Cup			Other			Total		
	Aps	Sub	Gls	Aps	Sub	Gls	Aps	Sub	Gls	Aps	Sub	Gls	Aps	Sub	Gls
1992-93										1			1		

NORMAN, Richard (Richie)

Left-back   *Newcastle, 5 September 1935*

An experienced left-back, Norman joined Posh in July 1968 after a distinguished career with Leicester, for whom he played over 300 League games in ten years. A veteran of two FA Cup finals with the Foxes, Norman failed to live up to Posh's expectations. He debuted at home to Exeter on the opening day of 1968-69, but made only a handful of appearances before retiring. He later spent many years as coach, trainer and physio at Derby, Northampton, Kettering and Nuneaton.

Season	League			FA Cup			League Cup			Other			Total		
	Aps	Sub	Gls	Aps	Sub	Gls	Aps	Sub	Gls	Aps	Sub	Gls	Aps	Sub	Gls
1968-69	9	1					3						12	1	

NORRIS, Derek
Wing-half   *Beighton, 19 June 1935, Died 1997*

After signing from Gainsborough in July 1960, Norris debuted in Posh's first Football League match, at home to Wrexham. He figured in the next four games but lost his place to new signing Keith Ripley. Jimmy Hagan released Derek on a free transfer at the end of 1960-61.

Season	League			FA Cup			League Cup			Other			Total		
	Aps	Sub	Gls	Aps	Sub	Gls	Aps	Sub	Gls	Aps	Sub	Gls	Aps	Sub	Gls
1960-61	5												5		

NUTTELL, Michael John (Mick)
Forward   *Boston, 22 November 1968*

Leaving Boston Grammar School with six O-levels, Mick debuted as a YTS trainee in the last weeks of 1985-86. A contract followed in August 1987, due to his goalscoring displays at youth and reserve-team level, but the tall striker struggled in Division Four and was often on the bench. He netted in Freight Rover Trophy ties against Colchester and Cambridge in 1987-88, but was released the following season after loan spells at Crewe and Carlisle. Mick has enjoyed a good career with non-League Cheltenham, Wycombe, Boston, Kettering, Dagenham & Redbridge, and Rushden & Diamonds. Released from a second spell at Kettering in July 1998, Nuttell spent 1998-99 with Dr Martens League side King's Lynn before returning for a third spell at his hometown club Boston. In 2001-02 he turned out for Bedford and Wisbech.

Season	League			FA Cup			League Cup			Other			Total		
	Aps	Sub	Gls	Aps	Sub	Gls	Aps	Sub	Gls	Aps	Sub	Gls	Aps	Sub	Gls
1985-86	1	2								1			2	2	
1986-87	5	2		1			1						5	4	
1987-88	6	5		1						3	2		9	6	2
Total	12	9		2			1			4	2		16	12	2

O'CONNOR, Martyn John
Midfielder   *Walsall, 10 December 1967*

Barry Fry paid a club record £350,000 to Walsall for their inspirational midfielder who had captained them to promotion from Division Three in 1995. Posh fans were given few chances to appreciate O'Connor's passing and finishing, owing to his rapid transfer to Fry's former club, Birmingham, five months into his London Road career. A West Midlander, Martyn had started with Bromsgrove Rovers before joining

Crystal Palace for £25,000 in 1992. After just two League appearances he moved to Walsall, where his 21 League goals in two seasons included two beauties in the Saddlers' 3-2 win at London Road in March 1996. He debuted for Posh on the opening day of 1996-97, captaining the side that lost 0-1 at Bristol Rovers. When cash-strapped Posh accepted Birmingham's bid of £500,000 it meant that O'Connor held both Posh's incoming and outgoing transfer records. Installed as captain at St Andrews, O'Connor suffered three successive play-off semi-final defeats before returning to his old club Walsall in February 2002.

Season	League			FA Cup			League Cup			Other			Total		
	Aps	Sub	Gls	Aps	Sub	Gls	Aps	Sub	Gls	Aps	Sub	Gls	Aps	Sub	Gls
1996-97	18		3	2			4						24		3

O'KEEFE, Patrick John (Paddy)
Midfielder   *Peterborough, 17 July 1967*

A product of the government-funded Youth Training Scheme, local lad O'Keefe made his Fourth Division debut as a sub in a 1-1 draw at Bury on the final day of 1984-85. He was retained the following season, but was restricted to two games in the Freight Rover Trophy. Released in 1986, he spent many years on the non-League circuit and helped Stamford win the United Counties League in 1997 and 1998. Paddy moved to Blackstones, then joined Wisbech as player-coach in 2001.

Season	League			FA Cup			League Cup			Other			Total		
	Aps	Sub	Gls	Aps	Sub	Gls	Aps	Sub	Gls	Aps	Sub	Gls	Aps	Sub	Gls
1984-85		1												1	
1985-86										2			2		
Total		1								2			2	1	

OAKES, Dennis Raymond
Midfielder   *Bedworth, 10 April 1946*

The older brother of former Posh defender and physio Keith Oakes, midfielder Dennis joined Posh from Notts County in May 1971, with whom he had made 120 League appearances. He served his apprenticeship with Coventry but joined the Magpies after failing to make the first team. Debuting for Posh in a 2-0 home win over Southend on the opening day of 1971-72, he claimed the No 4 jersey for two seasons before, in 1973, being released to Chelmsford City as part of Noel Cantwell's rebuilding plans. He later joined Nuneaton and Tamworth. A useful cricketer, Dennis played county matches for Warwickshire.

Season	League			FA Cup			League Cup			Other			Total		
	Aps	Sub	Gls	Aps	Sub	Gls	Aps	Sub	Gls	Aps	Sub	Gls	Aps	Sub	Gls
1971-72	44		2	4			1						49		2
1972-73	40	1	3	4			1						45	1	3
Total	84	1	5	8			2						94	1	5

OAKES, Keith Brian
Central Defender   Bedworth, 3 July 1956

Dennis's kid brother, Keith Oakes, graduated through the ranks and debuted as a 16-year-old in a 1-1 draw at Doncaster in February 1973. He was at the time the youngest player to represent Posh in League football. The tall centre-half had limited first-team chances, with players like Chris Turner around, making just 62 League appearances in six seasons. Keith came into his own following a move to Newport, where he played 232 League games between 1978 and 1984. He also helped County reach the quarter-finals of the European Cup-Winners' Cup in 1981. Spells with Gillingham and Fulham followed before he rejoined Posh in August 1988. He took his total League appearances past 500 before helping Posh to promotion from Division Four in 1991. After a spell with Boston, he retired to become Posh's physiotherapist until 1997, whereupon he performed the same role for Lincoln.

Season	League			FA Cup			League Cup			Other			Total		
	Aps	Sub	Gls	Aps	Sub	Gls	Aps	Sub	Gls	Aps	Sub	Gls	Aps	Sub	Gls
1972-73	2	2											2	2	
1973-74	1	3					1						2	3	
1974-75	9	2		3	1								12	3	
1975-76	9		1				2						11		1
1976-77	23		1	1			3						27		1
1977-78	4	6					1	2					5	8	
1988-89	41		5	4			4		1	2		1	51		7
1989-90	27	2	1				2			1			30	2	1
1990-91	27		3	4			2			2			35		3
Total	143	15	11	12	1		15	2	1	5		1	175	18	13

OKORIE, Chima Ephraim
Forward   Izomber (Nigeria), 8 October 1968

Chima Okerie scored 300+ goals in a 15-year career in India after arriving from Nigeria as a student in 1985. Chima acquired legendary status with Calcutta club East Bengal. In the 1990s he shuttled between playing in India and Europe, taking his talents to Denmark, Norway and England. He arrived at London Road in September 1993, recommended by Nigerian team-mate Dominic Iorfa. Though Chima made only one appearance in a Posh shirt, he scored in a 1-3 Anglo-Italian Cup defeat at WBA. The burly striker then spent six months with Grimsby before appearing in 36 League games for Torquay. After returning to India in 1995, Chima prospered with Mohun Bagan until the All-India Football Federation banned him for two years for assaulting a referee. Chima retired from football to concentrate on coaching youngsters and writing political documentaries for Indian television.

Season	League			FA Cup			League Cup			Other			Total		
	Aps	Sub	Gls	Aps	Sub	Gls	Aps	Sub	Gls	Aps	Sub	Gls	Aps	Sub	Gls
1993-94										1		1	1		1

OLDFIELD, David Charles

Midfielder   *Perth (Australia), 30 May 1968*

A hard-running midfielder, Australian-born David Oldfield was a free transfer from Stoke in March 2000. His League career spanned 13 years and had earned him a cap for England Under-21s. He began at David Pleat's Luton in 1986 before signing for Manchester City for £600,000. In January 1990 he joined Leicester, with whom he featured in three First Division play-off finals. Noted for his goal-poaching, David was at his best at Filbert Street, netting 26 times in 188 League games. He returned to Luton in 1995, and was loaned to Millwall before joining Stoke. He debuted for Posh in a 1-1 draw at Third Division leaders Rotherham, keeping his place until the end of the season and playing as an emergency striker in the Wembley final victory over Darlington. In 2000-01 David went from strength to strength, his tireless, driving displays belying his 32 years and earning him the Player of the Season award. He struggled to maintain that standard in 2001-02 but passed on his experience as part of the Posh coaching staff.

Season	League Aps	Sub	Gls	FA Cup Aps	Sub	Gls	League Cup Aps	Sub	Gls	Other Aps	Sub	Gls	Total Aps	Sub	Gls
1999-00	9									3			12		
2000-01	32	7	3	5		1	2						39	7	4
2001-02	27	3	1	3	2		1			1	1		32	6	1
Total	68	10	4	8	2	1	3			4	1		83	13	5

OLIVER, Darren

Full-back   *Liverpool, 1 November 1971*

Left-back Oliver celebrated his one Posh appearance with a goal. Signed on loan from Bolton, he capped an impressive debut in a Coca-Cola Cup clash against Barnsley with a 25-yarder for Posh's third goal in a 3-1 win. Three days later he signed for Rochdale for £30,000.

Season	League Aps	Sub	Gls	FA Cup Aps	Sub	Gls	League Cup Aps	Sub	Gls	Other Aps	Sub	Gls	Total Aps	Sub	Gls
1993-94							1		1				1		1

ORR, Henry (Harry)

Wing-half   *Lisburn, 31 July 1936*

This talented little Irishman had three seasons with Posh in the mid-1960s. Signed by Gordon Clark in July 1964, Orr began with Belfast club Distillery before making ten League appearances in five years with Sheffield United. After debuting for Posh at Hull in November 1964, 'Harry' kept his place for the rest of the season, during which Posh reached the FA Cup quarter-finals. His first-team opportunities were less frequent after that and he was released in May 1967.

Season	League			FA Cup			League Cup			Other			Total		
	Aps	Sub	Gls	Aps	Sub	Gls	Aps	Sub	Gls	Aps	Sub	Gls	Aps	Sub	Gls
1964-65	26			8									34		
1965-66	14			1									15		
1966-67	7	1		1		1	1						9	1	1
Total	47	1		10		1	1						58	1	1

OSBORNE, Steven Colin (Steve)

Forward   *Middlesbrough, 3 March 1969*

Osborne was a busy striker, admired for his direct running and powerful shooting. Known as 'Supersub' – a tag he hated – Osborne had a
knack of scoring goals after coming off the bench. He was helping to
build Chelsea Harbour and playing part-time for Northern League
side South Bank when Mick Jones won the race to sign him on transfer deadline day 1989. Steve was unable to claim a regular place and,
despite his popularity with the fans, later managers Mark Lawrenson
and Chris Turner also used him mainly as a substitute. Disillusioned,
Osborne left London Road for York in August 1991.

Season	League			FA Cup			League Cup			Other			Total		
	Aps	Sub	Gls	Aps	Sub	Gls	Aps	Sub	Gls	Aps	Sub	Gls	Aps	Sub	Gls
1988-89	3	6	1										3	6	1
1989-90	12	21	5	1	1			1		1	2		14	25	5
1990-91	3	16	1		1		2	1			1		5	19	1
Total	18	43	7	1	2		2	2		1	3		22	50	7

OTTO, Ricky

Winger   *Hackney, 9 November 1967*

A flamboyant left-winger, Ricky was loaned from Birmingham in February 1997, when his dazzling displays and spectacular goals offered
hope in the fight against relegation. Ricky also weighed in with goals
in the Auto Windscreens Shield, including one in the area final against
Colchester that gave Posh a 2-0 first leg lead. Injury kept him out of the
return leg at Layer Road, which Posh lost 0-3. Otto was a late starter in
League football, joining Leyton Orient from non-League Harringay
Borough in 1990 before starring for Southend under Barry Fry. Fry
took the dreadlocked extrovert to Birmingham in December 1994 for a
club record £800,000. In his first season there, Ricky won a Second
Division championship medal and the Auto Windscreens Shield final
at Wembley. He played his last League soccer at Notts County in 1997-
98 before dropping into non-League with Rhyl and Halesowen.

Season	League			FA Cup			League Cup			Other			Total		
	Aps	Sub	Gls	Aps	Sub	Gls	Aps	Sub	Gls	Aps	Sub	Gls	Aps	Sub	Gls
1996-97	15		4							2		2	17		6

OVERFIELD, Jack
Outside-left   *Leeds, 14 May 1932*

Yorkshireman Overfield enjoyed a distinguished career in the 1950s and early 1960s with Leeds and Sunderland, before spending eighteen months at London Road. Signed in February 1963 by Jack Fairbrother for £5,000, Overfield's only senior outing came in a 1-3 home defeat by Wrexham later that month. He moved on to Bradford City in July 1964 and played eleven more League games before hanging up his boots.

Season	League			FA Cup			League Cup			Other			Total		
	Aps	Sub	Gls	Aps	Sub	Gls	Aps	Sub	Gls	Aps	Sub	Gls	Aps	Sub	Gls
1962-63	1												1		

PARIS, Alan David
Right-back   *Slough, 15 August 1964*

A stylish defender with a good first touch and fine distribution skills, Paris was Posh's first choice right-back for three seasons following his arrival from Watford in August 1985. The Hornets had discovered him at Slough Town in November 1982 but, after he had failed to break through, he joined Posh on a free transfer. He debuted in Posh's 4-2 win at Preston on the first day of 1985-86 and scooped the Player of the Year award after being ever present. The following season his fellow professionals named him in the PFA select side for Division Four. Ever present again in 1987-88, he was signed by Leicester in an exchange deal that brought striker Nick Cusack to London Road. Alan quickly adjusted to life in the Second Division, playing 88 League games for the Foxes before being sold for £80,000 to Notts County in January 1991. The Magpies had a brief flirtation with top-flight soccer in 1991-92, but injury forced Paris's retirement from the game two years later.

Season	League			FA Cup			League Cup			Other			Total		
	Aps	Sub	Gls	Aps	Sub	Gls	Aps	Sub	Gls	Aps	Sub	Gls	Aps	Sub	Gls
1985-86	46			7			2			2			57		
1986-87	43	2		1			4			2			50	2	
1987-88	46		2	2			6			4			58		2
Total	135	2	2	10			12			8			165	2	2

PARK, Robert Clydesdale (Bobby)
Midfielder   *Edinburgh, 3 July 1946*

Scottish midfielder Park signed for Aston Villa in 1963, appearing 74 times in the First and Second Division. Having helped Wrexham to promotion in 1969-70, he joined Posh with forward Ray Smith in June 1972. Bobby was a regular in Jim Iley's side, but had limited chances under Noel Cantwell from October 1972. Released the following summer, Park ended his League career with Northampton and Hartlepool.

Season	League			FA Cup			League Cup			Other			Total		
	Aps	Sub	Gls	Aps	Sub	Gls	Aps	Sub	Gls	Aps	Sub	Gls	Aps	Sub	Gls
1972-73	15	3	1				1						16	3	1

PARKIN, Thomas Aitchison (Tommy)
Midfielder   *Gateshead, 1 February 1956*

Another of Noel Cantwell's many loan signings, Geordie midfielder Parkin arrived from Ipswich in July 1976. The long-haired 20-year-old had been unable to break into Ipswich's team but had gained League experience during an earlier loan spell at Grimsby. He made his Posh debut in a 3-2 League Cup victory at Reading in August 1976, and showed neat touches in four subsequent outings before returning to Portman Road. He stayed with Ipswich until 1987, making 70 League appearances, mainly as cover for Town's injured stars.

Season	League			FA Cup			League Cup			Other			Total		
	Aps	Sub	Gls	Aps	Sub	Gls	Aps	Sub	Gls	Aps	Sub	Gls	Aps	Sub	Gls
1976-77	3						2						5		

PARKINSON, Andrew James (Andy)
Forward   *Johannesburg, 5 May 1959*

A tall South African forward signed from Newcastle, Andy spent just four months at London Road before choosing to return to his homeland. Limited to just three substitute appearances on Tyneside, he joined Peter Morris's Posh team in August 1979 and debuted in a 3-1 League Cup-tie against Charlton. His first Posh goal came in the same competition, in a 1-1 home draw with First Division Bristol City. Andy endeared himself to fans by hitting five League goals in five games prior to his sudden departure. He later played for Philadelphia Fury.

Season	League			FA Cup			League Cup			Other			Total		
	Aps	Sub	Gls	Aps	Sub	Gls	Aps	Sub	Gls	Aps	Sub	Gls	Aps	Sub	Gls
1979-80	12	1	5	1			4		1				17	1	6

PARR, Trevor William
Forward   *Bradford, 21 December 1961*

Failing to break into League football with Birmingham, Bradford City and Huddersfield, Parr joined Yorkshire club Thackley. John Wile offered him another chance when signing him on a non-contract basis in November 1984. The fair-haired striker's Posh career was restricted to a brief substitute appearance in a 1-2 defeat at Southend. Parr's career was threatened in December 1984 by a bottle attack in his home town of Bradford, in which he nearly lost the sight of an eye.

Season	League			FA Cup			League Cup			Other			Total		
	Aps	Sub	Gls	Aps	Sub	Gls	Aps	Sub	Gls	Aps	Sub	Gls	Aps	Sub	Gls
1984-85		1												1	

PARSLOW, Linden
Goalkeeper   *Port Elizabeth (Australia), 1963*

RAF weapons mechanic Linden Parslow attracted several clubs following his performances for Stamford en route to the FA Vase Wembley final in 1984. His trial with Posh was curtailed by injury, but Parslow joined up with John Wile in April 1986 and appeared in a 2-0 Freight-Rover Trophy win against Aldershot at London Road.

Season	League			FA Cup			League Cup			Other			Total		
	Aps	Sub	Gls	Aps	Sub	Gls	Aps	Sub	Gls	Aps	Sub	Gls	Aps	Sub	Gls
1985-86										1			1		

PAYNE, Derek Richard
Midfielder   *Edgware, 26 April 1967*

A pint-sized, tenacious midfielder, Payne played under Barry Fry at Barnet and Southend before joining Watford in July 1994. After 36 League appearances in two seasons with the Hornets, he joined Posh on a free transfer in August 1996. His grit and enthusiasm helped him win the Player of the Year award after his first season. Unfortunately, the rest of Payne's Posh career was blighted by controversy. He found himself accused of stealing from assistant manager Phil Neal at the club's training ground. Although he was not charged, the incident badly affected Payne who was sent off within two minutes of a League Cup-tie with Reading the same day. Posh's League form collapsed later that season and Payne was often scapegoated by a section of Posh fans – a situation exacerbated when he went AWOL for a crunch game at Lincoln in April 1998. Although Payne figured early in 1998-99, the parting of the ways came in March 1999 when his contract was cancelled. He spent 1999-00 helping Dagenham & Redbridge win the Ryman Premier League, but has since joined Harrow Borough.

Season	League			FA Cup			League Cup			Other			Total		
	Aps	Sub	Gls	Aps	Sub	Gls	Aps	Sub	Gls	Aps	Sub	Gls	Aps	Sub	Gls
1996-97	36		2	6			3			5			50		2
1997-98	35	2	2	3			4			3			45	2	2
1998-99	8	1											8	1	
Total	79	3	4	9			7			8			103	3	4

PAYNE, John
Full-back   *Swansea, 1 April 1949*

Young Welshman Payne joined Posh in September 1969 following his release from Swansea. The 20-year-old right-back played just once when called upon as a last-minute replacement for Brian Potts in an FA Cup-tie at Gillingham, after Potts had missed the train to Kent.

Season	League			FA Cup			League Cup			Other			Total		
	Aps	Sub	Gls	Aps	Sub	Gls	Aps	Sub	Gls	Aps	Sub	Gls	Aps	Sub	Gls
1969-70				1									1		

PEARCE, Dennis Andrew
  Full-back   *Wolverhampton, 10 September 1974*
Failing to make the grade at Aston Villa, this left-sided defender joined hometown team Wolves in 1995, making nine League appearances before moving on a free transfer to Notts County in July 1997. He was an integral part of the Magpies side that won the Third Division title in 1988. Barry Fry added Pearce's pace and athleticism to the Posh squad in July 2001 but Dennis's first season was racked by injury.

Season	League			FA Cup			League Cup			Other			Total		
	Aps	Sub	Gls	Aps	Sub	Gls	Aps	Sub	Gls	Aps	Sub	Gls	Aps	Sub	Gls
2001-02	8	1		1									9	1	

PEARCE, Reginald Stanley (Reg)
  Wing-half   *Liverpool, 12 January 1930*
A defender who represented the English Football League during his early career, Liverpool-born Pearce joined Posh in August 1963. He was a key figure with Cambridge City before making a late entry to the professional ranks. He left Winsford for Luton in November 1954 and played 75 League games for the Hatters before serving Sunderland from 1958 to 1961. He debuted for Posh on the first day of 1963-64, helping Gordon Clark's side beat Wrexham 5-2. He remained a regular until returning to Cambridge City midway through the season.

Season	League			FA Cup			League Cup			Other			Total		
	Aps	Sub	Gls	Aps	Sub	Gls	Aps	Sub	Gls	Aps	Sub	Gls	Aps	Sub	Gls
1963-64	28		2	1			1						30		2

PETERS, Mark
  Central Defender   *St Asaph, 6 July 1972*
Though capped by Wales Under-21s, Peters could not break through at Manchester City or Norwich, so signed for Posh in August 1993. He began that season as centre-half before losing his place to Lee Howarth. In September 1994 he went on a free to Mansfield, whom he helped beat Leeds in the League Cup and reach the Third Division play-offs. Peters later teamed up with other former Posh players at Rushden & Diamonds, helping them into the Football League in 2001.

Season	League			FA Cup			League Cup			Other			Total		
	Aps	Sub	Gls	Aps	Sub	Gls	Aps	Sub	Gls	Aps	Sub	Gls	Aps	Sub	Gls
1993-94	17	2					2			2			21	2	

PHILLIPS, Brendan Ulysses
  Midfielder   *Jamaica, 16 July 1954*
Brendan arrived in the UK from Jamaica aged six. A free transfer signing from Leicester in August 1973, Brendan was given just one chance in the Posh team by Noel Cantwell, due to an abundance of midfield

talent at the club. Released at the end of the campaign, Phillips did so well with non-League Burton Albion, Nuneaton Borough, Kettering Town and Boston United – gaining England semi-pro international honours – that he rejoined the professional ranks with Mansfield in August 1980. He made 17 League appearances for the Stags, before returning to the semi-professional ranks with Scarborough, Shepshed Charterhouse, Corby, Aylesbury, and Bedworth United. He managed Stafford Rangers in 1990 before taking charge at Nuneaton, whom he guided to the Dr Martens Premier League title in 1998-99. Dismissed in 2000-01, Brendan is now in charge at Halesowen.

Season	League			FA Cup			League Cup			Other			Total		
	Aps	Sub	Gls	Aps	Sub	Gls	Aps	Sub	Gls	Aps	Sub	Gls	Aps	Sub	Gls
1973-74	1												1		

PHILLIPS, Ian Alexander
Left-back   *Edinburgh, 23 April 1959*

One of many former Mansfield players brought in by Peter Morris, Ian Phillips was a tenacious Scot who made 23 League appearances for the Stags before joining Posh in August 1979. A regular left-back in his first two seasons, Ian shared the No 3 shirt with Steve Collins in 1981-82 before moving on to Northampton. After a year with the Cobblers, he joined Colchester, where he completed 150 League games, prior to ending his League days with Aldershot. He returned to Colchester, where as player-coach Football League status was regained in 1991-92.

Season	League			FA Cup			League Cup			Other			Total		
	Aps	Sub	Gls	Aps	Sub	Gls	Aps	Sub	Gls	Aps	Sub	Gls	Aps	Sub	Gls
1979-80	39		1				3						42		1
1980-81	41			6			4						51		
1981-82	17		2	1									18		2
Total	97		3	7			7						111		3

PHILLIPS, Stephen Edward (Steve)
Forward   *Edmonton, 4 August 1954*

A prolific goalscorer with a good track record in the lower leagues, veteran Phillips arrived in November 1986 with 180 League goals to his name. The diminutive Londoner gained England Youth honours with Birmingham in the early 1970s but had to wait until joining Northampton in 1975 for regular first-team action. He scored eight goals in 51 League appearances for the Cobblers before hitting the heights during a three-year stint at Brentford. All-told he netted 65 League goals for the Bees and in 1977-78 was the country's leading marksman with 36 goals in all competitions. He was no less prolific in the 1980s, back with Northampton, then with Southend and Torquay, before Lil Fuccillo signed him on loan in November 1986, just after the sacking of John Wile. Phillips scored on his Posh debut to earn a 1-1 draw at Exeter, then hit the winner to beat Preston 2-1 at home, in the first game of Noel Cantwell's second spell. Cantwell rewarded him with a permanent contract soon afterwards, and Steve finished 1986-87 as top scorer. Surprisingly axed and loaned to Exeter and Chesterfield in 1987-88, he was recalled late that season and scored a hat-trick in a 4-0 win at Newport. After four more games with Posh, Steve graced non-League with Stamford, Baker Perkins, Molins and Warboys Town. Phillips is now the proprietor of 'Inchy's Bar' in Spain.

Season	League			FA Cup			League Cup			Other			Total		
	Aps	Sub	Gls	Aps	Sub	Gls	Aps	Sub	Gls	Aps	Sub	Gls	Aps	Sub	Gls
1986-87	30		11	1						2		1	33		12
1987-88	16	2	5	1			3			2			22	2	5
Total	46	2	16	2			3			4		1	55	2	17

PHILLISKIRK, Anthony (Tony)
Forward   *Sunderland, 10 February 1965*

A striker with a sweet left foot, Philliskirk was bought from Bolton for £85,000 in October 1992 to replace popular Ken Charlery. Free-kick specialist Tony was an England schoolboy international, who started out with Sheffield United, then served Rotherham (on loan), Oldham and Preston before joining Bolton, where he was top scorer for three consecutive seasons. His Posh career started brightly in front of the TV cameras at Leicester, where his curler helped record a 2-0 win. He soon added two more goals as Posh won 2-1 at Charlery's new club, Watford. Although not quick, Philliskirk knew the route to goal and his finishing was never in question. He remained a popular player during Posh's brief sojourn in Division One, forming a useful strike partnership with Tony Adcock. Philliskirk's five-goal haul against Kingstonian in the FA Cup was erased from the records after the tie had to be replayed after a coin-throwing incident. Although hampered by injury during 1993-94, Tony registered the first hat-trick by a Posh player in six years, at home to Oxford. He joined Burnley for £80,000 in January 1994, staying at Turf Moor for two years before ending his League career with Cardiff and Macclesfield. After considering a career as a referee, Tony became a coach at his old club Oldham.

Season	League			FA Cup			League Cup			Other			Total		
	Aps	Sub	Gls	Aps	Sub	Gls	Aps	Sub	Gls	Aps	Sub	Gls	Aps	Sub	Gls
1992-93	31	1	11	3		1							34	1	12
1993-94	6	5	4	1			2		1	2		1	11	5	6
Total	37	6	15	4		1	2		1	2		1	45	6	18

PHILPOTT, Lee
Winger   *Barnet, 21 February 1970*

A youth product, Philpott had limited opportunities – mostly as substitute – before finding success elsewhere. A left-footed wide player,

Lee left Posh under a cloud following an alleged incident at a night-club. In May 1989 he was signed by Cambridge and played a major part in their rise under John Beck. In November 1992 he earned a £350,000 fee from Leicester, playing 75 League games for the Foxes – some in the Premiership – before joining Blackpool, Lincoln and Hull.

Season	League			FA Cup			League Cup			Other			Total		
	Aps	Sub	Gls	Aps	Sub	Gls	Aps	Sub	Gls	Aps	Sub	Gls	Aps	Sub	Gls
1987-88		1												1	
1988-89	1	2		1						2			1	5	
Total	1	3		1						2			1	6	

PIKE, Martin Russell
Left-back   *South Shields, 21 October 1964*

Posh's Player of the Season in 1984-85, Pike started out as a midfielder before developing into an overlapping full-back. Pike followed John Wile into London Road from WBA in August 1983, but could not hold down a place until he was switched to left-back the following season. He went from strength to strength, and after missing just one match in 1984-85 was ever present the next season as Wile's side reached the fifth round of the FA Cup. Martin joined Second Division Sheffield United in August 1986 for £20,000, playing 129 League games before joining Fulham in 1990 via spells at Tranmere and Bolton. After 200+ games for the Cottagers, he ended his League career at Rotherham in 1996, returning to his native north-east with Blyth Spartans of the Unibond Premier League. Martin now scouts for Fulham.

Season	League			FA Cup			League Cup			Other			Total		
	Aps	Sub	Gls	Aps	Sub	Gls	Aps	Sub	Gls	Aps	Sub	Gls	Aps	Sub	Gls
1983-84	28	7	2	1			4			1		1	34	7	3
1984-85	45		4	2			2			2			51		4
1985-86	46		2	7			2			2			57		2
Total	119	7	8	10			8			5		1	142	7	9

PLEAT, David John
Winger   *Nottingham, 15 January 1945*

A respected figure in the modern game, as manager of Luton, Spurs, Leicester, and Sheffield Wednesday, Pleat had an undistinguished playing career. Despite earning England Schoolboy and Youth honours, he was released by Nottingham Forest in 1964 after six League appearances. He had spells with Luton, Shrewsbury and Exeter before joining Posh on a free transfer in July 1970. Pleat never established himself, leaving London Road after one season to begin his managerial career with non-League Nuneaton Borough.

Season	League			FA Cup			League Cup			Other			Total		
	Aps	Sub	Gls	Aps	Sub	Gls	Aps	Sub	Gls	Aps	Sub	Gls	Aps	Sub	Gls
1970-71	28	1	2	1			1						30	1	2

POLLARD, Gary
Central Defender   Staveley, 30 December 1959

Defensive stalwart Pollard spent two injury-ridden seasons with Posh in the late 1980s. Signed by Noel Cantwell to replace Wakeley Gage in August 1987, Pollard already had 170+ League games in the lower divisions with Chesterfield, Port Vale and Mansfield. A knee injury sustained in a home clash with Cardiff sidelined him for over a year. Though he returned briefly in 1988-89, he was released by Mick Jones.

Season	League			FA Cup			League Cup			Other			Total		
	Aps	Sub	Gls	Aps	Sub	Gls	Aps	Sub	Gls	Aps	Sub	Gls	Aps	Sub	Gls
1987-88	12						4						16		
1988-89	8												8		
Total	20						4						24		

POPE, Neil Lester
Midfielder   Ashton-under-lyne, 9 October 1972

Neil started as a trainee with Cambridge United before playing two games for Chris Turner's Posh as a non-contract player in March 1991. After debuting as a sub in a 1-4 defeat at Burnley, he made his full League debut three days later as Posh were held to a 0-0 home draw by Scunthorpe. Not retained that summer, Pope embarked upon a non-League career with, among others, Cambridge City and Kettering.

Season	League			FA Cup			League Cup			Other			Total		
	Aps	Sub	Gls	Aps	Sub	Gls	Aps	Sub	Gls	Aps	Sub	Gls	Aps	Sub	Gls
1990-91	1	1											1	1	

POTTS, Brian
Right-back   Sunderland, 3 September 1948

Brian Potts joined Posh in July 1969 from Leicester, where he had made ten League appearances after signing pro forms in September 1965. A dependable full-back, he missed just one League game in his first season, but lost his place early in 1970-71, following manager Jim Iley's decision to switch Frank Noble from left to right-back to accommodate new signing John Duncliffe. Potts was not retained at the end of the season and pursued his career with then non-League Hereford.

Season	League			FA Cup			League Cup			Other			Total		
	Aps	Sub	Gls	Aps	Sub	Gls	Aps	Sub	Gls	Aps	Sub	Gls	Aps	Sub	Gls
1969-70	45			3			2						50		
1970-71	4	1					1						5	1	
Total	49	1		3			3						55	1	

POWER, Lee Michael
Forward   Lewisham, 30 June 1972

Blond striker Lee Power burst onto the First Division scene as a teenager with Norwich in 1990-91. He won the Republic of Ireland's

Young Player of the Year award in 1992-93 after amassing a record number of Under-21 caps. The rise of fellow youngster Chris Sutton impeded Power's progress at Carrow Road and he was loaned to Charlton, Sunderland and Portsmouth before transferring to Bradford City for £200,000 in 1994. A victim of injury and illness after his arrival, he managed just five League goals in 30 games for the Bantams before switching to Posh in July 1995. His troubles persisted at London Road where, despite neat touches, he rarely looked like justifying his £80,000 price tag. Lee left Posh soon after Barry Fry arrived in 1996, joining Scottish Premier League Hibs for a small fee. He returned to England with Plymouth Argyle at the start of 1998-99, and later served Halifax and Boston United before concentrating on his business interests. These included an abortive attempt to buy Wisbech Town.

Season	League			FA Cup			League Cup			Other			Total		
	Aps	Sub	Gls	Aps	Sub	Gls	Aps	Sub	Gls	Aps	Sub	Gls	Aps	Sub	Gls
1995-96	25	13	6	1	2		2	2		1		1	29	17	7

PRICE, David James
Midfielder   *Caterham, 23 June 1955*

A former England Schoolboy and Youth cap, midfielder Price was loaned to Posh by Arsenal in January 1975. He played six League games and the FA Cup fifth round ties with Middlesbrough before returning to Highbury. He forced his way into the Gunners' first team, amassing nearly 150 games. These included three successive FA Cup finals between 1978-80. Price ended his professional career at Crystal Palace and Orient in the early 1980s and is now a mini-cab driver.

Season	League			FA Cup			League Cup			Other			Total		
	Aps	Sub	Gls	Aps	Sub	Gls	Aps	Sub	Gls	Aps	Sub	Gls	Aps	Sub	Gls
1974-75	6		1	2									8		1

PRICE, Paul Terence
Central Defender   *St Albans, 23 March 1954*

Capped 25 times by Wales, defender Price brought experience to Posh's defence for two years in the late 1980s. He had come to prominence with Luton, where he played 200+ League games before switching to Spurs for £200,000 in 1981. In his first season at White Hart Lane, Paul helped Spurs win the FA Cup by defeating QPR. After a period in America playing for Minnesota, Paul spent two seasons with Swansea prior to joining Posh in August 1986. At 5ft 11in, he was short for a central defender, but compensated with fine positional sense and an ability to read the game. A clear winner of the Player of the Season award in 1986-87, Price missed just two matches the following campaign to help take Posh to within a whisker of the Fourth Division play-offs. Price retired from League football in the summer of 1988 after 17 years as a professional. He turned out for Essex side Wivenhoe Town and was later joint player-manager at Hitchin Town.

Season	League			FA Cup			League Cup			Other			Total		
	Aps	Sub	Gls	Aps	Sub	Gls	Aps	Sub	Gls	Aps	Sub	Gls	Aps	Sub	Gls
1986-87	42						4			2			48		
1987-88	44			2			6			4			56		
Total	86			2			10			6			104		

PRICE, Peter William

Forward   *Wrexham, 17 August 1949*

Peter Price started out with Liverpool, but signed for Norman Rigby's Posh in July 1968 in a bid to kick-start his League career. The young Welshman proved to be a prodigious goalscorer during his four years at London Road. He scored on his debut to help beat First Division WBA in a League Cup-tie, but had to await the arrival of manager Jim Iley in January 1969 before really doing himself justice. Price formed a deadly double-act with Jim Hall that was feared throughout the lower divisions. Peter was at his most prolific in 1971-72, when he was the top marksman in the Fourth Division and the first Posh player to score 30 goals in a season since Terry Bly. Four of those goals came in a 4-2 win at Southport. That sort of form – which earned Peter four Welsh Under-23 caps – did not go unnoticed and in June 1972 he was sold to Second Division Portsmouth for £27,000. A back injury hindered his progress with Pompey, for whom he managed only 14 League games in two years before returning to London Road on loan early in 1974-75. He did better at Barnsley, linking up again with Jim Iley, until more back troubles forced his retirement in 1978. His back also cut short a career with the police. Peter lives on a medical pension in Barnsley, while helping out Emley in the Unibond League.

Season	League			FA Cup			League Cup			Other			Total		
	Aps	Sub	Gls	Aps	Sub	Gls	Aps	Sub	Gls	Aps	Sub	Gls	Aps	Sub	Gls
1968-69	24	2	11				1		1				25	2	12
1969-70	38		17	4		3	1		1				43		21
1970-71	13	3	6						1				13	4	6
1971-72	39		28	4		4	1						44		32
1974-75	2												2		
Total	116	5	62	8		7	3	1	2				127	6	71

PRUDHOE, Mark

Goalkeeper   *Washington, 8 November 1963*

Prudhoe served several lower division clubs during the 1980s before finding success at Darlington, who won the Vauxhall Conference in 1990 and the Fourth Division title a year later. His shot-stopping brought a £120,000 move to First Division Stoke in June 1993, but after losing his place early the following season he arrived at London Road on a month's loan in October 1994. He debuted in a 2-1 win at Cardiff and was well received by Posh fans before returning to the Victoria Ground, where he reclaimed the No 1 jersey in 1995-96. Prudhoe linked up with Bradford City in July 1997 before joining Southend – his 16th League club – in November 1999. Ever the wanderer, Mark returned to Bradford City on a free transfer in December 2001.

Season	League			FA Cup			League Cup			Other			Total		
	Aps	Sub	Gls	Aps	Sub	Gls	Aps	Sub	Gls	Aps	Sub	Gls	Aps	Sub	Gls
1994-95	6												6		

PULLEY, Gordon Albert
Outside-left   *Stourbridge, 18 September 1936*

A diminutive winger, Pulley played a handful of games for Posh during Gordon Clark's reign in the mid-1960s, debuting in an FA Cup second-round defeat at Shrewsbury. Pulley joined Posh from Gillingham, where he had scored 46 goals in 203 League appearances spanning eight years. After starting his career with Oswestry, he had joined the professional ranks when signing for Millwall in 1956, moving to Priestfield a couple of years later. Following his release from Posh the end of 1966-67, he returned to non-League with Chelmsford.

Season	League			FA Cup			League Cup			Other			Total		
	Aps	Sub	Gls	Aps	Sub	Gls	Aps	Sub	Gls	Aps	Sub	Gls	Aps	Sub	Gls
1965-66	12		3	1									13		3
1966-67	4	1	1				1						5	1	1
Total	16	1	4	1			1						18	1	4

PYATT, John Henry
Inside-forward   *Barnet, 26 September 1948*

Pyatt was given his chance in professional football after his displays for Chesham United were noted by Liverpool boss Bill Shankly, who took him to Anfield in 1967. Unable to break into the first team, Pyatt was recruited by Jim Iley on a free transfer in July 1968, debuting in a 1-1 home draw with Exeter City on the first day of 1968-69. Pyatt left the club after one season after losing his place in the side.

Season	League			FA Cup			League Cup			Other			Total		
	Aps	Sub	Gls	Aps	Sub	Gls	Aps	Sub	Gls	Aps	Sub	Gls	Aps	Sub	Gls
1968-69	15	1	1							3			18	1	1

QUINN, James Martin (Jimmy)
Forward   *Belfast, 18 November 1959*

Barry Fry signed 37-year-old Quinn in July 1997 and the charismatic Irishman repaid Fry's faith with a hatful of goals. Posh soared to the top of Division Three as Quinn found the net at a phenomenal rate early in 1997-98, particularly in front of his adoring home crowd. He scored in all but three of Posh's opening fifteen home League games, including a hat-trick against Barnet and a late winner against Cambridge. His goal in a 1-0 win over Rotherham in January 1998 took his tally to 20 in 29 League games, becoming the first Posh player to score a 'score' in 16 years. Quinn became Fry's number two following the sacking of Phil Neal in March 1998, but remained on the playing staff. When he left to manage his first club, Swindon, it should have signalled the end of a 17-year professional career that had yielded 210 League goals from 571 appearances but as Swindon plummeted into the Second Division in 1999-2000 Quinn was obliged to turn out as an occasional player. Swindon's relegation meant the sack for Jimmy. Having originally fled trouble-torn Belfast with his family and set up home in Salisbury, he had been spotted playing Sunday football by former Liverpool player Fred Morris and began playing for Oswestry Town. After joining Swindon at 22, Quinn played for Blackburn, Leicester and Bradford City before enjoying his biggest move, to West Ham for £320,000 in 1989. After leaving Upton Park two years later, he topped the scoring charts at Bournemouth and Reading before joining Posh. It was whilst at Reading that he first sampled management, leading the Royals to second spot in Division One alongside co-manager Mick Gooding and seeing his side lose the play-off final after leading Bolton 2-0 – and missing a penalty. Jimmy also won 46 international caps, notching twelve goals to become Northern Ireland's second highest scorer behind another ex-Posh player, Colin Clarke. Jimmy is fondly remembered for bringing quality to Posh's forward line and striking fear into Third Division defenders with his aerial expertise and fierce shooting. Since his dismissal from Swindon, Jimmy has gone non-League with Northwich Victoria, Hereford, Highworth Town and Hayes before becoming manager at Northwich.

Season	League			FA Cup			League Cup			Other			Total		
	Aps	Sub	Gls	Aps	Sub	Gls	Aps	Sub	Gls	Aps	Sub	Gls	Aps	Sub	Gls
1997-98	40	2	20	3		3	4		1	3	1	1	50	3	25
1998-99	7		5				2						9		5
Total	47	2	25	3		3	6		1	3	1	1	59	3	30

QUOW, Trevor

Midfielder   *Peterborough, 28 September 1960*

Peterborough-born Quow was a gifted midfielder whom many pundits thought would go a long way in the game, but whose career was punctuated by injuries. One of several youngsters to come through the ranks in the late 1970s, Quow made his League debut at 17 against Sheffield Wednesday on the first day of 1978-79. He was on the margins of the first team that season until breaking a leg. Returning to fitness during the following season, Trevor produced some sublime displays in 1980-81, his impudent skills assisting Posh to chase League and FA Cup glory under Peter Morris's leadership. Sadly, Quow broke his leg again in October 1981, and again in February 1983. Yet he bounced back to rediscover some of his early form during 1983-84 and, despite starting only 24 League games, was included in the PFA select side for Division Four. As the club's longest serving player, he was made captain at the start of 1984-85, but further injury sidelined him in 1985-86 and forced him to miss the FA Cup run. He later returned to the side but was released by John Wile in August 1986, joining Gillingham on a free transfer after having made 200+ appearances in eight seasons. Trevor spent two and a half years at Priestfield, then served a similar time at Northampton before going to Hong Kong, where he appeared for Instant Dict and Hong Kong Rangers. Upon his return to England in 1995, he played for Sudbury Town and Stamford, then followed Daniels' boss Steve Evans to Boston United in 1998.

Season	League			FA Cup			League Cup			Other			Total		
	Aps	Sub	Gls	Aps	Sub	Gls	Aps	Sub	Gls	Aps	Sub	Gls	Aps	Sub	Gls
1978-79	5	3						1					5	4	
1979-80	27	2	3				2						29	2	3
1980-81	44		4	5		1	4						53		5
1981-82	10		1				2						12		1
1982-83	17	1	1	2	1	1	2						21	2	2
1983-84	24	4	4	1			2		1	1		1	28	4	6
1984-85	35	1	1	1			2			2		1	40	1	2
1985-86	29	1	3	1			2						32	1	3
Total	191	12	17	10	1	2	16	1	1	3		2	220	14	22

Bobby Barnes (left) v Huddersfield in the play-offs, May 1992

Dick Tydeman

Mark Peters

Worrell Sterling v Newcastle, September 1992

Simon Davies

David Morrison (centre) v Hull, September 1994

Kevin Ashley (left)
v Hull, September 1994

RADCLIFFE, Vincent (Vince)
Centre-half   *Manchester, 9 June 1945*

Blond centre-back Radcliffe spent 1967-68 with Posh but was kept out of the side by the likes of Frank Rankmore. Signed by Norman Rigby in July 1967, Vince had spent four seasons with Portsmouth, where he made ten League appearances. After waiting until April 1968 for his Posh debut, he joined Rochdale three months later on a free transfer.

Season	League			FA Cup			League Cup			Other			Total		
	Aps	Sub	Gls	Aps	Sub	Gls	Aps	Sub	Gls	Aps	Sub	Gls	Aps	Sub	Gls
1967-68	2												2		

RAMAGE, Craig Darren
Midfielder   *Derby, 30 March 1970*

Capped three times by England Under-21s during his days at Derby, Craig had a disappointing spell on loan from Watford in February 1997 during Posh's relegation season. He arrived with a reputation as a talented, goalscoring midfielder but showed little of his ability. He debuted in a 0-1 home defeat by Wrexham but returned to Watford the following month before signing for Bradford City in June 1997. Craig spent two years at Valley Parade before moving on to Notts County.

Season	League			FA Cup			League Cup			Other			Total		
	Aps	Sub	Gls	Aps	Sub	Gls	Aps	Sub	Gls	Aps	Sub	Gls	Aps	Sub	Gls
1996-97	7									1			8		

RANKMORE, Frank Edward John
Centre-half   *Cardiff, 21 July 1939*

A tall Welsh centre-half, Frank Rankmore was Posh captain and the pivot of the defence during the cup runs of the mid-1960s. He was recommended to Posh by Derek Dougan in August 1963, after playing 67 League games for Cardiff and winning two Welsh Under-23 caps. He debuted for Posh in a 5-2 home win over Wrexham on the opening day of the 1963-64 season, in which he was ever present. His displays in the FA Cup in 1965 and the League Cup a year later earned him a full cap for Wales in their friendly with Chile in May 1966. By the time of his £12,000 move to Northampton in August 1968, Rankmore had made a Posh record 201 League appearances, including another ever present campaign. Frank played 103 League games for the Cobblers before retiring in 1971 to run a pub-restaurant in his home town, Cardiff.

Season	League			FA Cup			League Cup			Other			Total		
	Aps	Sub	Gls	Aps	Sub	Gls	Aps	Sub	Gls	Aps	Sub	Gls	Aps	Sub	Gls
1963-64	46		1	2			1						49		1
1964-65	29			8			2						39		
1965-66	42			2			6		1				50		1
1966-67	38	2		2			3						43		2
1967-68	46	4		3			1						50		4
Total	201	7		17			13		1				231		8

RAYMENT, Patrick John (Paddy)

Full-back   *Peterborough, 11 April 1965*

. A local lad who progressed through the ranks, Paddy debuted in the penultimate game of 1981-82. It was a baptism of fire for the 17-year-old former Jack Hunt pupil, as Posh were hammered 0-4 at Sheffield United. Paddy made his home debut against Tranmere a week later. He made 15 starts the following season, switching to the left wing, from where he netted his first goals. He never progressed as expected under new boss John Wile and – aside from a cracker in a 6-0 blitz of Northampton in April 1984 – he made little impact and was allowed to join Cambridge the following October. Playing for the U's in an FA Cup-tie against Posh, he went on to make 48 League appearances for Cambridge prior to joining Corby Town in November 1986. He spent many years there – latterly as player-manager – before turning out for Stamford, Kettering, Chelmsford and Raunds Town and Yaxley.

Season	League			FA Cup			League Cup			Other			Total		
	Aps	Sub	Gls	Aps	Sub	Gls	Aps	Sub	Gls	Aps	Sub	Gls	Aps	Sub	Gls
1981-82	2												2		
1982-83	14		2				1						15		2
1983-84	8	5	1					1			1		8	7	1
1984-85		1												1	
Total	24	6	3				1	1			1		25	8	3

RAYNER, James Patrick (Jim)

Wing-half   *Cornsay, 31 March 1935*

Rayner was an instant success when signed from Grantham by Jimmy Hagan in 1958. A prolific goalscorer when operating as an inside-forward, he proved to be a revelation when switching to wing-half. Formerly with Grimsby, Bury, Hartlepool and Barrow, Rayner helped Posh to the Fourth Division title in 1960-61, having formed – with Norman Rigby and Keith Ripley – the famous 'Three R's' half-back line that served Posh well during their formative League years. Jim helped Hagan's side establish themselves in Division Three in 1961-62 before new boss Jack Fairbrother switched him back to striker for part of the following season. His goals included a hat-trick in a 6-0 home drubbing of Millwall. Rayner re-joined Grantham as player-manager in July 1964, but within weeks he was back in the League with Notts County, for whom he hit 13 goals in 32 League games in 1964-65. He dropped into non-League football at the end of that season, performing player-manager roles at Ilkeston Town and Durham City, where he made occasional appearances until he was 50 years of age.

Season	League			FA Cup			League Cup			Other			Total		
	Aps	Sub	Gls	Aps	Sub	Gls	Aps	Sub	Gls	Aps	Sub	Gls	Aps	Sub	Gls
1960-61	43		1	5			1						49		1
1961-62	43		1	6			1						50		1

1962-63	33	10	2		35	10
Total	119	12	13	2	134	12

REA, Simon

Defender   *Coventry, 20 September 1976*

Heavily-built defender Rea initially had his sights set on professional rugby, but changed his mind after being taken on by Birm-ingham in the early 1990s under Terry Cooper. He debuted for the Blues in 1995-96 but had limited opportunities and was reunited with Barry Fry at London Road in August 1999, playing his first game that month in a League Cup-tie with Reading. Simon did not lay claim to a regular place until late in the season when – having recovered from problems with his calf, Achilles and wisdom teeth – he played a key role in Posh's promotion success. Rea's display in the final helped stifle the threat of Darlington's Marco Gabbiadini. Although not the most mobile of defenders, Rea's wholehearted commitment enabled him to continue to partner skipper Andy Edwards in central defence.

Season	League			FA Cup			League Cup			Other			Total		
	Aps	Sub	Gls	Aps	Sub	Gls	Aps	Sub	Gls	Aps	Sub	Gls	Aps	Sub	Gls
1999-00	11	3	1					1		2	1		13	5	1
2000-01	35	1	2	3			2			1			41	1	2
2001-02	27	3	1	5			1			1			34	3	1
Total	73	7	4	8			3	1		4	1		88	9	4

READ, John Anthony (Tony)

Goalkeeper   *Haydock, 5 July 1942*

Tony Read was one of a rare breed, who could operate either in goal or out of it. It was his goalkeeping that Gordon Clark sought when signing him from Sheffield Wednesday in May 1964. After playing just two games, conceding nine goals, Read moved on to Luton in March 1965. He enjoyed greater success at Kenilworth Road, making 198 League appearances and helping the Hatters lift the Fourth Division title in 1968. Tony also scored twelve League goals as a centre-forward prior quitting the game in 1972 to concentrate on his used car business.

Season	League			FA Cup			League Cup			Other			Total		
	Aps	Sub	Gls	Aps	Sub	Gls	Aps	Sub	Gls	Aps	Sub	Gls	Aps	Sub	Gls
1964-65	2												2		

REES, Anthony Andrew (Tony)

Forward   *Merthyr Tydfil, 1 August 1964*

Welsh international forward Tony Rees came on loan in October 1985, scoring twice in five games before returning to Birmingham. John Wile hoped to sign Rees on a permanent basis, but Posh could not meet the £15,000 valuation. A former Aston Villa apprentice, Tony went on to claim a regular spot at St Andrews, hitting twelve League goals in 95 games before moving to Barnsley in March 1988. He joined Grimsby in August 1989 and finished his League career by joining WBA in 1994.

Season	League			FA Cup			League Cup			Other			Total		
	Aps	Sub	Gls	Aps	Sub	Gls	Aps	Sub	Gls	Aps	Sub	Gls	Aps	Sub	Gls
1985-86	5		2										5		2

REGIS, David (Dave)
Forward   *Paddington, 3 March 1963*

A powerfully built forward, Regis spent October 1996 on loan from Barnsley. Despite scoring on his debut to earn a draw at Plymouth, Dave was soon back on the subs bench, then returned to Oakwell. Known to Barry Fry from his Birmingham days, Regis had also served Notts County, Plymouth, Bournemouth, Stoke and Southend before joining Posh. More recently, the much-travelled player has appeared for Notts County, Leyton Orient, Lincoln and Scunthorpe.

Season	League			FA Cup			League Cup			Other			Total		
	Aps	Sub	Gls	Aps	Sub	Gls	Aps	Sub	Gls	Aps	Sub	Gls	Aps	Sub	Gls
1996-97	4	3	1										4	3	1

REILLY, Daniel (Danny)
Midfielder   *Peterborough, 17 November 1966*

A local product of the YTS scheme, Reilly debuted in March 1985, coming off the bench in a Fourth Division game at Blackpool. Released by John Wile, Danny served non-League Stamford, Mirrlees Blackstones and Spalding before joining works Peterborough League side Perkins.

Season	League			FA Cup			League Cup			Other			Total		
	Aps	Sub	Gls	Aps	Sub	Gls	Aps	Sub	Gls	Aps	Sub	Gls	Aps	Sub	Gls
1984-85		1												1	

RENNIE, David
Defender   *Edinburgh, 29 August 1964*

Prior to joining Posh from Northampton in December 1997, tall Scot David Rennie had enjoyed a successful career with Leicester, Leeds, Bristol City, Birmingham and Coventry, where he tasted Premiership action. A veteran of nearly 400 League games, the balding defender debuted for Posh in a local derby with Cambridge, shining in a 1-0 win. He quickly became a regular – occasionally appearing in midfield – but rarely looked able to halt Posh's slide down the Fourth Division table. Omitted early in 1998-99, Rennie played a few games after Christmas before being told by Fry that he would be released at the end of the campaign. His last game was at Scarborough on the final day of the season. Rennie joined Boston United, then Burton Albion.

Season	League			FA Cup			League Cup			Other			Total		
	Aps	Sub	Gls	Aps	Sub	Gls	Aps	Sub	Gls	Aps	Sub	Gls	Aps	Sub	Gls
1997-98	18									4			22		
1998-99	9									1			10		
Total	27									5			32		

RETALLICK, Graham

Midfielder   *Cambridge, 8 February 1970*

A hard-working midfielder, Retallick arrived on a non-contract basis during Posh's first season in Division One but had few first-team opportunities. After debuting as a substitute in the televised 2-0 win at Leicester in October 1992, he was loaned to Boston United before being given his first Posh start in the return clash with Leicester six months later. Transferred to Corby at the end of 1992-93, he subsequently turned out for Cambridge City and Jewson League side Ely City.

Season	League			FA Cup			League Cup			Other			Total		
	Aps	Sub	Gls	Aps	Sub	Gls	Aps	Sub	Gls	Aps	Sub	Gls	Aps	Sub	Gls
1992-93	2	3											2	3	

RICHARDS, Carroll Lloyd (Carl)

Forward   *Jamaica, 1 December 1960*

Mick Jones paid Birmingham £37,500 for this giant, West Indian-born striker in the summer of 1989. After debuting in a 1-0 win over new-comers Maidstone on the first day of 1989-90, Richards hit his first Posh goals against Aldershot in the League Cup as Posh crashed out 4-6 on aggregate to earn Jones the sack. Left out by Mark Lawrenson, Carl joined Third Division Blackpool in January 1990 for a small fee.

Season	League			FA Cup			League Cup			Other			Total		
	Aps	Sub	Gls	Aps	Sub	Gls	Aps	Sub	Gls	Aps	Sub	Gls	Aps	Sub	Gls
1989-90	16	4	5	2		1	2		2	2			22	5	7

RICKETTS, Graham Anthony

Wing-half   *Oxford, 30 July 1939*

A former England Youth cap, Ricketts joined from Doncaster in March 1968 with 300+ League appearances to his credit. He started out at Bristol Rovers in 1956, playing 32 League games before moving to Doncaster via a three-year spell with Stockport. Signed for Posh by Norman Rigby in a £2,500 deal, Ricketts debuted in a 1-0 home win over Southport and scored in his next game a week later to earn Posh a 1-1 draw at Shrewsbury. He was an unsung hero of the League Cup run in 1968-69, when Posh knocked out First Division QPR and WBA before losing at Tottenham. First-team opportunities were few after Jim Iley's arrival in January 1969. Ricketts left the club in the summer, spending time with King's Lynn, March Town and Yaxley. He still lives in Yaxley and, despite having two steel kneecaps – a legacy of his 13-year professional career – he works in the timber trade.

Season	League			FA Cup			League Cup			Other			Total		
	Aps	Sub	Gls	Aps	Sub	Gls	Aps	Sub	Gls	Aps	Sub	Gls	Aps	Sub	Gls
1967-68	14		1										14		1
1968-69	32	3		1			5						38	3	
Total	46	3	1	1			5						52	3	1

RIGBY, Norman

Centre-half   *Newark, 23 May 1923, Died September 2001*

The oldest player to represent the club in a League match, Rigby was a rock in Posh's defence for over ten years. The tall, granite-faced centre-half captained the team to the Fourth Division title in 1961, aged 37. After 46 League appearances in four seasons at Notts County after the war, Norman joined Posh – then of the Midland League – in 1951. He became the backbone of the side that knocked on the Football League door throughout the 1950s, his rugged style helping Posh to five consecutive Midland League titles, as well as some famous FA Cup victories. When entry to the League was secured in 1960, Rigby was an inspiring captain in Posh's record-breaking debut season in Division Four. He played 40 League games that season but was less assured of his place in Division Three and was one of a clutch of players released on a free transfer – Rigby hearing the news in his sickbed as he recovered from injury. He joined Boston United in July 1962 and, after two years captaining the Pilgrims, Norman returned to London Road as trainer and manager. Installed into the hot-seat following Gordon Clark's resignation in September 1967, Rigby was in charge when Posh were demoted the following year for financial irregularities. Although unable to engineer a swift return to Division Three, Rigby signed future legends Jim Hall and Tommy Robson before stepping down in January 1969. He later became boss of March Town, Bourne Town and, most notably, Stamford, whom he guided to the 1976 FA Vase final.

Season	League			FA Cup			League Cup			Other			Total		
	Aps	Sub	Gls	Aps	Sub	Gls	Aps	Sub	Gls	Aps	Sub	Gls	Aps	Sub	Gls
1960-61	40			2			1						43		
1961-62	15												15		
Total	55			2			1						58		

RILEY, David Sydney

Forward   *Northampton, 8 December 1960*

Known as 'Biddy' – a nickname acquired from his father – Riley was born in Northampton but moved to Nottingham while a baby. Failing a trial with Forest as a 15-year-old, Riley spent eight years as a welder, builders' labourer and sales rep before Brian Clough offered him a professional contract in January 1984. With first-team opportunities in short supply, 'Biddy' was loaned to Posh in July 1987. He did well, but a permanent move was vetoed due to a cash crisis at London Road. Port Vale took him instead for £15,000 in October 1987 and, after Riley had scored eleven times in 76 League games for Vale, Posh finally got their man on a free transfer in March 1990. A tidy forward with a never-say-die attitude, Riley marked his second coming with a goal in a 3-1 home win over Wrexham. He developed a partnership with loa-nee forward Ronnie Jepson as Mark Lawrenson's side chased the play-offs. After playing a key role in Posh's 1990-91 promotion, and con-tributing to the League Cup run the next season, 'Biddy' missed the Wembley play-off glory in favour of Ken Charley and Tony Adcock. After a spell in the commercial office at London Road, David joined Boston United before heading off to play and work in New Zealand. On returning to Peterborough, he works in the kitchen industry.

Season	League Aps	Sub	Gls	FA Cup Aps	Sub	Gls	League Cup Aps	Sub	Gls	Other Aps	Sub	Gls	Total Aps	Sub	Gls
1987-88	12		2				4		1				16		3
1989-90	15		5										15		5
1990-91	35	6	9	5		2	2			1	1		43	7	11
1991-92	23	5	9	3		1	6	1	1	5	1	1	37	7	12
Total	85	11	25	8		3	12	1	2	6	2	1	111	14	31

RIOCH, Gregor James (Greg)
Defender   *Sutton Coldfield, 24 June 1975*

The son of former Derby and Scotland star Bruce Rioch, aggressive defender Greg arrived in August 1995 from Luton, where he hadn't made the grade. An injury to Tony Spearing gave Greg an early chance and he gave a committed display in a League Cup-tie with Swansea that saw Posh overturn a three-goal first-leg deficit. After initially keeping his place – creating an impression with his tough tackling – he was given few opportunities after Mick Halsall replaced John Still. In July 1996 Rioch signed for Hull, where he became captain and a big hit with Tigers' fans. He spent three seasons at Boothferry Park before taking his talents to Macclesfield and, after that, Shrewsbury.

Season	League Aps	Sub	Gls	FA Cup Aps	Sub	Gls	League Cup Aps	Sub	Gls	Other Aps	Sub	Gls	Total Aps	Sub	Gls
1995-96	13	5		2	1		2			2	1		19	7	

RIPLEY, Stanley Keith (Keith)
Wing-half   *Normanton, 29 March 1935*

A stylish wing-half, Ripley joined Posh from Mansfield in July 1960, at the start of their first season in League football. With Norman Rigby and Jim Rayner, Posh presented a formidable half-back trio – dubbed 'The three R's' – that played their part in winning the Fourth Division title in 1960-61. The big Yorkshireman debuted in a 2-0 win at Crystal Palace, and he retained a regular place as Posh took Division Four by storm. His physique enabled him to dominate in the air and brush aside most challenges, but he was more than just a stopper. He scored vital goals, including one in a 2-1 FA Cup win at Portsmouth in January 1961. Keith missed just three Third Division matches in 1961-62 before joining Doncaster, where he played 128 League games. Prior to joining Posh he had made 100+ League appearances during spells with Leeds, Norwich and Mansfield.

Season	League			FA Cup			League Cup			Other			Total		
	Aps	Sub	Gls	Aps	Sub	Gls	Aps	Sub	Gls	Aps	Sub	Gls	Aps	Sub	Gls
1960-61	39		5	5		2							44		7
1961-62	43		7	6			1						50		7
Total	82		12	11		2	1						94		14

ROBERTS, Darren Anthony
Forward   *Birmingham, 12 October 1969*

After starting with Burton Albion, Roberts was given his chance in League football in April 1992 by Wolves, for whom he played 21 First Division games, scoring five goals, two of them at London Road in Wolves' 3-2 win. He later had a spell with Chesterfield before joining Darlington in 1996. Brought to Posh in February 1998 by Barry Fry in an attempt to boost a flagging promotion bid, Roberts' hopes of a contract were dashed by injury in his second game. He returned to Feethams, then joined Scarborough, and was part of their side relegated to the Conference by Posh on the last day of 1998-99. After returning to the League with Exeter, Roberts played for Barrow and Tamworth.

Season	League			FA Cup			League Cup			Other			Total		
	Aps	Sub	Gls	Aps	Sub	Gls	Aps	Sub	Gls	Aps	Sub	Gls	Aps	Sub	Gls
1997-98	2	1											2	1	

ROBERTSON, Archibald Lamond (Lammie)
Midfielder   *Paisley, 27 September 1947*

Lammie joined Posh – his seventh League club – in August 1978. By then the Scottish midfielder had amassed nearly 350 League appearances in a career that began at Burnley in 1966. He never made the first team at Turf Moor but saw action with Bury, Halifax, Brighton, Exeter and, in the top flight, Leicester. His Posh career was brief, lasting only five months until his departure in January 1979 to Bradford City, where he played 43 League games before turning out for Darwen.

Season	League			FA Cup			League Cup			Other			Total		
	Aps	Sub	Gls	Aps	Sub	Gls	Aps	Sub	Gls	Aps	Sub	Gls	Aps	Sub	Gls
1978-79	12	3	1	1			1	1					14	4	1

ROBINSON, Brian Thomas Arthur
Goalkeeper   *Paddington, 2 April 1946*

London-born Robinson was one of four keepers used by Gordon Clark in 1964-65. Emerging through the ranks, Brian played in a League Cup draw at League Cup-holders Leicester, where he kept a clean sheet. His League debut came later that season, but he was released in 1966 after being unable to dislodge the No 1 jersey from Willie Duff.

Season	League			FA Cup			League Cup			Other			Total		
	Aps	Sub	Gls	Aps	Sub	Gls	Aps	Sub	Gls	Aps	Sub	Gls	Aps	Sub	Gls
1964-65	5						2						7		
1965-66	3												3		
Total	8						2						10		

ROBINSON, David Alan (Dave)
Centre-half   *Middlesbrough, 14 January 1965*

Mick Jones paid a club record £100,000 to Halifax in July 1989 for this classy central defender. At 6ft 1in, the former Hartlepool man was rarely beaten in the air and, despite his slender frame, he was a fierce tackler. He made his Posh debut in a 1-0 home win over newcomers Maidstone in August 1989, and subsequently impressed to the extent of being voted Player of the Year at the end of 1989-90. An Achilles injury ruled him out for much of 1990-91, although he played a few late-season games and scored a vital goal in the decisive final match at Chesterfield. He was back to his best during the surge through Division Three the following season, missing just three League games and starring in the Wembley play-off final against Stockport. A knee injury forced Dave out of action again as Posh made an encouraging start in the new First Division, but that did not stop Notts County paying £450,000 – another club record – to sign him in October 1992. Sadly, Robinson never regained fitness and after a handful of matches for the Magpies he retired from professional football in 1994. He still lives in the Peterborough area and, after a brief period working for a cable television company, Dave now earns his living as a lorry driver.

Season	League			FA Cup			League Cup			Other			Total		
	Aps	Sub	Gls	Aps	Sub	Gls	Aps	Sub	Gls	Aps	Sub	Gls	Aps	Sub	Gls
1989-90	45		4	3		1	2			3			53		5
1990-91	6		2				1						7		2
1991-92	43		3	3			8			7			61		3
1992-93	1									1			2		
Total	95		9	6		1	11			11			123		10

ROBINSON, David John
Forward   *Newcastle, 27 November 1969*

Robinson's League career began at his hometown club Newcastle, where he made eight League appearances before coming to Posh on loan in February 1991. An all-action forward, David scored three goals for Chris Turner's promotion-chasers before returning to Newcastle, who released him soon afterwards. After a spell at Reading he played for Blackpool, Gateshead, Bishop Auckland and, in July 1996, Scottish League side Berwick Rangers. In February 1997 he joined Whitley Bay.

Season	League			FA Cup			League Cup			Other			Total		
	Aps	Sub	Gls	Aps	Sub	Gls	Aps	Sub	Gls	Aps	Sub	Gls	Aps	Sub	Gls
1990-91	7		3										7		3

ROBINSON, Ronald (Ronnie)
Defender   *Sunderland, 22 October 1966*

A solid, left-footed defender, Ronnie joined Posh on a free transfer from Rotherham in December 1991. He was soon an automatic choice at left-back and was part of the side that sealed promotion to Division One via the Wembley play-off win over Stockport. He lost his place to new arrival Tony Spearing midway through 1992-93 and was sold for £25,000 to Exeter in August 1993. After two seasons in Devon and a year at Scarborough he ended a twelve-year playing career that had taken him to Ipswich, Leeds, Doncaster and WBA. No longer involved in football, Ronnie now works as a car salesman in Sunderland.

Season	League			FA Cup			League Cup			Other			Total		
	Aps	Sub	Gls	Aps	Sub	Gls	Aps	Sub	Gls	Aps	Sub	Gls	Aps	Sub	Gls
1991-92	24	3								8			32	3	
1992-93	20			3			3			2			28		
Total	44	3		3			3			10			60	3	

ROBINSON, Steven (Steve)
Midfielder   *Nottingham, 17 October 1975*

This energetic midfielder came on loan from Barry Fry's Birmingham in March 1996. Though slight of frame, Steve adapted well to Second Division football, showing crisp tackling and strong running. A permanent move never materialised, and after returning to St Andrews he went from strength to strength. He played 81 League games for the Blues before joining Swindon for £50,000 in February 2001.

Season	League			FA Cup			League Cup			Other			Total		
	Aps	Sub	Gls	Aps	Sub	Gls	Aps	Sub	Gls	Aps	Sub	Gls	Aps	Sub	Gls
1995-96	5												5		

ROBSON, Thomas Henry (Tommy)
Winger   *Gateshead, 31 July 1944*

Posh's favourite son, dynamic winger Tommy Robson, signed for a club record £20,000 in November 1968. He was a loyal servant for 13 seasons and made a record 482 League appearances. Born in Gateshead, Tommy left school at 15 to work as a garage mechanic after Newcastle had told him he would not make the grade. Within a year he had joined Northampton and in August 1961 he was taken on as a full professional. He made his Cobblers' League debut at London Road as a 17-year-old in March 1962, scoring in the visitors' 2-0 win. After assisting Northampton's spectacular rise to the First Division, Tommy was snapped up by Chelsea boss Tommy Docherty for the then considerable sum of £35,000. Robson might have enjoyed a longer stay in the top flight had it not been for two twists of fate. After seven League games he fell victim to jaundice and was sidelined for almost a year. Unable to regain his place, he was sold to Newcastle in December 1966. It was a dream move for Tommy – back in his home town to play for the team he had supported as a boy. He scored eleven times in 48 League games, until a freak gardening accident left him with a broken foot and two months out of action. Once fit, he was transferred in November 1968 to Posh, debuting in a 0-1 defeat at Workington. Whilst his debut may have been undistinguished, the ensuing years saw Tommy regularly warm the London Road crowd with his ball skills, spectacular goals and zest for the game. Possessed with a competitive streak, 'Robbo' was at his peak in 1973-74, when his dazzling wing-play helped secure the Fourth Division title and earned him the Player of the Season award. That honour was bestowed on Tommy again in 1977-78 when, as a 33-year-old in his tenth season with the club, he hit a career-best 14 League goals to finish the campaign as top scorer. It was a testament to his dedication and professionalism that he remained in contention for a first-team place for another three seasons before calling time on his Posh career in 1981. He played non-League football for Nuneaton and Stamford, finishing his career with a fairytale trip to Wembley with the Daniels in the 1984 FA Vase final. Tommy returned to London Road for two years as youth-team coach in the late 1980s before working in the advertising department of a local newspaper. These days Tommy is regularly seen at London Road in his capacity as chief summariser for BBC Radio Cambridgeshire.

Season	League			FA Cup			League Cup			Other			Total		
	Aps	Sub	Gls	Aps	Sub	Gls	Aps	Sub	Gls	Aps	Sub	Gls	Aps	Sub	Gls
1968-69	28		10										28		10
1969-70	46		13	4		1	2		1				52		15
1970-71	40	3	11	2									42	3	11
1971-72	40	2	9	4		1	1						45	2	10
1972-73	35	1	9	4		2	1						40	1	11
1973-74	46		9	4		1	2		1				52		11
1974-75	36	3	9	8			1						45	3	9
1975-76	39	3	13	5			5		2				49	3	15
1976-77	23	3	2	2		1	3		2				28	3	5
1977-78	31	6	14	3	1	1	3						37	7	15
1978-79	29	7	4	1			8			1			38	7	5
1979-80	29	11	4		1		3	1					32	13	4
1980-81	18	3	4	6		3	2						26	3	7
Total	440	42	111	43	2	10	31	1	7				514	45	128

ROCHE, David
Midfielder   *Newcastle, 13 December 1970*

David Roche came up through the ranks at Newcastle where he made 36 League appearances in five seasons. After struggling to make headway under Kevin Keegan, the aggressive midfielder was loaned to Posh in January 1993. Following his debut in a 1-1 home draw with Barnsley, David's next appearance was at Newcastle. The game ended in controversy when Lil Fuccillo, having seen Posh lose 0-3, accused Keegan of loaning him an unfit player! Roche was not offered a permanent contract and later joined Doncaster on a free transfer before moving on to Southend in 1995. Off the field, Roche has had his controversial moments. He was shot in the leg and sprayed with ammonia during a nightclub 'incident' and, late in 1995, was imprisoned for wounding with intent during an incident in Newcastle city centre.

Season	League			FA Cup			League Cup			Other			Total		
	Aps	Sub	Gls	Aps	Sub	Gls	Aps	Sub	Gls	Aps	Sub	Gls	Aps	Sub	Gls
1992-93	4												4		

RODAWAY, William Vincent (Billy)
Central Defender   *Liverpool, 26 September 1954*

Defensive strongman Rodaway was an England Schoolboy international before joining Burnley, with whom he turned professional in September 1971. He made 200+ League appearances for the Clarets before joining Posh on a free transfer in July 1981. His Posh debut came in a 1-0 home win over Mansfield on the opening day of 1981-82. His experience made him a key figure at London Road for two seasons and in 1982-83 he was made captain and also had a spell as player-coach under Martin Wilkinson. In August 1983 he surprisingly rejected a new contract and signed for Blackpool. Billy spent one season there and a further two with Tranmere before ending his League career back at Burnley in 1986-87. These days Rodaway is a scaffolder in Liverpool while being part of the management team at Runcorn.

Season	League			FA Cup			League Cup			Other			Total		
	Aps	Sub	Gls	Aps	Sub	Gls	Aps	Sub	Gls	Aps	Sub	Gls	Aps	Sub	Gls
1981-82	42			2			2						46		
1982-83	38	1		4			4						46	1	
Total	80	1		6			6						92	1	

ROGERS, Andrew (Andy)
Winger   *Chatteris, 1 December 1956*

Fenland-born Rogers made 250+ League appearances during the 1980s after beginning his professional career at London Road. Noel Cantwell plucked Andy from local side Chatteris Town as a teenager in July 1975, nurturing the young winger's talent until he had earned himself a regular first-team place by the end of 1976-77. No sooner did he appear to be established than he made only five starts the following campaign, prompting his release in 1978. He returned to non-League football with Hampton, before Andy resurfaced with First Division Southampton in February 1980. He made five substitute appearances for the Saints, then moved to Plymouth, where he enjoyed four good years and scored the goal that took the Pilgrims to the semi-finals of the 1984 FA Cup. Rogers played 163 League games for Argyle, scoring 15 goals, prior to joining Reading, with whom he collected a Third Division champions medal in 1985-86. After 44 League appearances for the Berkshire side, he signed for Southend, where he finished his League career in 1988. He spent several years on the semi-profession-al circuit, tuning out for Carshalton, Farnborough and Basingstoke. He is now a consultant for a West Midlands building products company.

Season	League			FA Cup			League Cup			Other			Total		
	Aps	Sub	Gls	Aps	Sub	Gls	Aps	Sub	Gls	Aps	Sub	Gls	Aps	Sub	Gls
1975-76	1	4											1	4	
1976-77	22		1										22		1
1977-78	2						3						5		
Total	25	4	1				3						28	4	1

ROGERS, David Raymond (Dave)
Defender *Liverpool, 25 August 1975*

Everton fan Rogers was saddened when released by them as a school-boy. Neighbours Tranmere gave him a two-year YTS and a twelve-month professional contract, but it was not until Rogers joined Chester on a free transfer in March 1995 that he achieved first-team football. He spent two years at the Deva Stadium before trying his luck with Dundee, helping them to promotion to the Scottish Premier League. He later had an unhappy spell with Ayr, which prompted a three-month loan to Posh in October 2000. He appeared short of match fit-ness on the few occasions that he sampled first-team action. He played one game for Scunthorpe before joining Carlisle in September 2001.

Season	League			FA Cup			League Cup			Other			Total		
	Aps	Sub	Gls	Aps	Sub	Gls	Aps	Sub	Gls	Aps	Sub	Gls	Aps	Sub	Gls
2000-01	1	2								1			2	2	

RONSON, Brian
Goalkeeper *Durham, 7 August 1935*

Keen to strengthen his squad for the Third Division in 1961, Jimmy Hagan signed Ronson from Norwich as cover for regular custodian Jack Walls. Formerly of Fulham and Southend, Ronson waited in the wings until Walls' departure in 1962-63, when he played well enough to keep former Scotland Under-23 newcomer Dick Beattie out of the side. In the summer of 1963 Ronson left to become player-coach with Spalding United, a job he held until retiring four years later.

Season	League			FA Cup			League Cup			Other			Total		
	Aps	Sub	Gls	Aps	Sub	Gls	Aps	Sub	Gls	Aps	Sub	Gls	Aps	Sub	Gls
1961-62	14						1						15		
1962-63	36			3			1						40		
Total	50			3			2						55		

ROONEY, James (Jimmy)

Outside-left   *Dundee, 10 December 1945*

Young Scot Rooney joined Posh from Scottish amateur side Lochee Harp in July 1965 in a deal that also landed striker Tommy Ross. Forced to wait until February 1966 for his League debut – a 3-1 home win over Scunthorpe – Rooney bagged his first goal in a 5-2 win at Exeter seven days later. He struggled to earn a regular place under Gordon Clark and was released in 1967 after only seven appearances in two seasons. Rooney had a spell with Scottish side Montrose before emigrating in 1968 to Australia. A star with several Australian league sides, Rooney won his first cap in 1971 and completed a rags-to-riches story when appearing for the Socceroos in the 1974 World Cup finals in West Germany. His performances for club side Marconi Fairfield earned him Australia's Player of the Season award in 1977, while three years later he earned his 100th and final cap for his adopted country.

Season	League			FA Cup			League Cup			Other			Total		
	Aps	Sub	Gls	Aps	Sub	Gls	Aps	Sub	Gls	Aps	Sub	Gls	Aps	Sub	Gls
1965-66	5		1										5		1
1966-67	2		1										2		1
Total	7		2										7		2

ROSS, Ian

Central Defender   *Glasgow, 26 January 1947*

Ross was a defender whose class and commitment made him a popular figure for Posh during the late 1970s. Glasgow-born Ian began his career at Liverpool, where Bill Shankly often used him to mark specific dangermen. It was in that role that, in March 1971, Ross marked Franz Beckenbauer in a UEFA Cup quarter-final at Bayern Munich so tightly that the German star hardly got a kick. Ross even found time to score and earn the Reds a 1-1 draw. Despite his talent, he made only 42 League appearances in six seasons at Anfield and was transferred to Aston Villa in February 1972. At Villa Park he made 175 League appearances and captained the side that won the League Cup and promotion to the First Division in 1975. Posh were having a lean spell when 'Rosco' joined, initially on loan, in December 1976. His arrival sparked a late-season revival, helped by the understanding that Ross developed alongside Chris Turner in central defence. A permanent move was completed in the close season, and Ian became an important member of John Barnwell's team that missed promotion to Division Two on goal-difference, despite conceding just 33 League goals in that

1977-78 campaign. Ross was appointed captain during his final season with Posh, then moved into coaching with Wolves and his former club, Aston Villa. Similar posts followed in the Middle East, South Africa and Australia, before he returned to England as player-assistant manager at Hereford in 1982-83. He was named manager of Icelandic club FC Valur the following season, while more recently he has taken charge of Huddersfield and been reserve-team boss at Sunderland.

Season	League			FA Cup			League Cup			Other			Total		
	Aps	Sub	Gls	Aps	Sub	Gls	Aps	Sub	Gls	Aps	Sub	Gls	Aps	Sub	Gls
1976-77	21												21		
1977-78	46			5			5						56		
1978-79	45	1		1			8						54		1
Total	112	1		6			13						131		1

ROSS, Thomas (Tommy)

Forward   *Tain, 27 February 1947*

A Scot from the Highland town of Tain, diminutive forward Ross was signed by Gordon Clark in July 1965 from Scottish amateurs Lochee Harp, along with fellow striker Jimmy Rooney. Ross waited until April 1966 for his League debut in a 5-2 home win over Bristol Rovers, then scored his first goal in a 1-1 draw at Workington five days later. He made just one other first-team appearance that season, and after making only three starts in 1966-67, scoring one goal, he moved to York in June 1967. He stayed for two seasons at Bootham Crescent, scoring twenty goals in 61 League games in a forward line that included future internationals Ted MacDougall and Phil Boyer. Released from York in 1969, he joined Wigan, then Scarborough.

Season	League			FA Cup			League Cup			Other			Total		
	Aps	Sub	Gls	Aps	Sub	Gls	Aps	Sub	Gls	Aps	Sub	Gls	Aps	Sub	Gls
1965-66	3		1										3		1
1966-67	2	2	1	1									3	2	1
Total	5	2	2	1									6	2	2

ROWE, Ezekiel Bartholomew (Zeke)

Forward   *Stoke Newington, 30 October 1973*

In three years with Posh, Rowe showed little of the ability that gave him four years on Chelsea's books as a youngster. His Posh debut came in a 2-1 win at Bournemouth in August 1996. He scored in consecutive home games against Millwall and York the following month but lost his place soon afterwards. Thereafter he featured rarely and was loaned to Doncaster and Welling United, who signed him on a permanent basis in June 1999. Nowadays Zeke lives in Stanground , having played in 2001-02 for Dr Martens Premier side King's Lynn.

Season	League			FA Cup			League Cup			Other			Total		
	Aps	Sub	Gls	Aps	Sub	Gls	Aps	Sub	Gls	Aps	Sub	Gls	Aps	Sub	Gls
1996-97	10	12	3	3	1		2				1		15	14	3
1997-98	3	3			1						2		3	6	
1998-99		7		1									1	7	
Total	13	22	3	4	2		2				3		19	27	3

RUSH, David

Forward   *Sunderland, 15 January 1971*

After coming to prominence with his hometown club, Sunderland, for whom he played in the 1992 FA Cup final defeat by Liverpool, Rush never secured a place on Wearside and this nippy, blond striker was loaned to Posh in October 1993. He weighed in with two goals for a side struggling at the foot of the First Division, but a lack of funds ended hopes of a permanent move. David later spent a month on loan to Cambridge before joining Oxford in a £100,000 deal in September 1994. His goals helped Oxford to promotion to the First Division in 1995-96, after which he took his talents to York and Hartlepool.

Season	League			FA Cup			League Cup			Other			Total		
	Aps	Sub	Gls	Aps	Sub	Gls	Aps	Sub	Gls	Aps	Sub	Gls	Aps	Sub	Gls
1993-94	2	2	2				1						3	2	2

RUSSELL, Allan

Midfielder   *Aberdeen, 16 November 1953*

Signed as a 17-year-old in August 1971 from Leicester, where he was an apprentice, Russell captained Posh's youth side before making his League debut at Scunthorpe in March 1972. He never established himself, however, and after adding a handful of appearances to his tally in 1972-73 the young Scot moved into non-League with Stamford. He was part of the Daniels side that reached the FA Vase Wembley final in 1976 under the guidance of former Posh stalwart Norman Rigby.

Season	League			FA Cup			League Cup			Other			Total		
	Aps	Sub	Gls	Aps	Sub	Gls	Aps	Sub	Gls	Aps	Sub	Gls	Aps	Sub	Gls
1971-72	1	1											1	1	
1972-73	6	7	1	1									7	7	1
Total	7	8	1	1									8	8	1

RUSSELL, Kevin John

Forward   *Brighton, 6 December 1966*

Known as 'Rooster', hard-working striker Kevin Russell was a former England Youth cap who joined Posh on loan from Leicester in September 1990. A prolific scorer for Wrexham in the late 1980s, he scored on his Posh debut in a 1-1 draw at Scunthorpe. His hit two more goals in his next three games, including the winner in a 2-1 win at Northampton. Sadly for Posh fans, Russell returned to Leicester, where his goals helped keep the Foxes in the Second Division. Released from Filbert

Street in 1992 Kevin served Stoke, Burnley, Bournemouth and Notts County before enjoying a second spell at Wrexham, whom he helped to FA Cup glory in 1997 by scoring against West Ham and Posh en route to the quarter-finals. Rooster has completed close to 200 League games for the Welsh club, where he is assistant boss to Denis Smith.

Season	League			FA Cup			League Cup			Other			Total		
	Aps	Sub	Gls	Aps	Sub	Gls	Aps	Sub	Gls	Aps	Sub	Gls	Aps	Sub	Gls
1990-91	7		3										7		3

SALMAN, Danis Mahmut Mehmet
Defender   *Famagusta (Cyprus), 12 March 1960*

A veteran of 500 League games, Cypriot-born Salman was an England Youth international whose career began at Brentford in the late 1970s. After 325 League games for the Bees he joined Millwall in August 1986. After four years at the Den – as part of John Docherty's side that reached the First Division in 1988 – he joined Plymouth in 1990. Loaned to Posh in March 1992, Danis debuted in a Third Division defeat at Wigan. Injured in his next game – a 3-3 draw at Stoke in an Autoglass Trophy area final – he returned to Home Park but was forced to retire shortly afterwards. Danis became commercial manager at Torquay before coaching youngsters in Plymouth with his former boss at Argyle, Dave Smith.

Season	League			FA Cup			League Cup			Other			Total		
	Aps	Sub	Gls	Aps	Sub	Gls	Aps	Sub	Gls	Aps	Sub	Gls	Aps	Sub	Gls
1991-92	1									1			2		

SANSBY, Clifford Palmer (Cliff)
Defender   *Peterborough, 24 November 1934*

The first Peterborough-born player to represent Posh in the Football League, Cliff Sansby was signed by Jimmy Hagan in July 1959 from March Town. A versatile defender, he played once in Posh's Fourth Division title season, 1960-61, standing in for Jim Walker at left-back. Cliff celebrated his inclusion by helping Posh thrash Doncaster 6-2 in September 1960. Sansby joined Spalding in the summer of 1962.

Season	League			FA Cup			League Cup			Other			Total		
	Aps	Sub	Gls	Aps	Sub	Gls	Aps	Sub	Gls	Aps	Sub	Gls	Aps	Sub	Gls
1960-61	1												1		

SARGENT, Gary Stewart
Forward   *Bedford, 11 September 1952*

After a handful of League appearances as a youth with Norwich and Scunthorpe, Sargent dropped into the Southern League with home-town club Bedford Town, where his goals earned him another chance in the League, this time with Posh in August 1977. Although never prolific, he hit two on his debut in a 4-1 League Cup win over Bradford City. He is perhaps best remembered for his goal in a 1-1 draw with Newcastle in a home FA Cup-tie in January 1978. Sargent spent two seasons with Posh before joining Northampton in June 1979. He later returned to the non-League with Barnet, Wellingborough and Irthlingborough Diamonds, whom he managed in the 1980s.

Season	League			FA Cup			League Cup			Other			Total		
	Aps	Sub	Gls	Aps	Sub	Gls	Aps	Sub	Gls	Aps	Sub	Gls	Aps	Sub	Gls
1977-78	18	5	3	4		2	5		2				27	5	7
1978-79	9	2	2		1								9	3	2
Total	27	7	5	4	1	2	5		2				36	8	9

SCOTT, Richard Paul
Midfielder/Full-back   Dudley, 29 September 1974

West Midlander Scott began his career at Birmingham, for whom he made twelve League appearances – mainly as a full-back – before his desire for regular first-team football took him to Shrewsbury in March 1995. At Gay Meadow, his goals from midfield caught the eye of Posh boss Barry Fry, his former manager at St Andrews, and resulted in the player's £10,000 move to London Road in July 1998. Scott experienced mixed fortunes in his first season but gave notice of his potential with late-season strikes at Carlisle, Scunthorpe and Scarborough as Posh narrowly missed the play-offs. After struggling to win a regular place at the start of 1999-2000, Scott benefited from the sale of Simon Davies to Tottenham by claiming a midfield slot after Christmas. He was a regular until the end of the season, by which time he was operating at full-back in place of the injured Dean Hooper. Scott also demonstrated his awesome shooting with long-range goals against Hull, home and away. He finished the campaign in the side that celebrated promotion to the Second Division with a play-off victory over Darlington. But Scott spent much of the following season in the wings and, rejecting a one-year contract extension, he joined Telford in July 2001.

Season	League			FA Cup			League Cup			Other			Total		
	Aps	Sub	Gls	Aps	Sub	Gls	Aps	Sub	Gls	Aps	Sub	Gls	Aps	Sub	Gls
1998-99	19	8	4	1			1	1		1	1		22	10	4
1999-00	28	6	3							4			32	6	3
2000-01	18	2						2		1			19	4	
Total	65	16	7	1			1	3		6	1		73	20	7

SEAMAN, David Andrew
Goalkeeper   Rotherham, 19 September 1963

A name familiar to football fans across the globe, Seaman began his League career as a teenager with Posh. Released by Leeds in August 1982 without making a first-team appearance, the big Yorkshire lad made his League debut at Stockport on the opening day of 1982-83, whereupon his emerging talent was visible to all. After an encouraging first season, he produced many inspired displays in 1983-84, when his safe handling, sharp reflexes and knack of saving penalties earned a call-up to the England Under-21 squad. An inevitable move upwards began with his £100,000 sale to Birmingham in October 1984. Seaman helped the Blues to promotion to the old First Division in 1985, but joined QPR following the Blues' relegation a year later. After four seasons with Rangers – during which time he made his full England debut, against Saudi Arabia – Seaman joined Arsenal in May 1990 for £1.3 million, a world record fee for a goalkeeper. He helped to make a solid Arsenal defence even more watertight and in 1991 the Gunners swept to their second League title in three years. Since then, David has continued to accumulate domestic honours whilst establishing himself as England's first-choice keeper. He won League and FA Cup winners' medals in 1993, then helped the Gunners lift the European Cup Winners' Cup a year later. Under Arsene Wenger he helped Arsenal win the League and Cup double in 1998 and again in 2002. At international level he has remained England's No 1 ever since his Wembley heroics during Euro 96, when he attained hero status with penalty saves against Scotland and Spain. An unflappable, reliable goalkeeper who makes difficult saves look easy, Seaman appeared in all of England's matches in the World Cup finals in France in 1998 and Japan in 2002.

Season	League			FA Cup			League Cup			Other			Total		
	Aps	Sub	Gls	Aps	Sub	Gls	Aps	Sub	Gls	Aps	Sub	Gls	Aps	Sub	Gls
1982-83	38			4			4						46		
1983-84	45			1			4						50		
1984-85	8						2						10		
Total	91			5			10						106		

SEDGEMORE, Benjamin Redwood (Ben)

Midfielder   *Wolverhampton, 5 August 1975*

Mick Halsall signed England Schoolboy international Ben from Barry Fry's Birmingham in January 1996. The player debuted in a 4-5 home loss to Bournemouth later that month, and featured in a handful of games over the rest of that season. Ironically, it was Fry's arrival at London Road that signalled the end of Sedgemore's brief Posh career. Omitted at the start of 1996-97, the young midfielder joined Mansfield on a free transfer, spending two years at Field Mill before going on to Macclesfield. He joined Lincoln City in February 2001.

Season	League			FA Cup			League Cup			Other			Total		
	Aps	Sub	Gls	Aps	Sub	Gls	Aps	Sub	Gls	Aps	Sub	Gls	Aps	Sub	Gls
1995-96	13	4		1									14	4	

SEMPLE, Ryan

Midfielder   *Derry, 2 July 1977*

One of several Irish lads brought in by Youth Development Officer Kit Carson, Ryan was still a trainee when he debuted in April 1995 as a sub in a 1-0 home win over Blackpool. The right-sided midfielder lined up from the start in the final game, a 1-1 home draw with York. Not offered a contract, he returned to Northern Ireland with Derry City.

Season	League			FA Cup			League Cup			Other			Total		
	Aps	Sub	Gls	Aps	Sub	Gls	Aps	Sub	Gls	Aps	Sub	Gls	Aps	Sub	Gls
1994-95	1	1											1	1	

SENIOR, Vincent Roy (Roy)

Winger   *Barnsley, 21 June 1940*

A pacy, all-action wide player, Senior was signed by Jimmy Hagan in September 1961 from Doncaster, where he netted five League goals in thirteen games. Senior showed early promise with Posh, keeping out fans' favourite Peter McNamee after scoring in his first two appearances. Thereafter, Roy struggled to establish himself, joining Millwall in March 1964. By November he was off again, returning to his home town, Barnsley, with whom he ended his League career in 1964-65.

Season	League			FA Cup			League Cup			Other			Total		
	Aps	Sub	Gls	Aps	Sub	Gls	Aps	Sub	Gls	Aps	Sub	Gls	Aps	Sub	Gls
1961-62	19		6	5									24		6
1962-63	15		5				1						16		5
1963-64	4			2		1							6		1
Total	38		11	7		1	1						46		12

SHARKEY, Patrick Gerald (Pat)

Midfielder   *Omagh, 26 August 1953*

Sharkey was capped by Northern Ireland whilst with Ipswich in the 1970s. He made 18 League appearances for the Portman Road club and seven on loan to Millwall prior to joining Mansfield in 1977. He scored five League goals in 32 appearances for the Stags, had an unfulfilled time at Colchester, then followed manager Peter Morris to Posh in March 1979. Pat kept his place for the rest of the season but struggled for form as Posh were relegated. After seeing first-team action just six times in the next two seasons, Sharkey quit professional soccer in 1981.

Season	League			FA Cup			League Cup			Other			Total		
	Aps	Sub	Gls	Aps	Sub	Gls	Aps	Sub	Gls	Aps	Sub	Gls	Aps	Sub	Gls
1978-79	11												11		
1979-80	4			1			1						6		
Total	15			1			1						17		

SHAW, Paul
Midfielder   *Burnham, 4 September 1973*

A goalscoring midfielder, this England Youth international was a big favourite whilst on loan from Arsenal. He debuted in October 1995 in Posh's 0-3 defeat at Brentford – that proved to be John Still's last game, then scored in his first home outing as Mick Halsall's reign began with a 6-1 demolition of York. After bringing quality to Posh's midfield and having his loan spell extended to three months, Shaw signed off by scoring twice in a 2-1 win at Brighton before returning to High-bury. Given a run in the Gunners' first team in 1996-97, he scored twice in eight League games before joining Millwall in September 1997. After 25 League goals in 109 games, Shaw joined Gillingham in 2000 for £450,000 following the Gills' promotion to Division One.

Season	League			FA Cup			League Cup			Other			Total		
	Aps	Sub	Gls	Aps	Sub	Gls	Aps	Sub	Gls	Aps	Sub	Gls	Aps	Sub	Gls
1995-96	12		5							2			14		5

SHEAVILLS, James Edward (Jimmy)
Winger   *Aylesham, 28 July 1940*

Jimmy Hagan snapped up this pacy winger from Holbeach United near the end of 1959-60 – Posh's last season in the Midland League. Despite hitting five goals in as many games, Jimmy was unable to command a place in the side that went on to lift the Fourth Division title. The former Leeds apprentice stayed two more seasons at London Road, enjoying his best run on the right wing after Billy Hails' departure early in 1962-63. After leaving Posh in June 1963, Sheavills joined Barnsley, where he played 65 League games before joining the exodus of English players to South Africa in the mid-1960s. When his football career finished he stayed in South Africa, working in the sports clothing industry. He returned to England in 1985 and lives in Barnsley.

Season	League			FA Cup			League Cup			Other			Total		
	Aps	Sub	Gls	Aps	Sub	Gls	Aps	Sub	Gls	Aps	Sub	Gls	Aps	Sub	Gls
1960-61	1												1		
1961-62	11		2				1						12		2
1962-63	18		6	3			1						22		6
Total	30		8	3			2						35		8

SHEFFIELD, Jonathan (Jon)
Goalkeeper   *Bulkington, 1 February 1969*

John Still paid £150,000 to Cambridge for this highly rated goalkeeper in July 1995. A year later it appeared money well spent. Sheffield was ever present and won Posh's Player of the Season award. Although reluctant to leave his line for crosses, Jon proved to be a fine shot-stopper and played a major role in ensuring Posh's Second Division survival. However, he seemed to lose confidence under new boss Barry

Fry, and after losing his place he was loaned to Watford and Oldham, then sold to Plymouth for £100,000 in July 1997. Jon spent four years at Home Park before joining Yeovil. In a career that began at Norwich in 1987, he also played for Aldershot, Colchester, Hereford and Swindon.

Season	League Aps	Sub	Gls	FA Cup Aps	Sub	Gls	League Cup Aps	Sub	Gls	Other Aps	Sub	Gls	Total Aps	Sub	Gls
1995-96	46			4			4			5			59		
1996-97	16			2			4						22		
Total	62			6			8			5			81		

SHEFFIELD, Laurence Joseph (Laurie)
Centre-forward   *Swansea, 27 April 1939*

This well-travelled striker had seen League action at six different clubs before signing in August 1970. Posh proved to be his last League club as a broken ankle brought a premature end to his career. The stocky Welshman was a regular scorer during earlier spells with Newport, Doncaster, Norwich, Rotherham, Oldham and Luton, notching 100+ League goals. He became youth team coach at Doncaster. After some years as a car dealer, he is now an independent financial advisor.

Season	League Aps	Sub	Gls	FA Cup Aps	Sub	Gls	League Cup Aps	Sub	Gls	Other Aps	Sub	Gls	Total Aps	Sub	Gls
1970-71	17	1	6				1						18	1	6

SHEPHERD, Jamie Greig (Greig)
Forward   *Edinburgh, 29 September 1960*

Blond striker Greig started his League career at Norwich, scoring twice in 16 League games before joining Southend via a season in Hong Kong. He played 53 League games for the Shrimpers – alongside several former Posh men – then joined Peterborough in December 1984. He made his Posh debut in a 1-0 win at Exeter and scored his first goal in a 3-0 Boxing Day drubbing of Northampton. Injury disrupted Greig's progress the following season, but he recovered to play a part in Posh's run to the fifth round of the FA Cup. Appearing as a substitute in the third round home tie with Leeds, the Scottish marksman scored the winner in a 1-0 win, then repeated the feat in the next round as Posh beat Carlisle by the same score. Brighton finally put an end to the Cup run with a replay win at the Goldstone Ground, but only after Greig had headed Posh in front at London Road. He dropped out of the professional game in 1986-87 to run a pub, but has since taken up employment with the Cambridgeshire Constabulary and has been spotted in the Moys End enclosure looking after visiting fans!

Season	League			FA Cup			League Cup			Other			Total		
	Aps	Sub	Gls	Aps	Sub	Gls	Aps	Sub	Gls	Aps	Sub	Gls	Aps	Sub	Gls
1984-85	27		7							1			28		7
1985-86	23	2	6	5	1	3				1			29	3	9
1986-87	3		1				2						5		1
Total	53	2	14	5	1	3	2			2			62	3	17

SHIELDS, Anthony Gerard (Tony)
Midfielder   *Londonderry, 4 June 1980*

A combative, red-haired Irishman, Tony was given a run in the first team at the end of 1998-99. His mature performances belied his tender years. What the diminutive midfielder lacks in height, he makes up in tenacity. One of a crop of talented lads to emerge from the club's burgeoning youth policy, Shields was a member of the side that reached the last four of the FA Youth Cup in 1998. Capped by Northern Ireland at Under-18 and Under-21 level, he made a bright start to 1999-00 until injuries disrupted his progress. Tony established himself during 2000-01, when his battling performances won admirers. The 2001-02 campaign was an unhappy one for Shields. He was stricken by injuries and personal problems caused by homesickness for Northern Ireland.

Season	League			FA Cup			League Cup			Other			Total		
	Aps	Sub	Gls	Aps	Sub	Gls	Aps	Sub	Gls	Aps	Sub	Gls	Aps	Sub	Gls
1997-98		1												1	
1998-99	6	3											6	3	
1999-00	15	9	1	1			2		1	1			18	10	2
2000-01	28	5	1	1	3	1	1	1					30	9	2
2001-02	6	9		1						1			7	10	
Total	55	27	2	3	3	1	3	1	1	2			61	33	4

SHIELS, Dennis Patrick
Centre-forward   *Belfast, 24 August 1938*

A Northern Ireland 'B' cap, Shiels debuted for Posh at Brentford in October 1964. He signed from Sheffield United, where he scored eight League goals in 32 games. After one season at London Road, as understudy to Derek Dougan and Peter Deakin, he moved to Notts County in July 1965, finishing his League career a year later with seven goals from 28 League games. Shiels joined Retford in July 1966.

Season	League			FA Cup			League Cup			Other			Total		
	Aps	Sub	Gls	Aps	Sub	Gls	Aps	Sub	Gls	Aps	Sub	Gls	Aps	Sub	Gls
1964-65	12		4				1						13		4

SHOEMAKE, Kevin Paul
Goalkeeper   *Wickford, 28 January 1965*

Essex-born Shoemake enjoyed a colourful career, most of it spent serving a host of non-League clubs. After making four League appearances for Orient in 1983-84, he had spells with Harlow, Chelmsford and

Welling before, in September 1986, John Wile offered him a second stab at a League career. Kevin debuted in a 1-2 home defeat by Cardiff early in 1986-87, whereupon he stayed Posh's first-choice keeper until Joe Neenan's arrival the following season. Shoemake returned to non-League football with Kettering in 1988, then moved to Dagenham & Redbridge, Rushden & Diamonds, Chelmsford, and Kettering again.

Season	League			FA Cup			League Cup			Other			Total		
	Aps	Sub	Gls	Aps	Sub	Gls	Aps	Sub	Gls	Aps	Sub	Gls	Aps	Sub	Gls
1986-87	34			1			1			2			38		
1987-88	6						1			2			9		
Total	40			1			2			4			47		

SIMPSON, Terence John Norman (Terry)
Wing-half   *Southampton, 8 October 1938*

Simpson was an elegant wing-half who had a fine season with Posh in 1962-63, missing just one League match and impressing with his cultured defending. He was signed from his hometown club, Southampton, for £5,000 by Jimmy Hagan after playing 22 League games for the Saints in four seasons. Simpson's Posh debut came in a 3-3 draw at Bournemouth in August 1962, and his first goal in a 3-2 success at Northampton a month later. Posh fans were sad to see him leave for WBA in June 1963 in a swap for striker Keith Smith. The move reunited Terry with former boss Hagan, who had taken the manager's job at The Hawthorns after being dismissed by Posh. Terry played 71 League games for Albion, whom he helped win the League Cup in 1966 after defeating Posh in the semi-finals. He then had spells with Walsall and Gillingham, where a broken leg ended his League career in 1969. He stayed at Priestfield as trainer and assistant coach until 1972, when he made a brief comeback as a player with Swaythling Athletic.

Season	League			FA Cup			League Cup			Other			Total		
	Aps	Sub	Gls	Aps	Sub	Gls	Aps	Sub	Gls	Aps	Sub	Gls	Aps	Sub	Gls
1962-63	45		4	3			1						49		4

SIMS, David Nigel (Nigel)
Goalkeeper   *Coton-in-Elms, 9 August 1931*

An experienced keeper known from his Aston Villa days, Sims finished his League career with Posh in 1964-65. Sims had started out with Wolves in 1948 but joined Villa in March 1956. He had made just 38 League appearances for Wolves, but enjoyed greater success at Villa, appearing in nearly 250 League matches and picking up FA Cup and League Cup winners medals in 1957 and 1961 respectively. The tall keeper also had a spell with Toronto Falcons in Canada before joining Posh. One of four keepers on the books in 1964-65, the 34-year-old veteran was unable to claim a regular spot and returned to Canada.

Season	League			FA Cup			League Cup			Other			Total		
	Aps	Sub	Gls	Aps	Sub	Gls	Aps	Sub	Gls	Aps	Sub	Gls	Aps	Sub	Gls
1964-65	16			3									19		

SINGLETON, Thomas Wilfred (Tommy)

Full-back   *Blackpool, 8 September 1940*

A full-back noted for his speedy excursions upfield, former Blackpool apprentice Singleton arrived at Posh in June 1962 as a replacement for ageing right-back Dick Whittaker. Tommy debuted in a 3-3 draw at Bournemouth on the first day of 1962-63 and was the regular No 2 in his first season at the club. His involvement lessened over the next couple of seasons, although his versatility allowed him to play right or left-back, and even take on Derek Dougan's forward role at Port Vale in October 1964. Tommy signed for Chester in June 1965, joining Bradford three years later before going part-time with Fleetwood in 1969.

Season	League			FA Cup			League Cup			Other			Total		
	Aps	Sub	Gls	Aps	Sub	Gls	Aps	Sub	Gls	Aps	Sub	Gls	Aps	Sub	Gls
1962-63	37			2			1						40		
1963-64	27			2			1						30		
1964-65	21	1					1						22		1
Total	85	1		4			3						92		1

SISSONS, John Graham (Graham)

Defender   *Chester-le-Street, 20 May 1934*

Sissons signed in December 1962 after making 91 League appearances in eight years with Birmingham. Signed by Jimmy Hagan as a replacement for veteran Jim Walker, Sissons commanded a regular place until November 1964, when he joined Walsall. He played 100 League games for the Saddlers, then in 1969 went non-League with Stourbridge.

Season	League			FA Cup			League Cup			Other			Total		
	Aps	Sub	Gls	Aps	Sub	Gls	Aps	Sub	Gls	Aps	Sub	Gls	Aps	Sub	Gls
1962-63	22			1									23		
1963-64	40			2			1						43		
1964-65	6			1			1						8		
Total	68			4			2						74		

SLACK, Trevor Colin

Central Defender   *Peterborough, 26 September 1962*

As a child, Slack used to stand on the London Road terraces with his dad, little knowing that he would make over 200 League appearances for his favourite team. Peterborough-born Slack was ideally built for a central defender, standing 6ft 2in and weighing nearly 13st. He was competitive, strong, and determined in the tackle. An England Youth cap, Trevor signed professional forms as a 17-year-old in August 1980, and days later made his League debut against Lincoln on the opening day of 1980-81. He was an instant success and kept his place throughout the campaign, helping Posh reach the fifth round of the FA Cup and challenge for promotion to Division Three. After making only a handful of appearances the following season, Slack returned to regular action in 1982-83, when he shared the club's Player of the Season award with Micky Gynn. Trevor remained a popular figure at London Road for three more seasons – helping Posh to further FA Cup success in 1985-86 – before John Wile let him go. Slack had spells with Rotherham, Grimsby, Northampton and Chesterfield before he was reunited with former Posh boss Peter Morris at Kettering. Slack later turned out for Boston United and Corby Town in the early 1990s. Now retired from football, he drives vans for Peterborough-based frozen food company King Brothers, along with another former Posh star, Bob Doyle.

Season	League			FA Cup			League Cup			Other			Total		
	Aps	Sub	Gls	Aps	Sub	Gls	Aps	Sub	Gls	Aps	Sub	Gls	Aps	Sub	Gls
1980-81	35		4	6		1	4						45		5
1981-82	7		2				2		1				9		3
1982-83	40		1	4			3						47		1
1983-84	39		3	1			4			1			45		3
1984-85	41		3	2						1		1	44		4
1985-86	39	1	5	7						2			48	1	5
Total	201	1	18	20		1	13		1	4		1	238	1	21

SLOUGH, Alan Peter

Midfielder/Defender   Luton, 24 September 1947

Utility man Slough joined his hometown club, Luton, as a professional in May 1965. He spent eight years at Kenilworth Road and helped the Hatters win the Fourth Division title in 1968 and promotion to the Second two years later. After 275 League appearances, in August 1973 he joined Fulham for a substantial fee of £45,000. A part of the side that reached the 1975 FA Cup final, he had four years at Craven Cottage, playing alongside George Best, Bobby Moore and Rodney Marsh. In September 1976, Slough scored Fulham's 'other' goal in a 2-1 League Cup win over Posh – Best having scored a beauty. Alan transferred to Posh for £25,000 in July 1977 and missed just one match in his first season, which ended with Posh missing promotion to Division Two. Towards the end of that season, Slough achieved the rare feat of a hat-trick of penalties, in a 3-4 defeat at Chester. Injury sidelined him for much of 1978-79 and by the time he resurfaced in September 1979 Posh were back in the Fourth Division. Although best remembered for his busy midfield displays, Alan played the rest of his time with Posh in central defence, alongside Colin Foster, before assisting the progress of young Trevor Slack. Slough had a brief spell with Millwall in 1981-82 before taking up coaching posts with Torquay, Weymouth, Yeovil and Minehead. Nowadays he runs a cleaning business in Devon, while managing a football side for the Christians in Sport movement.

Season	League			FA Cup			League Cup			Other			Total		
	Aps	Sub	Gls	Aps	Sub	Gls	Aps	Sub	Gls	Aps	Sub	Gls	Aps	Sub	Gls
1977-78	45		6	5		2	5		2				55		10
1978-79	10	1	4				6		2				16	1	6
1979-80	22						1						23		
1980-81	27			6									33		
Total	104	1	10	11		2	12		4				127	1	16

SMALL, Michael Anthony (Mike)
Forward   *Birmingham, 2 January 1962*

A loan signing from Luton in October 1982, this tall, strong England Youth cap played four times for Posh, scoring in a 2-1 home win over Halifax. A permanent move never materialised and after returning to Kenilworth Road he left England to try his luck abroad, representing Dutch sides Go Ahead Eagles and FC Twente, Standard Liege of Belgium and Greek outfit PAOK Salonika. He returned home in 1990, whereupon a useful season with Brighton led to a £400,000 move to West Ham. He top-scored for the Hammers and earned a call-up to the England squad in 1991-92 before a sequence of injuries led to his gradual demise. After ending up at non-League Stevenage Borough, whom he helped into the Conference, he rejoined former Luton team-mate Brian Stein at Dr Martens League side Baldock Town in July 1996.

Season	League			FA Cup			League Cup			Other			Total		
	Aps	Sub	Gls	Aps	Sub	Gls	Aps	Sub	Gls	Aps	Sub	Gls	Aps	Sub	Gls
1982-83	2	2	1										2	2	1

SMELT, Lee Adrian
Goalkeeper   *Edmonton, 13 March 1958*

This former Gravesend & Northfleet and Colchester goalkeeper joined Posh on loan from Nottingham Forest, where he was understudy to Peter Shilton in 1981-82, and tasted Fourth Division action five times. Smelt went on to make a solitary First Division start for Forest but later figured in 119 League games during a three-year stint with Halifax. His next move was to Cardiff, where his League career ended in 1985.

Season	League			FA Cup			League Cup			Other			Total		
	Aps	Sub	Gls	Aps	Sub	Gls	Aps	Sub	Gls	Aps	Sub	Gls	Aps	Sub	Gls
1981-82	5						2						7		

SMEULDERS, John
Goalkeeper   *Hackney, 28 March 1957*

Smeulders was a well-travelled goalkeeper who arrived on loan from Torquay. Stepping in for regular custodian Kevin Shoemake, Smeulders helped Posh to a 1-1 draw at Aldershot in January 1987. The former England Youth international made 18 League appearances for Torquay and nearly 100 in three spells with Bournemouth, as well as serving Brentford, Weymouth and Poole Town.

Season	League			FA Cup			League Cup			Other			Total		
	Aps	Sub	Gls	Aps	Sub	Gls	Aps	Sub	Gls	Aps	Sub	Gls	Aps	Sub	Gls
1986-87	1												1		

SMITH, Anthony (Tony)

Central Defender   *Sunderland, 20 February 1957*

This Sunderland-born, former England Youth team captain, served his apprenticeship at rivals Newcastle. After progressing to the first team and playing two First Division games in 1977-78, Smith joined Posh in March 1979, along with team-mate Alan Guy. Tony was unable to prevent Posh's dive into Division Four and was limited to just 18 appearances over the next couple of seasons. He fared better in 1981-82, establishing himself as a regular in central defence alongside Billy Rodaway. Despite this success, Tony joined Halifax in August 1982 He played 83 League games in two seasons at the Shay before adding another 200 appearances to his tally with Hartlepool. Tony later worked with the Nissan car plant in his home town, Sunderland.

Season	League			FA Cup			League Cup			Other			Total		
	Aps	Sub	Gls	Aps	Sub	Gls	Aps	Sub	Gls	Aps	Sub	Gls	Aps	Sub	Gls
1978-79	15		2										15		2
1979-80	9			1			3						13		
1980-81	5												5		
1981-82	39		3	3									42		3
Total	68		5	4			3						75		5

SMITH, Harold Raymond (Ray)

Inside-forward   *Hull, 13 September 1934*

This speedy forward was an unsung hero of Posh's Fourth Division title-winning side of 1960-61. Perhaps lacking the flair or eye for goal of Dennis Emery and Billy Hails, Ray missed only one match that season and weighed in with hat-tricks against Millwall and Aldershot. Born in Hull, Smith joined his hometown club in 1952 but made only 23 League appearances in four years as a professional at Boothferry Park. He dropped into non-League soccer with Posh in July 1956 and helped the club to four Midland League titles plus some memorable FA Cup triumphs. Smith hit 17 League goals in 1960-61 and remained a regular until Jimmy Hagan surprisingly transfer-listed him in October 1962. Smith responded with a goal in a 2-0 win against Bradford before signing for Northampton after the match. Within days, Posh colleague Billy Hails had joined him at the County Ground, while troubled boss Hagan was sacked the following week. Ray hit seven goals in 21 League games as the Cobblers stormed to the Third Division title in 1962-63 and was among the scorers in their 4-0 win at London Road on the penultimate Saturday of the campaign. The following season was Ray's last in professional football. After losing his place at Northampton, in October 1963 he moved to Luton.

Season	League			FA Cup			League Cup			Other			Total		
	Aps	Sub	Gls	Aps	Sub	Gls	Aps	Sub	Gls	Aps	Sub	Gls	Aps	Sub	Gls
1960-61	45		17	5			1						51		17
1961-62	37		11	4			1						42		11
1962-63	10		5										10		5
Total	92		33	9			2						103		33

SMITH, Keith Wilson

Centre-forward   *Swadlincote, 15 September 1940*

Keith Smith arrived at London Road in May 1963 in a swap for WBA's wing-half Terry Simpson. Smith had scored 30 goals in 63 Division One appearances, but despite scoring a superb solo goal on his debut, he had trouble winning over the Posh crowd. He spent much of his first season in the shadow of Derek Dougan, but hit the goal-trail at the start of 1964-65, outscoring the Irish legend. Unfortunately his exploits also attracted the attention of bigger clubs and in November 1964 he was sold to Crystal Palace for £12,000. Smith struck 14 times in 50 League games for the Eagles, his goal at Derby in December 1964 being timed at six seconds – equalling that for the fastest ever goal in the Football League. In November 1966 Keith joined Darlington before later serving Leyton Orient, Notts County and non-League Tamworth.

Season	League			FA Cup			League Cup			Other			Total		
	Aps	Sub	Gls	Aps	Sub	Gls	Aps	Sub	Gls	Aps	Sub	Gls	Aps	Sub	Gls
1963-64	37		14	2			1						40		14
1964-65	18		14										18		14
Total	55		28	2			1						58		28

SMITH, Raymond James (Ray)

Centre-forward   *Islington, 18 April 1943*

Bustling Ray Smith was given his League debut by Southend, who snapped him up from Basildon in December 1961. He scored over 50 League goals in six seasons at Roots Hall before following manager Alvan Williams to Wrexham in a £8,000 deal in July 1967. Ray hit 62 goals in 172 League games to become a firm favourite in north Wales. Jim Iley hoped Smith would continue in such form when signing him for £5,000 in July 1972, but after a disastrous start Posh slumped to the foot of the Fourth Division and sacked their manager. Despite hitting two goals in Noel Cantwell's first game in charge – a 3-1 win over Doncaster – Smith was given few further opportunities following John Cozens' arrival from Notts County and was released after one season.

Season	League			FA Cup			League Cup			Other			Total		
	Aps	Sub	Gls	Aps	Sub	Gls	Aps	Sub	Gls	Aps	Sub	Gls	Aps	Sub	Gls
1972-73	22		8	2			1						23	2	8

SMITH, Robert Nisbet (Bobby)
Midfielder/Left-back   Dalkeith, 21 December 1953
After 150+ games for Hibs, this stocky midfielder joined Leicester in December 1978 and debuted in the Football League alongside fellow debutant Gary Lineker. Bobby won a Second Division winners' medal with City in 1980 before losing his place and coming on loan to Posh in February 1982. His first game was memorable as Peter Morris's promotion chasers shared eight goals with Hartlepool. Smith returned to Filbert Street a month later and reclaimed a first-team spot at left-back. He played 181 League games for Leicester before returning to Hibs in October 1986. After spells with Dunfermline, Partick and Berwick, he retired to his home town, Dalkeith where he is a pub landlord.

Season	League			FA Cup			League Cup			Other			Total		
	Aps	Sub	Gls	Aps	Sub	Gls	Aps	Sub	Gls	Aps	Sub	Gls	Aps	Sub	Gls
1981-82	5												5		

SOLOMAN, Jason Rafael
Midfielder   Welwyn Garden City, 6 October 1970
A former England Youth cap, Jason was highly regarded as a teenager with Watford, with whom he won the FA Youth Cup in 1989. After graduating to the Hornets' first team he made 100 League appearances before being loaned to Posh in January 1995. A permanent move did not follow, and Soloman joined Wycombe on a free transfer. He later had spells with Fulham and Stevenage Borough of the Conference.

Season	League			FA Cup			League Cup			Other			Total		
	Aps	Sub	Gls	Aps	Sub	Gls	Aps	Sub	Gls	Aps	Sub	Gls	Aps	Sub	Gls
1994-95	4												4		

SORRELL, Anthony Charles (Tony)
Midfielder   Hornchurch, 17 October 1966
After starting his career with Bishop's Stortford and Barking, competitive midfielder Sorrell helped Maidstone into the Football League in 1989. He had a trial with Posh in 1992 following the demise of the Kent club, making just one appearance in a League Cup-tie at Barnet. Tony almost had a League debut for Posh when named as a substitute for a First Division trip to Barnsley, but he was not called upon. He later had spells with Colchester, Barnet and Brentford before returning to the non-League arena with Dagenham & Redbridge and Romford.

Season	League			FA Cup			League Cup			Other			Total		
	Aps	Sub	Gls	Aps	Sub	Gls	Aps	Sub	Gls	Aps	Sub	Gls	Aps	Sub	Gls
1992-93							1						1		

SPEARING, Anthony (Tony)

Left-back — *Romford, 7 October 1964*

Tenacious and enthusiastic, Spearing was liked by Posh fans, who dubbed him 'Psycho' in recognition of his never-say-die spirit. A former England Youth captain, he began his League career at Norwich, for whom he signed professional terms in October 1983. Despite an own-goal on his First Division debut at Tottenham, he spent five successful years at Carrow Road, making 69 League appearances and winning a Second Division winners' medal in 1985-86. He was loaned to Stoke and Oxford before transferring to Leicester for £100,000 in July 1988. After three years at Filbert Street he joined Plymouth, from where Posh picked him up on a free transfer in January 1993. Signed as a replacement for the departing Ronnie Robinson, Tony made his Posh debut at Birmingham and was an automatic left-back until 1995-96, when he stood aside following Simon Clark's successful switch from central defence. Tony stayed with Posh for one season under Barry Fry, his fifth different manager in four years with the club, then joined King's Lynn, where he later progressed to the manager's chair.

Season	League			FA Cup			League Cup			Other			Total		
	Aps	Sub	Gls	Aps	Sub	Gls	Aps	Sub	Gls	Aps	Sub	Gls	Aps	Sub	Gls
1992-93	21	1											21	1	
1993-94	33	1	1		1		4			2			39	2	1
1994-95	31	2		2						3			36	2	
1995-96	9		1	1	1		1			1			12	1	1
1996-97	11	2			1		2			2			15	3	
Total	105	6	2	3	3		7			8			123	9	2

SPEED, Adrian

Central Defender — *Newark, 30 January 1971*

A tall central defender, Speed was a Posh trainee in the late 1980s. He made one substitute appearance, coming on for Phil Crosby in a 1-0 home win over Fulham in the Leyland Daf Trophy in November 1989. Released shortly afterwards, Speed turned out for Holbeach United before joining Grantham Town in July 1990. He is a loyal servant to the Gingerbreads, for whom he has now made over 500 appearances.

Season	League			FA Cup			League Cup			Other			Total		
	Aps	Sub	Gls	Aps	Sub	Gls	Aps	Sub	Gls	Aps	Sub	Gls	Aps	Sub	Gls
1989-90											1			1	

STAFFORD, Ellis

Right-back — *Sheffield, 17 August 1929*

A regular in the side that dominated the Midland League in the late 1950s, Stafford was still first-choice right-back when Posh began life in the Football League. He played 13 League games at the start of 1960-61, but was unable to regain his place after injury and ended the season having played one game fewer than the minimum required to earn a Fourth Division championship medal. Ellis remained on the playing staff for three more years. His release to Corby in 1964 ended a Posh career that had begun with his signing from Scarborough ten years earlier. Returning to London Road in 1968, Stafford gave 20 years more service as pools manager and commercial manager.

Season	League			FA Cup			League Cup			Other			Total		
	Aps	Sub	Gls	Aps	Sub	Gls	Aps	Sub	Gls	Aps	Sub	Gls	Aps	Sub	Gls
1960-61	13												13		
1961-62							1						1		
1962-63	4												4		
Total	17						1						18		

STANHOPE, Andrew
Midfielder   *Boston, 21 January 1976*

Stanhope appeared in Posh's line-up for an Anglo-Italian Cup defeat at WBA in September 1993 while still a trainee. Unable to secure a professional contract, the goalscoring midfielder joined former Posh manager Peter Morris at King's Lynn, then transferred to Boston in January 1997. After helping his hometown club re-establish themselves in the Conference in 2000-01, Stanhope moved to Gainsborough Trinity.

Season	League			FA Cup			League Cup			Other			Total		
	Aps	Sub	Gls	Aps	Sub	Gls	Aps	Sub	Gls	Aps	Sub	Gls	Aps	Sub	Gls
1993-94										1			1		

STEELE, Eric Graham
Goalkeeper   *Newcastle, 14 May 1954*

At 5ft 11in, Eric Steele was not the tallest of goalkeepers, but he was not short of agility and bravery. Loaned from Newcastle in December 1973, Eric played his part in helping Posh lift the Fourth Division title. Noel Cantwell moved quickly to ensure the 20-year-old Geordie signed a permanent deal that summer, after which Steele was ever present until October 1976, establishing a club record 148 consecutive appearances. Confident and extrovert, Eric was a favourite with the Posh faithful during a happy era of big crowds and memorable cup runs. He commanded an £18,000 fee in February 1977 when joining Brighton, whose talented side reached the top flight in 1979. After 87 League games for the Seagulls, Eric transferred to Graham Taylor's Watford for £100,000 and added a further 51 appearances to his total before joining Derby in July 1984. After two promotions with the Rams, Eric finished his playing career at Southend in 1988, before leaving football to run a pub-restaurant in Derby. He later returned to Derby as goalkeeping coach, a role he now performs at Aston Villa.

Season	League			FA Cup			League Cup			Other			Total		
	Aps	Sub	Gls	Aps	Sub	Gls	Aps	Sub	Gls	Aps	Sub	Gls	Aps	Sub	Gls
1973-74	20												20		
1974-75	46			8			1						55		
1975-76	46			5			5						56		
1976-77	12						5						17		
Total	124			13			11						148		

STEELE, Luke

Goalkeeper   *Peterborough, 24 September 1984*

This local lad from Glinton progressed through the Posh ranks before completing a fairytale move to Manchester United – the team he supported as a boy – in May 2002. Steele's displays in Posh's second string during 2001-02 earned him a call-up to the England Under-18 squad and prompted Sir Alex Ferguson to offer the 17-year-old a month's loan at Old Trafford. Buoyed by the experience, Luke was handed his League debut by Barry Fry upon his return to London Road. After impressing in a 2-2 draw at Reading's Majedski Stadium he retained his place for the final game of the season at home to Bury, scooping Man of the Match awards on both occasions. An offer of a permanent switch to Old Trafford swiftly followed. Manchester United paid an initial £500,000 in a deal that could ultimately net Posh £2.5 million.

Season	League			FA Cup			League Cup			Other			Total		
	Aps	Sub	Gls	Aps	Sub	Gls	Aps	Sub	Gls	Aps	Sub	Gls	Aps	Sub	Gls
2001-02	2												2		

STENSON, John Andrew

Midfielder   *Catford, 16 December 1949*

A former England Schoolboy and Youth cap, Stenson started his League career at Charlton in the late 1960s. He made eleven League appearances before moving to Mansfield, from where he was loaned to Posh in January 1972. He figured in first-team action on just two occasions, wearing No 10 in consecutive 1-1 draws at Darlington and Northampton, where he received an injury that led to his quick return to Field Mill. Stenson later joined Aldershot and played 45 League games for the Shots until dropping out of League soccer in 1974.

Season	League			FA Cup			League Cup			Other			Total		
	Aps	Sub	Gls	Aps	Sub	Gls	Aps	Sub	Gls	Aps	Sub	Gls	Aps	Sub	Gls
1971-72	2												2		

STERLING, Worrell Ricardo

Winger   *Bethnal Green, London, 8 June 1965*

Worrell became Posh's most expensive player when Mick Jones paid Watford £70,000 for the tricky right-winger in March 1989. Sterling's value to the team was probably not fully appreciated until after he had left London Road. Born in London, he began his League career at Watford, signing professional forms in June 1983 and making close to 100 top-flight appearances for Graham Taylor's team. In just over four seasons at London Road he missed only a handful of games and was part of Chris Turner's team that rose from Division Four to the new First Division in two seasons. Noted for his crossing ability, Worrell was a hard-working player whose defensive contribution – sometimes overlooked by supporters – proved a real asset. Perhaps his finest contribution came at Huddersfield, where he scored the vital equaliser in the 2-1 play-off win that earned Posh a Wembley final place in 1992. During the following season – his last at London Road – Sterling continued to hit important goals, including the winner in a local derby win over Cambridge. He left Posh in July 1993 for Bristol Rovers in a £140,000 deal. After 119 League appearances for Rovers, he finished his League career with Lincoln in July 1996. Worrell returned to the Peterborough area soon afterwards, working as a van driver and helping local sides Spalding United, Bourne Town and Deeping Rangers.

Season	League			FA Cup			League Cup			Other			Total		
	Aps	Sub	Gls	Aps	Sub	Gls	Aps	Sub	Gls	Aps	Sub	Gls	Aps	Sub	Gls
1988-89	12		3										12		3
1989-90	46		4	3		1	2		1	3			54		6
1990-91	46		9	5		1	4		1	2			57		11
1991-92	43	2	4	3		1	6		1	10		2	62	2	8
1992-93	43	1	8	3		2	3						49	1	10
Total	190	3	28	14		5	15		3	15		2	234	3	38

STYLES, Arthur (Archie)
Left-back   *Liverpool, 3 September 1949*
Styles won England Schoolboy and then Youth caps whilst at his first club Everton, where he later progressed to play 23 First Division games during the early 1970s. He continued his career in the top flight with Birmingham, playing 74 League games in four years before joining Posh on a free transfer in July 1978. Archie settled into the No 3 shirt and in October 1978 netted in three consecutive matches. He lost his place shortly after Peter Morris took charge in March 1979, which led to his departure that summer. After helping Portsmouth gain promotion to Division Three in 1979-80, injury forced Styles' retirement, whereupon he continued to serve Pompey as youth-team coach.

Season	League			FA Cup			League Cup			Other			Total		
	Aps	Sub	Gls	Aps	Sub	Gls	Aps	Sub	Gls	Aps	Sub	Gls	Aps	Sub	Gls
1978-79	32		1	1			8		2				41		3

SUTTON, Richard Melvyn

Defender   *Gravesend, 21 August 1965*

Martin Wilkinson gambled in handing 17-year-old Sutton his League debut at Aldershot in September 1982. Suspensions to central defenders Neil Firm and Trevor Slack forced Wilkinson to pitch the teenager into action just hours after he had returned from England's Under-18 game in Yugoslavia. An exhausted Sutton struggled to adjust to the pace and was substituted after just 28 minutes. It proved to be the only taste of senior action for the lad, who was released at the end of 1982-83. After a spell with Norwich, he joined Dagenham, and was a member of the Daggers side that dumped Posh from the FA Cup in 1984.

Season	League			FA Cup			League Cup			Other			Total		
	Aps	Sub	Gls	Aps	Sub	Gls	Aps	Sub	Gls	Aps	Sub	Gls	Aps	Sub	Gls
1982-83	1												1		

SWINDLEHURST, David (Dave)

Forward   *Edgware, London, 6 January 1956*

A striker who stood 6ft 2in tall and weighed over 13st, Swindlehurst found fame as part of Terry Venables' exciting young Crystal Palace side that was dubbed the 'team of the eighties' following their Second Division championship triumph in 1979. An England Under-21 cap, Swindlehurst used his powerful frame to good effect to score 73 League goals in 237 games for Palace before joining Derby, West Ham and Sunderland. After playing in Cyprus, he returned to England in 1988 and played twice for Wimbledon before dropping into Division Four with Colchester in June 1988. Despite hitting five goals in twelve games for the Essex club, he found himself out of favour and was loaned to Posh midway through the campaign. Dave's four games for a poor Posh side all ended in defeat. Included in that miserable run was a 1-5 home drubbing by Cambridge, when he scored his solitary goal for the club. Swindlehurst quit the professional game in 1989 and these days combines coaching football and cricket at Old Harrodian school in Barnes, London, with managing Ryman League Molesey.

Season	League			FA Cup			League Cup			Other			Total		
	Aps	Sub	Gls	Aps	Sub	Gls	Aps	Sub	Gls	Aps	Sub	Gls	Aps	Sub	Gls
1988-89	4		1										4		1

SYRETT, David Kenneth (Dave)

Forward   *Salisbury, 20 January 1956*

Peter Morris paid Walsall £50,000 for this lively forward in August 1979. An England Youth cap, Syrett gained a reputation as a hard-working goalscorer during earlier spells with Swindon and Mansfield, for whom he hit 16 Second Division goals in 1977-78, including a hat-trick against Tottenham. His Posh career got off to an unfortunate start when he sustained an ankle injury on his debut at Port Vale but, after returning to the side later in the season, he hit a terrific patch that yielded eleven goals from 14 games. Syrett began 1980-81 as striking partner to new signing Robbie Cooke, but was later dropped when his goalscoring touch deserted him. Recalled in October 1981, Dave hit another purple patch, bagging six goals in as many games, including two in the 7-1 home thrashing of Aldershot. Nevertheless, Dave played only a small part in Posh's promotion push that season before joining Northampton on a free transfer in July 1982. He scored 13 League goals in 44 games for the Cobblers, with whom he established a front pairing with former Posh team-mate Steve Massey. Syrett quit League football in 1984 and is now a milkman in Towcester.

Season	League			FA Cup			League Cup			Other			Total		
	Aps	Sub	Gls	Aps	Sub	Gls	Aps	Sub	Gls	Aps	Sub	Gls	Aps	Sub	Gls
1979-80	29		11	1									30		11
1980-81	30	3	4		1		4		1				34	4	5
1981-82	16	1	8	3		1							19	1	9
Total	75	4	23	4	1	1	4		1				83	5	25

Alan Waddle (left) v Bristol City, February 1984

Alan Morton

Paddy Rayment

Paul Culpin scores against Wrexham, March 1990

John Wile   Steve Massey

Andy Clarke v Notts Co, October 2000

Tommy Robson with his son, Ian, for Tommy's testimonial in 1976

Trevor Quow

Chris Turner

TAYLOR, John
Winger   *Cresswell, 11 January 1939*

Left-winger Taylor joined Posh as a 20-year-old from Mansfield in July 1960. He had broken into the Stags' team during 1959-60, scoring two goals in five League games, but added just one appearance to his tally during Posh's first League season. Standing in for the injured Peter McNamee, Taylor wore No 11 in a Fourth Division game at Doncaster in September 1960 but was released at the end of the campaign.

Season	League			FA Cup			League Cup			Other			Total		
	Aps	Sub	Gls	Aps	Sub	Gls	Aps	Sub	Gls	Aps	Sub	Gls	Aps	Sub	Gls
1960-61	1												1		

TAYLOR, Stuart James
Goalkeeper   *Romford, 28 November 1980*

Stuart Taylor experienced mixed fortunes whilst guarding Posh's net for a month in Mark Tyler's absence in 2000-01. With Tyler sidelined by a heel injury, 6ft 4in Taylor came in on loan from Arsenal, where he was behind Seaman and Manninger in the pecking order. Despite having started only a couple of games for the Gunners – a Champions League group trip to Ukrainian side Shakhtar Donetsk and a League Cup-tie with Ipswich – Taylor had sampled League action on loan to Bristol Rovers and Crystal Palace. He made his Posh debut in a 1-1 draw at Reading and played in five subsequent games, the last of which saw him beaten five times in a crushing defeat at Port Vale.

Season	League			FA Cup			League Cup			Other			Total		
	Aps	Sub	Gls	Aps	Sub	Gls	Aps	Sub	Gls	Aps	Sub	Gls	Aps	Sub	Gls
2000-01	6												6		

TELFORD, William Albert (Billy)
Centre-forward   *Carlisle, 5 March 1956*

Billy made an impact when scoring within a minute of his Posh debut as a sub against Aldershot in September 1975. Signed from Manchester City, where he made a solitary First Division appearance, Billy scored against Rotherham the same month before going on loan to Colchester later in the season. It took him three minutes to find the net on his U's debut but after just one further appearance as a substitute he returned to London Road, where he finished the season as Posh's top scorer in the reserves. Telford left professional football for Bangor City in 1976.

Season	League			FA Cup			League Cup			Other			Total		
	Aps	Sub	Gls	Aps	Sub	Gls	Aps	Sub	Gls	Aps	Sub	Gls	Aps	Sub	Gls
1975-76	3	1	2										3	1	2

THOMAS, Glen Andrew

Central Defender   Hackney, 6 October 1967

Big, blond centre-back Thomas began his career with Fulham where he came up through the ranks to make 250+ League appearances. His spell with Posh lasted only four months following his free transfer arrival in November 1994. After appearing in only a handful of games, he moved on to Barnet in March 1995, Gillingham ten months later, and then Aveley and Bishop's Stortford of the Ryman League. Outside of football, Glen runs a sandwich bar in Upminster, Essex.

Season	League			FA Cup			League Cup			Other			Total		
	Aps	Sub	Gls	Aps	Sub	Gls	Aps	Sub	Gls	Aps	Sub	Gls	Aps	Sub	Gls
1994-95	6	2			1					2			8	3	

THOMPSON, Peter Colin

Winger   Kenya, 25 July 1942

A slender, versatile winger signed from Grantham in March 1964, African-born Thompson scored on his League debut against Coventry in front of over 26,000 fans at London Road. His career stuttered over the next couple of seasons, and it was not until the late 1960s that he was given an extended run in the side. His best season was 1967-68, when he scored vital goals from his preferred role on the left wing, though he also made a huge contribution to Posh's League Cup run the following season. After scoring in giant-killing wins over First Division QPR and WBA, Peter was nearly a hero in the next round at Spurs, where his 'equaliser' was ruled out for offside. A loyal Posh servant for five years, Thompson later served Nuneaton and Grantham.

Season	League			FA Cup			League Cup			Other			Total		
	Aps	Sub	Gls	Aps	Sub	Gls	Aps	Sub	Gls	Aps	Sub	Gls	Aps	Sub	Gls
1963-64	2		1										2		1
1964-65	7		2										7		2
1965-66	3												3		
1966-67	16	2	1				1						17	2	1
1967-68	29	3	8	2		1							31	3	9
1968-69	22	1	3	1			5		2				28	1	5
Total	79	6	15	3		1	6		2				88	6	18

TOMLINSON, David Ian

Winger   Rotherham, 13 December 1968

This speedy Yorkshire right-winger was loaned to Posh from Barnet in September 1992. Starting out at Sheffield Wednesday, he gained further League experience with Rotherham and had a spell at Boston prior to joining Barry Fry's Barnet in December 1990. He played in an Anglo-Italian Cup defeat at Wolves before returning to Underhill.

Season	League			FA Cup			League Cup			Other			Total		
	Aps	Sub	Gls	Aps	Sub	Gls	Aps	Sub	Gls	Aps	Sub	Gls	Aps	Sub	Gls
1992-93										1			1		

TONER, Ciaran

Midfielder   *Craigavon, 30 June 1981*

A stocky midfielder, Toner spent a month on loan from Spurs midway through 2001-02. Having been unable to break into Spurs' first team, his League debut was Posh's 1-3 Boxing Day defeat at Huddersfield. He made little impact in six subsequent appearances, which included an FA Cup-tie at Darlington. After being loaned to Bristol Rovers in April 2002, Ciaran joined Leyton Orient on a free transfer.

Season	League			FA Cup			League Cup			Other			Total		
	Aps	Sub	Gls	Aps	Sub	Gls	Aps	Sub	Gls	Aps	Sub	Gls	Aps	Sub	Gls
2001-02	6			1									7		

TURLEY, John William

Centre-forward   *Bebington, 26 January 1939*

Turley was plucked from Ellesmere Port by Sheffield United in 1956, hitting three goals for the Blades in five League games in 1957-58. Yet he was omitted for the next three seasons and joined Posh in July 1961. Turley had little more joy in three seasons at London Road, most of his time being spent as cover for regular strikers Terry Bly, George Hudson and Derek Dougan. He proved to be a capable deputy, averaging close to a goal every two games, but in May 1964 he joined Rochdale, scoring five League goals in 22 games before joining Cambridge.

Season	League			FA Cup			League Cup			Other			Total		
	Aps	Sub	Gls	Aps	Sub	Gls	Aps	Sub	Gls	Aps	Sub	Gls	Aps	Sub	Gls
1961-62	3		3										3		3
1962-63	16		6										16		6
1963-64	13		5										13		5
Total	32		14										32		14

TURNER, Christopher James (Chris)

Central Defender   *St Neots, 3 April 1951*

Considered by many to be the finest central defender in Posh history, Turner played 350+ games for Posh before later returning and achieving legendary status as a manager. Born at nearby St Neots, Chris first came to London Road as a young Arsenal fan in January 1965. The Gunners were in town for an FA Cup-tie and 13-year-old Turner left the ground in tears after seeing Arsenal beaten 2-1 by Third Division Posh! The memories of that afternoon were long forgotten by the time Chris signed professional terms for Posh in November 1969. He made his League debut the following month as a raw, 18-year-old alongside John Wile for a Fourth Division game at Notts County, and helped the side gain a 2-2 draw, despite conceding the penalty that led to the Magpies' second goal. He did not become a regular until 1971-72 when he formed a strong partnership with Jack Carmichael. Ever present the following season, Turner reached his peak under Noel Cantwell's tutelage in 1973-74 when Posh won the Fourth Division title, and over the next couple of seasons captained an experienced side that enjoyed long cup runs. After another superb season in 1977-78, when Posh conceded just 33 League goals to set a new club record, Chris was sold to Second Division Luton for £100,000 – a then record fee received by the club. Posh's drop to Division Four in 1978-79 showed that Turner's strength and leadership had been badly missed. A commanding figure, good in the air, he was a threat from set-pieces and his tally of 43 goals is the most ever scored for Posh by a defender. Chris spent just one season at Luton, scoring five goals in 30 League games before rejoining Cantwell at American side New England Teamen. Upon his return to England in 1980, Turner made 90 League appearances for Cambridge and was loaned to Swindon before finishing his League career at Southend in 1983-84. After working as a van driver and managing United Counties League side Ramsey Town, Turner returned to the professional game as manager of Cambridge in 1986. He laid the foundations for unprecedented success at the Abbey, before repeating the trick with Posh in the early 1990s, guiding the club from Division Four to the new First Division to become the most successful manager in Posh history. In December 1992, Chris fulfilled an ambition when he headed a consortium that purchased the club. He became chairman whilst managerial duties were handed to his assistant, Lil Fuccillo. Despite suffering ill health, Turner took over team affairs following Fuccillo's resignation in December 1993. His love for the club undiminished, Chris returned to a role behind the scenes the following year, acting as chief executive before serving as sales manager. A victim of cash constraints, he finally left London Road in May 2001.

Season	League			FA Cup			League Cup			Other			Total		
	Aps	Sub	Gls	Aps	Sub	Gls	Aps	Sub	Gls	Aps	Sub	Gls	Aps	Sub	Gls
1969-70	6	6											6	6	
1970-71	15		1	1									16		1
1971-72	35		2	4									39		2
1972-73	46		7	4			1						51		7
1973-74	44		4	4			2						50		4
1974-75	46		8	8	2		1						55		10
1975-76	31		5	5	1		3	1	1				39	1	7
1976-77	39		5	2			4						45		5
1977-78	46		5	5			5		2				56		7
Total	308	6	37	33		3	16	1	3				357	7	43

TURNER, John Graham Anthony
Goalkeeper   *Peterlee, 23 December 1954*

Signed from Burnley in October 1984 to replace David Seaman, Turner performed well until injury forced his retirement in 1986. He began his professional career at First Division Derby in December 1972, from where he gained League experience on loan to Doncaster and Huddersfield. He was also loaned to Posh during 1974-75 but did not make the first team. Leaving the Baseball Ground for Reading in 1975, Turner spent three seasons at Elm Park before serving Torquay, Chesterfield and Weymouth. In August 1984 he returned to League football with Burnley but joined Posh two months later. Unspectacular but dependable, John debuted in a Sunday fixture at Swindon and did not miss a match until breaking his leg in a collision with Leeds' Andy Ritchie at a snowy London Road in January 1986. His career over, Turner settled in Devon to run the 'Fortune of War' public house.

Season	League			FA Cup			League Cup			Other			Total		
	Aps	Sub	Gls	Aps	Sub	Gls	Aps	Sub	Gls	Aps	Sub	Gls	Aps	Sub	Gls
1984-85	38			2						2			42		
1985-86	22			4			2						28		
Total	60			6			2			2			70		

TURPIE, Robert Paul (Bob)
Midfielder   *Hampstead, 13 November 1949*

Hampstead-born Turpie was offered an apprenticeship by QPR in 1965. The hard-working midfielder turned professional two years later but with Rangers' team boasting Rodney Marsh, Terry Venables and Gerry Francis he was restricted to two League outings in three years, and moved on a free transfer switch to Posh in July 1970. Turpie debuted in a 0-1 defeat at Bournemouth, and was more often in the side than out for the rest of the season. Turpie's second season with Posh was less productive, and he was loaned out to Southern League Nuneaton Borough – then managed by former Posh colleague David Pleat. A permanent switch to Manor Park followed in 1972 and Bob did well for three seasons until being forced to retire after losing the sight in an eye due to an accident at work. He has remained active in football, most recently as a scout for Birmingham City and Stoke City.

Season	League			FA Cup			League Cup			Other			Total		
	Aps	Sub	Gls	Aps	Sub	Gls	Aps	Sub	Gls	Aps	Sub	Gls	Aps	Sub	Gls
1970-71	27	6	1	1			1						29	6	1
1971-72	4		2										4		2
Total	31	6	3	1			1						33	6	3

TUTTLE, David Phillip
Central Defender   *Reading, 6 February 1972*

Big centre-back Tuttle was a member of Tottenham's FA Youth Cup winning side of 1990. He then played 13 League games for Spurs before being loaned to Posh in January 1993. He made enough of an impression to have his spell extended to a second month, but was injured in a 2-1 home win over Birmingham and returned to White Hart Lane. Fit again, he was sold for £350,000 to Sheffield United, where he was a regular for two years before joining Crystal Palace in March 1996. David subsequently played for Barnsley and Millwall.

Season	League			FA Cup			League Cup			Other			Total		
	Aps	Sub	Gls	Aps	Sub	Gls	Aps	Sub	Gls	Aps	Sub	Gls	Aps	Sub	Gls
1992-93	7												7		

TYDEMAN, Richard (Dick)
Midfielder   *Chatham, 25 May 1951*

Tydeman arrived from Gillingham in October 1983 as John Wile tried to cover injuries to Trevor Quow and Kenny Beech. The 32-year-old midfielder was a veteran of 500+ League games from a 14-year career that incorporated two spells with Gillingham either side of a five-year stint at Charlton. His Posh debut saw a 2-0 home win over Tranmere, after which he was a regular throughout 1983-84, despite failing to win over Posh fans who doubted his willingness to mix it in the hurly-burly Fourth Division. Released at the end of the season, he retired from professional soccer and now works for Prudential Insurance.

Season	League			FA Cup			League Cup			Other			Total		
	Aps	Sub	Gls	Aps	Sub	Gls	Aps	Sub	Gls	Aps	Sub	Gls	Aps	Sub	Gls
1983-84	29			1									30		

TYLER, Mark Richard
Goalkeeper   *Norwich, 2 April 1977*

Since debuting as a 17-year-old in a televised 0-4 defeat at Birmingham Tyler matured into one of the finest young keepers in English football. A product of Posh's youth policy, Mark understudied Jon Sheffield and Bart Griemink before claiming the No 1 jersey in 1997-98. He was ever present that season when his displays attracted several big clubs and earned him a call-up to the England Under-21 squad. After sharing goalkeeping duties with Griemink at the start of 1998-99, Tyler was sidelined with broken ribs before re-establishing himself as first choice later in the season. He was at his best in 1999-2000 until a dislocated shoulder kept him out for two months. He returned in time for the play-offs, making a famous save from Darlington's Marco Gabbiadini in the final moments before Andy Clarke fired Posh into Division Two. Posh's longest serving current player, Tyler continues to attract transfer speculation. Often cited by manager Barry Fry as 'the best goalkeeper outside the Premier League' Tyler was voted into the PFA select side for Division Two for his displays during 2001-02.

Season	League			FA Cup			League Cup			Other			Total		
	Aps	Sub	Gls	Aps	Sub	Gls	Aps	Sub	Gls	Aps	Sub	Gls	Aps	Sub	Gls
1994-95	4	1								2			6	1	
1996-97	3									1			4		
1997-98	46			3			4			4			57		

Season	League Aps	Sub	Gls	FA Cup Aps	Sub	Gls	League Cup Aps	Sub	Gls	Other Aps	Sub	Gls	Total Aps	Sub	Gls
1998-99	27			1			1			2			31		
1999-00	32			2			2			4			40		
2000-01	40			5			2						47		
2001-02	44			6			1			2			53		
Total	196	1		17			10			15			238	1	

VICKERS, Ashley James Ward

Central Defender   *Sheffield, 14 June 1972*

After failing to make the grade as a schoolboy with Sheffield United, Vickers turned to a teaching career combined with non-League action. A tall, slim centre-back, he impressed with Worcester City, Malvern Town and Heybridge Swifts, but his brief spell as a professional with Posh is one he will want to forget. Signed by Barry Fry in December 1997, Ashley's League debut saw him sent off following a rash challenge in a 1-2 home defeat by Brighton. He never got another chance. After twice being an unused sub he quit full-time football. He joined Ryman League St Albans City, and then Dagenham & Redbridge.

Season	League Aps	Sub	Gls	FA Cup Aps	Sub	Gls	League Cup Aps	Sub	Gls	Other Aps	Sub	Gls	Total Aps	Sub	Gls
1997-98	1												1		

WADDLE, Alan Robert

Forward   *Wallsend, 9 June 1954*

A cousin of England star Chris Waddle, 6ft 3in Alan was a bludgeoning centre-forward in the old-fashioned mould who arrived in October 1983. Prior to joining Posh, he had served Halifax, Liverpool, Leicester, Swansea, Newport, Mansfield and Hartlepool. His biggest claim to fame was when – during his Liverpool days in the early 1970s – he scored the only goal of a Merseyside derby watched by a Goodison crowd of 57,000. Despite an awkward, ungainly style, Waddle proved to be an effective target-man during 1983-84, hitting twelve goals for John Wile's side to finish as top scorer. Injury restricted his progress the following season, prompting his release and subsequent return to Hartlepool in January 1985. Two months later he rejoined another of his former clubs, Swansea, where his goals helped to avoid relegation to Division Four. He remained at the Vetch Field for one more season before retiring from League soccer in 1986. After gaining a HND in computing, Alan now works for an IT company based in Merseyside.

Season	League Aps	Sub	Gls	FA Cup Aps	Sub	Gls	League Cup Aps	Sub	Gls	Other Aps	Sub	Gls	Total Aps	Sub	Gls
1983-84	33		12	1									34		12
1984-85	2	1					1						2	2	
Total	35	1	12	1			1						36	2	12

WALKER, James Frederick (Jim)

Left-back   *Sheffield, 1 July 1931*

Left-back Walker joined his local club Sheffield United from school, signing professional forms in November 1948. He played just four League games before moving to Huddersfield in August 1955. After one season at Leeds Road, George Swindin persuaded him to try his luck with Posh, who were celebrating their first Midland League title. Although quiet and unassuming, Jim proved to be a fierce competitor, strong and tenacious in the tackle. He was a regular member of the side that continued to flourish after Jimmy Hagan replaced Swindin in 1958, and helped Posh to a fifth consecutive Midland League title in 1960. Jim missed just three League games in the club's record-breaking first season in the Fourth Division. He was ever present the following season as Posh finished fifth in Division Three. Despite being dislodged by newcomer Graham Sissons in 1962-63, Walker remained on the playing staff until 1965, providing cover for a variety of defensive roles. He later returned as trainer and coach until 1972 before being invited back as youth-team manager by Chris Turner in 1993.

Season	League			FA Cup			League Cup			Other			Total		
	Aps	Sub	Gls	Aps	Sub	Gls	Aps	Sub	Gls	Aps	Sub	Gls	Aps	Sub	Gls
1960-61	43			5			1						49		
1961-62	46			6			1						53		
1962-63	27			2			1						30		
1963-64	3												3		
1964-65	6						2						8		
Total	125			13			5						143		

WALKER, James McIntyre (Jim)

Left-back   *Northwich, 10 June 1947*

A reliable, experienced left-back, Walker was signed from Brighton in October 1975 after impressing while on loan. Discovered playing for his hometown team Northwich Victoria by Derby boss Brian Clough, Jim signed professional terms for the Rams in February 1968 and made 42 League appearances before joining Brighton in September 1974. He came to London Road the following season, but found his chances limited by the excellence of Jeff Lee at left-back. Walker proved to be a capable deputy when injury ruled Lee out of the FA Cup replay win over Nottingham Forest in January 1976. He kept his place for the subsequent trip to Manchester United and provided reliable defensive cover throughout his time with Posh. He left in November 1976 to join Chester, where he stayed for five seasons, adding 172 League appearances to his tally. These days Jim is physiotherapist at Aston Villa.

Season	League			FA Cup			League Cup			Other			Total		
	Aps	Sub	Gls	Aps	Sub	Gls	Aps	Sub	Gls	Aps	Sub	Gls	Aps	Sub	Gls
1975-76	13	7		2									15	7	
1976-77	7	4	1				3		1				10	5	1
Total	20	11	1	2			3		1				25	12	1

WALKER, Paul Graham

Midfielder *Bradford, 3 April 1949*

A free-transfer signing from Wolves, for whom he played 26 games in the old First Division, midfield workhorse Walker played a vital part in Posh's Fourth Division title success of 1973-74. His tireless running and strong tackling complemented the creative talents of Freddie Hill and earned Paul the respect of the Posh crowd and his fellow professionals, who voted him into the PFA select side. Yorkshireman Paul maintained his high standards the following season – helping Posh to seventh place in Division Three – before leaving for Barnsley in July 1975. He spent one season at Oakwell and had a spell with Canadian side Ottawa before ending his League career at Huddersfield.

Season	League			FA Cup			League Cup			Other			Total		
	Aps	Sub	Gls	Aps	Sub	Gls	Aps	Sub	Gls	Aps	Sub	Gls	Aps	Sub	Gls
1973-74	37		2	2			2						41		2
1974-75	38	3	1	6	1		1						45	4	1
Total	75	3	3	8	1		3						86	4	3

WALLS, John (Jack)

Goalkeeper *Seaham, 8 May 1932*

Durham-born Walls was Posh's regular keeper for six seasons during the late 1950s and early 60s. Signed from Barnsley in May 1956 by George Swindin, Jack debuted for Posh on the opening day of 1956-57, keeping a clean sheet in a 1-0 Midland League win over Boston United watched by a 13,000 London Road crowd. He became a permanent fixture with all-conquering Posh, helping secure Midland League titles in each of his first four seasons. In 1960-61 he was ever present as Jimmy Hagan's men won the Fourth Division title at the first attempt. A reliable custodian whose contribution was often overshadowed by events at the other end of the pitch, Walls helped Posh establish themselves in Division Three. He joined King's Lynn in 1962, and later Wisbech.

Season	League			FA Cup			League Cup			Other			Total		
	Aps	Sub	Gls	Aps	Sub	Gls	Aps	Sub	Gls	Aps	Sub	Gls	Aps	Sub	Gls
1960-61	46			5									51		
1961-62	32			6									38		
Total	78			11									89		

WALSH, Colin David

Winger *Hamilton, 22 July 1962*

'Borrowed' from Charlton in February 1989, Walsh played five times for Posh, scoring in a 1-5 loss at York. A winger with a trusty left foot,

Colin had joined Charlton for £125,000 in July 1986 from Nottingham Forest, where he played 139 League games and gained Scottish Under-21 honours. After a loan to Middlesbrough, he returned to Charlton, where he completed almost 250 League games before retiring in 1996.

Season	League			FA Cup			League Cup			Other			Total		
	Aps	Sub	Gls	Aps	Sub	Gls	Aps	Sub	Gls	Aps	Sub	Gls	Aps	Sub	Gls
1988-89	5		1										5		1

WATKINS, Dale Allan

Forward   *Peterborough, 4 November 1971*

Watkins was a teenaged striker who tasted League action with Posh before settling at non-League level. Although born in Peterborough, Watkins was a trainee with Rotherham before signing for his home-town club in March 1990. He debuted as a substitute in a 1-2 home defeat by Southend on the last day of 1989-90. Upon his release a year later, Watkins joined Grantham before transferring to Rushden & Diamonds, where his scoring feats led to a £10,000 move to Gloucester City in 1996. Later moves took him to Cheltenham, where he briefly returned to League football following their Conference title in 1998-99, and Kettering, for whom he appeared in the FA Trophy final.

Season	League			FA Cup			League Cup			Other			Total		
	Aps	Sub	Gls	Aps	Sub	Gls	Aps	Sub	Gls	Aps	Sub	Gls	Aps	Sub	Gls
1989-90		1												1	
1990-91	5	4		1			1			1			6	6	
Total	5	5		1			1			1			6	7	

WATSON, Thomas (Tommy)

Winger   *Lesmahagow, 23 August 1943*

A speedy winger, on the left or right, little Tommy Watson was a match winner with a keen eye for goal. Signed from Stevenage in May 1965, Tommy made an impact in his first season, despite not establishing himself as a regular. He appeared in every match of Posh's run to the semi-finals of the League Cup, dazzled in the 4-0 eclipse of Division One leaders Burnley, and notched a hat-trick in a 7-1 League win at Mansfield. He was amongst the goals again in 1966-67, most memorably in the FA Cup, when he hit another treble as Posh crushed Bedford Town 6-2. Tommy was also on target in the next round at Sunderland, where Posh suffered a 1-7 mauling. The impish Scot left Posh in September 1967, days before the resignation of Gordon Clark, joining Walsall for £12,000. He played 100+ games for the Saddlers, then moved to Gillingham before going part-time with Maidstone.

Season	League			FA Cup			League Cup			Other			Total		
	Aps	Sub	Gls	Aps	Sub	Gls	Aps	Sub	Gls	Aps	Sub	Gls	Aps	Sub	Gls
1965-66	28		8	1			6		1				35		9
1966-67	39		11	4		6	2						45		17
1967-68	8		1				1						9		1
Total	75		20	5		6	9		1				89		27

WAUGH, Keith
Goalkeeper   *Sunderland, 27 October 1956*

This agile goalkeeper joined in July 1976 after failing to break into the team at his hometown club, Sunderland. He spent five years with Posh, making 195 League appearances and becoming a popular figure with fans. Reliable and consistent, he was ever present in 1978-79 and 1979-80 and missed just one game from February 1978 through to his departure in August 1981 to Sheffield United for £90,000. Keith settled into the Blades side that dealt Posh two 4-0 hammerings on their way to the Fourth Division title. During 1984-85 Waugh spent time on loan to Cambridge and Bristol City, before joining the Robins on a permanent basis in July 1985. He enjoyed two trips to Wembley for Freight Rover Trophy finals in 1986 and 1987, and was Bristol City's first-choice keeper for four years. He made 167 League appearances before his departure on a free transfer to Coventry in 1989. He played one League game for the Sky Blues – his first in the top flight – before ending his playing career with Watford in 1993. After spending 1993-94 as youth-team manager at Vicarage Road, Keith quit football for a career in the police. He is currently a detective based in Dunstable.

Season	League			FA Cup			League Cup			Other			Total		
	Aps	Sub	Gls	Aps	Sub	Gls	Aps	Sub	Gls	Aps	Sub	Gls	Aps	Sub	Gls
1976-77	32			2									34		
1977-78	26						4						30		
1978-79	46			1			8						55		
1979-80	46			1			6						53		
1980-81	45			6			4						55		
Total	195			10			22						227		

WEBSTER, Kenny
Right-back   *London, 2 March 1973*

A former England Youth cap, Webster arrived on a free transfer from Arsenal in 1994. After playing in two Auto Windscreens Shield games, one of which brought a 3-5 home defeat by Birmingham, in which he was shredded by Portuguese winger Jose Dominguez, Kenny left the club for Conference side Stevenage Borough in January 1995.

Season	League			FA Cup			League Cup			Other			Total		
	Aps	Sub	Gls	Aps	Sub	Gls	Aps	Sub	Gls	Aps	Sub	Gls	Aps	Sub	Gls
1994-95										2			2		

WELSH, Stephen George (Steve)
Central Defender   Glasgow, 19 April 1968

Gutsy Scottish defender Welsh won many friends at London Road during the early 1990s with his grit and never-say-die spirit. An ex-soldier, Steve joined Posh in August 1991 from Cambridge, for whom he made just one substitute appearance. His first season with Posh saw Welsh play a key role in Chris Turner's battlers that reached the quarter-finals of the League Cup before winning promotion to the First Division via the play-offs. Named captain following Ken Charlery's departure early in 1992-93, Steve led Posh to tenth place in Division One – the club's highest ever League finish. That same season saw him open his goalscoring account with a close-range effort at Bristol City, where his exuberant celebration epitomised his passion for the game. Posh were relegated a year later, but Welsh was one of the few to emerge with any credit, his committed displays earning him the club's Player of the Season award. After suffering a surprise loss of form early in 1994-95, he was transferred to Scottish Premier side Partick Thistle in December 1994. A loan spell at London Road under Barry Fry from July 1996 never worked out and after three months and a handful of games he returned to Scotland, this time to Dunfermline, then Ayr. Welsh came back to England, to Lincoln, in August 1999.

Season	League			FA Cup			League Cup			Other			Total		
	Aps	Sub	Gls	Aps	Sub	Gls	Aps	Sub	Gls	Aps	Sub	Gls	Aps	Sub	Gls
1991-92	42			3			8			10			63		
1992-93	45		1	2			4			2			53		1
1993-94	45		1	2			6			2			55		1
1994-95	14						2						16		
1996-97	6						3						9		
Total	152		2	7			23			14			196		2

WHITE, Christopher Jason (Chris)
Right-back   Chatham, 11 December 1970

Unable to break through during two years at Portsmouth, White joined Posh on a free transfer in May 1991. He began 1991-92 as first choice right-back but struggled to impress Chris Turner and spent the remainder of the campaign in the reserves. He briefly returned to first-team action at the start of the following season before being loaned to Doncaster in January 1993. A permanent move to Exeter followed. Chris moved to Yeovil in March 1994, then Farnborough and Slough.

Season	League			FA Cup			League Cup			Other			Total		
	Aps	Sub	Gls	Aps	Sub	Gls	Aps	Sub	Gls	Aps	Sub	Gls	Aps	Sub	Gls
1991-92	7	1					2			1			10	1	
1992-93	3	2					1	2		1	1		5	5	
Total	10	3					3	2		2	1		15	6	

WHITE, Dale

Forward   *Sunderland, 17 March 1968*

Restricted to four League appearances in two years at his hometown club, Sunderland, White was loaned to Posh in December 1987. The teenage forward showed potential during his three-month stay, hitting four goals and injecting pace into Posh's front line. Although available on a free transfer, Dale returned to Sunderland in March 1988 after Posh could only offer him terms until the end of the season.

Season	League			FA Cup			League Cup			Other			Total		
	Aps	Sub	Gls	Aps	Sub	Gls	Aps	Sub	Gls	Aps	Sub	Gls	Aps	Sub	Gls
1987-88	14		4										14		4

WHITTAKER, Richard (Dick)

Right-back   *Dublin, 10 October 1934, Died December 1998*

Capped by the Republic of Ireland during his Chelsea days, stylish right-back Whittaker was the final piece in Jimmy Hagan's jigsaw as Posh built their Fourth Division title-winning side of 1961. After being lured over to Stamford Bridge in 1952, Whittaker played 48 League games for Chelsea before joining Posh soon after the start of 1960-61 – Posh's first season in the League. Dick debuted in October in the League Cup at Preston and kept his place throughout the season. He maintained his high level of performance the next season, in which he was ever present, but played only occasionally in 1962-63 after losing his place to Tommy Singleton. Released in July 1963, Whittaker spent a year at QPR before quitting full-time football to go non-League.

Season	League			FA Cup			League Cup			Other			Total		
	Aps	Sub	Gls	Aps	Sub	Gls	Aps	Sub	Gls	Aps	Sub	Gls	Aps	Sub	Gls
1960-61	31			5			1						37		
1961-62	46			6			1						53		
1962-63	5			1									6		
Total	82			12			2						96		

WHITTINGHAM, Guy

Forward   *Evesham, 10 November 1964*

Whittingham arrived at London Road in August 2000, on loan as cover for injured striker Jason Lee. A former soldier, Guy first shot to prominence with Yeovil, where his goals persuaded Portsmouth to part with £450 to buy him out of the Army in 1989. Whittingham bagged 88 League goals in four seasons for Pompey, including a club-record 42 from 46 games in the new First Division in 1992-93. A £1.2 million move to Premier League Aston Villa followed, but Guy scored only five times in 25 League games. After rediscovering his scoring touch on loan to Wolves, he prospered in midfield at Sheffield Wednesday before returning to Portsmouth in 1999. A change of management at Fratton Park saw him out of favour at the start of 2000-01, prompting his loan to London Road. It did not take him long to make his mark, scoring in Posh's 4-1 win at Oldham after coming on as a substitute. Despite his dream start, the years had caught up with the 35-year-old player and he returned to Portsmouth after making only a handful of appearances. He later went on loan to Oxford before joining Wycombe on a free transfer in March 2001. Guy was player-manager of Dr Martens side Newport (IOW) until he was sacked in May 2002.

Season	League			FA Cup			League Cup			Other			Total		
	Aps	Sub	Gls	Aps	Sub	Gls	Aps	Sub	Gls	Aps	Sub	Gls	Aps	Sub	Gls
2000-01	1	4	1				1						2	4	1

WHYMARK, Trevor John

Forward   *Diss, 4 May 1950*

Trevor Whymark played four times for Posh as a 35-year-old. Signed in August 1985 on a weekly contract from Southend, the Norfolk-born striker had an illustrious past. He represented England at Under-21 and full international level whilst at his first club, Ipswich, for whom he scored 74 goals in 260 League games and played in Europe. He left Portman Road for Dutch side Sparta Rotterdam in 1978 and had spells with Derby, Vancouver Whitecaps and Grimsby before linking up with several former Posh men at Roots Hall. After leaving London Road, he appeared a couple of times for Colchester, then retired from playing to coach youngsters and run soccer courses at holiday camps.

Season	League			FA Cup			League Cup			Other			Total		
	Aps	Sub	Gls	Aps	Sub	Gls	Aps	Sub	Gls	Aps	Sub	Gls	Aps	Sub	Gls
1985-86	3						1						4		

WICKS, Matthew Jonathan

Central Defender   *Reading, 8 September 1978*

A tall, young centre-back, Wicks arrived on a free transfer from Crewe in March 1999 following the departure of Mick Bodley. The son of former Chelsea and QPR player Steve Wicks, Matthew gained England Youth honours during an early career that saw spells on the books of both Manchester United and Arsenal. He slotted straight into the heart of Posh's defence where he remained until the end of 1998-99, forming an effective partnership with Andy Edwards. Wicks was unable to claim a regular place the following season but nevertheless played his part in Posh's promotion success. Matthew joined Brighton for a nominal fee in October 2000 but has since moved on to Hull City.

Season	League			FA Cup			League Cup			Other			Total		
	Aps	Sub	Gls	Aps	Sub	Gls	Aps	Sub	Gls	Aps	Sub	Gls	Aps	Sub	Gls
1998-99	11												11		
1999-00	17	3		1			2			1			21	3	
Total	28	3		1			2			1			32	3	

WILE, John David
Central Defender   Sherburn, 9 March 1947

It was in his native north-east that young John Wile first tried to establish himself as a footballer in the 1960s. After a spell with Durham City, First Division Sunderland offered him a professional contract in June 1966. He was unable to make the break into their first team and joined Posh a year later after impressing Norman Rigby during a brief trial. It took Wile several months to win a regular first-team place, but eventually he became a permanent fixture in the centre of defence and for more than two years he was ever present. WBA had noted his progress and in December 1970 he was transferred to the Hawthorns for £35,000 – a record fee received by Posh at that time. A tall, unflappable centre-half, he soon established himself as one of the most reliable defenders in the First Division and many observers felt he was unlucky never to be capped by England. In 1978, during an FA Cup semi-final at Highbury against Ipswich, he received an ugly gash after colliding heads with Town's Brian Talbot. Showing typical bravery, John soldiered on, sporting a blood-soaked headband that left him looking like a war hero. Wile spent 13 years at the Hawthorns, playing 500 League games and not missing any between April 1978 and May 1982, a run of 131 consecutive League matches. He returned to London Road in 1983 as a popular successor to Martin Wilkinson in the manager's chair and, despite his advancing years, he continued to play for another couple of years, taking his total number of League appearances past 700. A move into management was almost inevitable for a player who, as a long-serving captain of WBA, led by example and was an inspiration to those around him. Before returning to Posh, John had twice taken temporary charge of affairs at the Hawthorns when the club was between managers. Managing Posh, however, was not a success. After an encouraging first season, Wile took the club perilously close to a first ever application for re-election in 1985-86. His reign was terminated following a poor start to 1986-87, whereupon John quit football to run an indoor cricket stadium in Lichfield. He has since returned to the game as a director at his former club, WBA.

Season	League Aps	Sub	Gls	FA Cup Aps	Sub	Gls	League Cup Aps	Sub	Gls	Other Aps	Sub	Gls	Total Aps	Sub	Gls
1967-68	3	2											3	2	
1968-69	46		1	1			5						5		1
1969-70	46		4	4			2						52		4
1970-71	21		2	1			1						23		2
1983-84	32		2	1			4						37		2
1984-85	41		1	2			2			1			46		1
1985-86	13	1		5			2						20	1	
Total	202	3	10	14			16			1			233	3	10

WILKINS, Steven (Steve)

Midfielder   *Hillingdon, 1958*

The least successful of four footballing brothers – one of which is ex-England star Ray, midfielder Steve Wilkins played one game for Posh on a non-contract basis during 1984-85. A former Chelsea apprentice, he was described by John Wile as being 'just like his brother Ray, only with more hair!' Wilkins did well enough in a handful of reserve outings and scored with a neat volley in a 7-2 mauling of Northampton. He was given a run-out in a Freight Rover Trophy tie at Cambridge in February 1985, but was released soon afterwards with Wile stating that the club could no longer afford the player's hotel bills. Wilkins was not amused, claiming he had not been given a fair chance. Steve was last known to be working for German airline Lufthansa.

Season	League			FA Cup			League Cup			Other			Total		
	Aps	Sub	Gls	Aps	Sub	Gls	Aps	Sub	Gls	Aps	Sub	Gls	Aps	Sub	Gls
1984-85										1			1		

WILLIAMS, Lee

Midfielder   *Birmingham, 3 February 1973*

A free transfer from Aston Villa, Lee arrived as a midfielder but proved his versatility by often appearing at right-back. Neat and tidy with two good feet, Williams had failed to break into the first team in four seasons at Villa Park but made his League debut while on loan at Shrewsbury in 1992. He had originally joined Posh on loan in February 1994, making his first appearance in a 1-0 Division One home win over Middlesbrough. The move was made permanent the following summer, after which Lee enjoyed two good seasons, taking his total number of Posh appearances past 100. One unfortunate moment occurred in September 1995, when on his return to Villa Park with Posh he was sent off during a 0-6 League Cup debacle. Williams left for Dublin side Shamrock Rovers in July 1996. Then, after completing an unsuccessful trial at Tranmere, he joined Mansfield in February 1997. After 173 League games for the Stags, Lee joined Cheltenham Town late in 2001.

Season	League			FA Cup			League Cup			Other			Total		
	Aps	Sub	Gls	Aps	Sub	Gls	Aps	Sub	Gls	Aps	Sub	Gls	Aps	Sub	Gls
1993-94	16	2											16	2	
1994-95	35	5	1	2		1	1	1		2			40	6	2
1995-96	32	1		3	1		3			5			43	2	
Total	83	8	1	5	1	1	4	1		7			99	10	2

WILLIAMS, Martin Keith

Midfielder   *Luton, 12 July 1973*

A wide midfield player, Williams spent the second half of 2000-01 on loan from Swindon. A former Leicester trainee, he made his League debut following a move to his hometown club, Luton, in September 1991. He went on to make 40 League appearances for the Hatters and later spent five years at Reading before switching to Swindon in 2000. Martin made no secret of his desire to leave the County Ground and his eagerness to impress Barry Fry saw his Posh career off to a bright start. He netted a couple of smartly taken goals, including a 25-yard free-kick against Wigan. He struggled to maintain his early form, however, and after failing to earn a permanent contract he signed a three-year deal with Conference outfit Stevenage Borough in July 2001.

Season	League			FA Cup			League Cup			Other			Total		
	Aps	Sub	Gls	Aps	Sub	Gls	Aps	Sub	Gls	Aps	Sub	Gls	Aps	Sub	Gls
2000-01	13	1	2										13	1	2

WILLIAMS, Michael Anthony
Midfielder   *Bradford, 21 November 1969*

A loanee from Sheffield Wednesday in March 1997, Williams made his Posh debut in a 1-2 home defeat by Bristol Rovers near the end of 1996-97. The tall, right-sided midfielder struggled to make any impact as Barry Fry's team slipped towards relegation from Division Two, and he returned to Sheffield after four weeks at London Road. He had previously served five seasons at Hillsborough, where he appeared just 23 times in the Premier League. He joined Burnley in July 1997.

Season	League			FA Cup			League Cup			Other			Total		
	Aps	Sub	Gls	Aps	Sub	Gls	Aps	Sub	Gls	Aps	Sub	Gls	Aps	Sub	Gls
1996-97	6												6		

WILLIAMS, Steven Robert (Steve)
Forward   *Sheffield, 3 November 1975*

A tall, left-sided forward, Williams made 17 League appearances for Lincoln before being released in 1995. Brought to London Road for a trial by Mick Halsall in February 1996, he made three substitute appearances before seeing out the season with Cambridge City. He moved on to Boston and had later spells with Stamford, Corby, King's Lynn, Gainsborough, Kettering, Spalding, and Hucknall Town.

Season	League			FA Cup			League Cup			Other			Total		
	Aps	Sub	Gls	Aps	Sub	Gls	Aps	Sub	Gls	Aps	Sub	Gls	Aps	Sub	Gls
1995-96		3												3	

WILLIAMS, Tom Andrew
Left-back/Midfielder   *Carshalton, 8 July 1980*

A fast, skilful defender, Tom signed for Posh in July 2001 after coming on loan from West Ham. Spotted by Hammers boss Harry Redknapp whilst playing for Walton & Hersham, Williams was unable to break into the first team at Upton Park ahead of England defenders Stuart Pearce and Nigel Winterburn. Loaned to Posh to gain League experience, Tom debuted as substitute in Posh's 1-2 defeat at Swindon before making his London Road bow against promoted Rotherham on the final day of 2000-01. Barry Fry persuaded Tom to sign a permanent contract and the youngster proved to be an inspired signing. A big hit with the fans, Tom performed equally well in midfield or as a marauding left-back. With his sweet left foot he became one of the best players at set pieces ever seen at London Road. Sadly, bigger clubs were soon on the prowl and Williams joined Birmingham City in a complicated deal which earned Posh an initial £350,000 in March 2002.

Season	League			FA Cup			League Cup			Other			Total		
	Aps	Sub	Gls	Aps	Sub	Gls	Aps	Sub	Gls	Aps	Sub	Gls	Aps	Sub	Gls
2000-01	1	1											1	1	
2001-02	31	3	2	4	1		1	1		1			37	5	2
Total	32	4	2	4	1		1	1	0	1			38	6	2

WILLIS, Roger Christopher
Midfielder   *Islington, 17 June 1967*

One of many players to follow Barry Fry to Posh after spells at Barnet and Birmingham, Roger 'Harry' Willis was one of the better performers during Posh's relegation season of 1996-97. A tall, strong midfielder who was good in the air, he had a keen eye for goal as demonstrated when he scored twice in a 6-2 November thrashing of Rotherham, then repeated the dose when Bristol City were beaten 3-1 in February. Willis began his League career with Grimsby in 1989-90 before linking up with Fry at Barnet, whom he helped acquire Football League status in 1991. His impressive goalscoring from midfield earned a £175,000 move to Watford in October 1992 and a transfer to Birmingham for a similar fee a year later. Roger's next move took him to Southend, from where Posh signed him in August 1996. He left London Road after one season, signing for Second Division Chesterfield in 1997 for £40,000.

Season	League			FA Cup			League Cup			Other			Total		
	Aps	Sub	Gls	Aps	Sub	Gls	Aps	Sub	Gls	Aps	Sub	Gls	Aps	Sub	Gls
1996-97	34	6	6	5	1		3			5			47	7	6

WINFIELD, Bernard John (John)
Left-back   *Draycott, 28 February 1943*

A tall, well-built defender, Winfield joined Posh from Nottingham Forest in July 1974, as Noel Cantwell looked to strengthen his squad in readiness for Posh's return to Division Three. Winfield brought with him the experience gained during 14 years with Forest, for whom he had made 355 League appearances. His Posh career was less distinguished and after playing just eleven games towards the end of 1974-

75 he left the club and retired from professional soccer. These days John can be found running a newsagency in Nottingham.

Season	League			FA Cup			League Cup			Other			Total		
	Aps	Sub	Gls	Aps	Sub	Gls	Aps	Sub	Gls	Aps	Sub	Gls	Aps	Sub	Gls
1974-75	11												11		

WINTERS, John Mark
Right-back   *Wisbech, 24 October 1960*

A local lad from Wisbech, this aggressive right-back came up through the ranks before breaking into the first team in 1980-81. After initially sharing the No 2 jersey with Dave McVay, he was edged out by experienced player-coach Geoff Butler in 1981-82 before making the right-back position his own the following campaign. Surprisingly relegated to reserve-team football following John Wile's appointment as manager in 1983-84, Winters was released from the club midway through the season. He has since popped up at several clubs, including Ramsey Town and Peterborough League outfits Eye United and Leverington.

Season	League			FA Cup			League Cup			Other			Total		
	Aps	Sub	Gls	Aps	Sub	Gls	Aps	Sub	Gls	Aps	Sub	Gls	Aps	Sub	Gls
1980-81	22		1										22		1
1981-82	7						2						9		
1982-83	31		2	4			2		1				37	1	2
Total	60		3	4			4		1				68	1	3

WOOF, William (Billy)
Forward   *Gateshead, 16 August 1956*

Striker Billy Woof played three times for Posh in March 1977 on loan from First Division Middlesbrough. A permanent deal was not forthcoming, and Billy returned to Boro, where he made 46 League appearances, scoring five goals. He dropped out of the League in 1981, but his impressive displays for Blyth Spartans resulted in a move to Cardiff. His stay at Ninian Park was short and after a return to the north-east with Gateshead he found fleeting success with Hull in February 1983, where his goals helped the Tigers to promotion from Division Four.

Season	League			FA Cup			League Cup			Other			Total		
	Aps	Sub	Gls	Aps	Sub	Gls	Aps	Sub	Gls	Aps	Sub	Gls	Aps	Sub	Gls
1976-77	2		1										2		1

WORRALL, Gary George
Winger   *Salford, 4 November 1961*

An orthodox winger, Worrall made his League debut in February 1984 while on loan from Manchester United. He had spent six years at Old Trafford without tasting first-team action. Gary was an instant hit, scoring on his Posh debut with a long-range drive to help John Wile's team to a 4-1 win over Bristol City. He signed a permanent contract soon afterwards and provided many entertaining moments during what were depressing years for Posh in the mid-1980s. Gary enjoyed a rapport with the London Road crowd who would urge his team-mates to pass to him on the left wing. The side's only ever present in 1984-85, Worrall finished the season as second highest scorer with nine League goals. Although starring in the 1985-86 FA Cup run, he was hampered by injuries and signed for Carlisle in July 1986. He played 32 League games for the Brunton Park club before joining Altrincham.

Season	League			FA Cup			League Cup			Other			Total		
	Aps	Sub	Gls	Aps	Sub	Gls	Aps	Sub	Gls	Aps	Sub	Gls	Aps	Sub	Gls
1983-84	18	1	2									1	18	2	2
1984-85	46		9	1			2			2			51		9
1985-86	29	1	5	7		1	2			1			39	1	6
Total	93	2	16	8		1	4			3	1		108	3	17

WOSAHLO, Roger Frank

Winger   *Cambridge, 11 September 1947*

Wosahlo began his career at Chelsea in the mid-1960s but struggled to break into the Blues' star-studded line-up, appearing just once in First Division action during 1966-67. He spent a season with Ipswich, again playing one game, before re-launching his career with Fourth Division Posh in July 1968. A winger capable of playing on either flank, he appeared in 18 League and Cup games, scoring in a 6-1 demolition of Bradford, before rejoining Ipswich, then going to South Africa.

Season	League			FA Cup			League Cup			Other			Total		
	Aps	Sub	Gls	Aps	Sub	Gls	Aps	Sub	Gls	Aps	Sub	Gls	Aps	Sub	Gls
1968-69	13	2	1	1			2						16	2	1

WRIGHT, George Brian (Brian)

Wing-half   *Sunderland, 16 September 1939*

Giant wing-half Wright was born in Sunderland but it was with rivals Newcastle that he began his professional career in 1956. He made 45 League appearances for the Magpies before starting a nine-year association with Posh in May 1963. It took Brian until 1966-67 to establish himself as a first-choice defender, but from that point he was a mainstay, providing experience whilst aiding the development of fledgling centre-backs John Wile and Chris Turner. A model of consistency, he missed just three matches between October 1967 and May 1971, during which time he broke Frank Rankmore's League appearance record for the club. Brian's service was recognised by Posh fans when they voted him Player of the Season for 1970-71. The following season was his last at London Road. The arrival of Jack Carmichael from Arsenal cost Wright his place. He quit in July 1972 and joined Scarborough.

Season	League			FA Cup			League Cup			Other			Total		
	Aps	Sub	Gls	Aps	Sub	Gls	Aps	Sub	Gls	Aps	Sub	Gls	Aps	Sub	Gls
1963-64	24		1	1			1						26		1
1964-65	21		2										21		2
1965-66	20						2						22		
1966-67	32	2		2			1						35	2	
1967-68	39		4	3									42		4
1968-69	46		1	1			5						52		1
1969-70	45			4			2						51		
1970-71	44		1	2			1						47		1
1971-72	20			4									24		
Total	291	2	9	17			12						320	2	9

YOUNG, Eric Royston

Midfielder   *Stockton, 26 November 1952*

Signed on loan from Manchester United by Noel Cantwell in November 1972, this former England Youth cap stayed with Posh for the rest of that season. After debuting in a 2-2 draw at Darlington, he went on to appear in 25 League games, plus three in the FA Cup, including the home defeat by champions Derby. After returning to Old Trafford, Eric went on loan to Walsall before making a permanent move to Stockport. He was at Edgley Park for six months before moving to Darlington, then went non-League before trying his luck in Australia.

Season	League			FA Cup			League Cup			Other			Total		
	Aps	Sub	Gls	Aps	Sub	Gls	Aps	Sub	Gls	Aps	Sub	Gls	Aps	Sub	Gls
1972-73	24	1	2	3									27	1	2

ZENCHUCK, Steven John (Steve)

Goalkeeper   *Peterborough, 20 November 1966*

A locally born keeper, Zenchuck received a fairytale call-up as a 17-year-old YTS trainee. His moment of glory came in a Fourth Division match at Blackpool in December 1983. When regular custodian David Seaman went sick, John Wile was left without experienced goalkeeping cover. Showing few nerves, Zenchuk pulled off some fine stops to help Posh record a 2-1 victory. He was not retained that summer and, after appearing for United Counties League sides Stamford and Holbeach, converted to a central defender in the Peterborough League, most notably with works side Perkins and Eye United.

Season	League			FA Cup			League Cup			Other			Total		
	Aps	Sub	Gls	Aps	Sub	Gls	Aps	Sub	Gls	Aps	Sub	Gls	Aps	Sub	Gls
1983-84	1												1		

Lee Williams v Cardiff, February 1995

Tommy Watson   Ken Charlery

Marcus Ebdon v Tranmere, May 1993

Dave Longhurst

Robbie Cooke

Ray Atkins	Bobby Doyle	Graham Kisby	Jim Hall
Ken & Ian Ball	Billy Hails	Pete Lane	Dennis Emery
J L Batterham		John Lawrence	Tommy Robson
Paul Bloodworth	Freddie Hill	Peter Mabbutt	Tommy Robson
R Brackley (Oundle)	Bobby Doyle	Don Maddams	Tommy Robson
Graham Bradshaw	Mick Quinn	John Marlow	Bobby Doyle
Bryn Brothers	Tommy Robson	C N Marsh	
Darren Michael Butcher		John Martin	
	Noel Luke	Pete McCray	Tommy Robson
Arthur Catchpole	Tommy Robson	Steve Oxlee	David Seaman
Bob Chamberlain	Bobby Doyle	Adam Palmer	Adam Drury
David Cox	Simon Davies	John Pickard	Mick Halsall
Tim & Ian Davison	Andy Edwards	John Pilgrim	Mark Tyler
Christopher Paul Day		Ian Porteous	Ken Charlery
	Leon McKenzie	Rob Redhead	Jim Hall
Robin Desborough	Tommy Robson	Mick Robinson	Tommy Robson
Dave Drage		Tony Scarr	Tommy Robson
Carl Drewery	Tommy Robson	Brian Seaton	Dennis Emery
Robert Eddington	Dennis Emery	Peter J Sindall	Adam Drury
Ian Espinosa	Tommy Robson	Craig 'fat man' Skinner	
David Fountain	Jim Hall		Robbie Cooke
Lee Garrett	Mark Tyler	Dave Smith	Mick Gooding
Anthony John Geary	Ken Charlery	Keith Smith	Tony Adcock
James B Hamilton	Derek Dougan	R F Smith	Ken Charlery
John Henson	Ken Charlery	D J Stimpson	
Derek Hyde	Ollie Hopkins	Richard Stocken	
Kevin & Adam Jackson		Dave Sugarman	
	Adam Drury	Jim Swales	Tommy Robson
David James	Freddie Hill	Harry Sykes	Tommy Robson
David Jarman	Ken Charlery	Peter Thompson	Peter Deakin
Paul Kidston	Tommy Robson	Graham Watson	Billy Kellock
Jon King	Dennis Emery	Roger M York	Mick Halsall